Praise for A BILLIO

"[Rinder's] voice is crisp, urgent, and vivi... ... ...
assessing his years as a compliant member, his breathless escape, or his
promise to continue exposing Scientology as a 'unique and vengeful
monster.' An intensely personal, cathartic memoir of blind allegiance,
betrayal, and liberation."

—*Kirkus Reviews* (starred review)*

"Few people understand Scientology like Mike Rinder does. In *A Billion Years*, he tells the gripping, harrowing account of growing up in
Scientology, serving founder L. Ron Hubbard, and rising to the top
of its ranks. Mike has found purpose in his pain, and his book offers
not only a cautionary tale but also an inspiring story of resilience."

—Leah Remini, *New York Times* bestselling author of *Troublemaker*

"A candid and deeply felt memoir of a life lost to false belief—and
courageously regained."

—Lawrence Wright, *New York Times* bestselling author of *Going Clear*

"*A Billion Years* is an extraordinarily powerful book. It is an essential
account from the inside, and while it's a devastating exposé of the abuses
of the church, the tone is measured and deeply humanistic. Rinder lets
us feel what it's like to fall into a state of blind faith, and how hard it
is to break free and see the truth for what it is. Nothing could be more
relevant to our current moment."

—Alex Gibney, Oscar Award–winning director
of *Taxi to the Dark Side* and *Going Clear*

"Mike Rinder has written the definitive book on the great threat of
Scientology in the twenty-first century. It's a flamethrower of a read,
burning up the organization's wicked nonsense so all that is left is like
so much ash in the ashtray. Read it."

—John Sweeney, investigative journalist and presenter of BBC
Panorama's *Scientology and Me* and *The Secrets of Scientology*

* A *Kirkus Reviews* Best Nonfiction Book of 2022

A
BILLION
YEARS

MY ESCAPE FROM
A LIFE IN THE
HIGHEST RANKS
OF SCIENTOLOGY

MIKE RINDER

GALLERY BOOKS

NEW YORK   LONDON   TORONTO   SYDNEY   NEW DELHI

G

Gallery Books
An Imprint of Simon & Schuster, LLC
1230 Avenue of the Americas
New York, NY 10020

First Gallery Books trade paperback edition February 2024

GALLERY BOOKS and colophon are registered trademarks of Simon & Schuster, LLC

Simon & Schuster: Celebrating 100 Years of Publishing in 2024

For information about special discounts for bulk purchases, please contact Simon & Schuster Special Sales at 1-866-506-1949 or business@simonandschuster.com.

The Simon & Schuster Speakers Bureau can bring authors to your live event. For more information or to book an event, contact the Simon & Schuster Speakers Bureau at 1-866-248-3049 or visit our website at www.simonspeakers.com.

Interior design by Jaime Putorti

Manufactured in the United States of America

10 9 8 7 6 5 4 3 2 1

Library of Congress Control Number: 2022942777

ISBN 978-1-9821-8576-3
ISBN 978-1-9821-8577-0 (pbk)
ISBN 978-1-9821-8578-7 (ebook)

Dedicated to my wife, Christie.

Written for my children, Taryn, Benjamin, and Jack.

CONTENTS

For what it's worth: it's never too late or, in my case, too early to be whoever you want to be. There's no time limit, stop whenever you want. You can change or stay the same, there are no rules to this thing. We can make the best or the worst of it. I hope you make the best of it. And I hope you see things that startle you. I hope you feel things you never felt before. I hope you meet people with a different point of view. I hope you live a life you're proud of. If you find that you're not, I hope you have the courage to start all over again.

—SOMETIMES ATTRIBUTED TO F. SCOTT FITZGERALD

AUTHOR'S NOTE

This is my recollection of my life.

With the passage of so many years, it is of course possible that I have some facts wrong. I may misremember some small details—being in Paris in December 1982 when in fact it was February 1983, for example—but this is of little consequence to my life's story. Memories of events are distorted by time and perspective, and they become especially hazy when you suffer the dimmed perceptions of sleep deprivation. I, like many around me, experienced the dull fog of exhaustion on a daily basis in my many years in the Sea Org. What I don't have wrong are my impressions, feelings, and emotions about my experiences, and how they affected me.

It may be odd to offer a disclaimer at the outset, but it is made necessary by the fact that scientology is a unique and vengeful monster. Obsessed with keeping records, scientologists have maintained diligent files of my days in the Sea Org, as well as reports from private investigators and spies and surveillance video from my life after leaving. They will no doubt respond to this book by nitpicking facts that they deem false to try to color everything I have written as a lie. I know, because it's a standard technique that I employed when dealing with people who said things scientology didn't like. What they will not do is respond to the substance of my experiences and observations. Such silence speaks volumes.

I use the term "scientology" throughout this book, rather than "Scientology," which is the trademark registered name preferred by the organization. The capitalization puts it in the same category as Catholicism or Judaism. I prefer to invoke a broader concept of the general subject, more in keeping with the terms "philosophy" or "sociopathy."

Though I've tried to use scientology jargon only when necessary, it is often unavoidable. A glossary of those terms can be found at the back of this book.

A LETTER TO MY CHILDREN

Dear Taryn and Benjamin,

Let me start with this: I am truly sorry for placing you in a world where your future was preordained. It is difficult and painful to contemplate that I brought you into a life where, from your earliest years, you were denied any meaningful free will. If I had known then what I know now, I would never have let that happen.

A few days after you were born, you were turned over to the nannies in the "nursery." Your mother and I rarely saw you as you grew up, but that was justified in our minds—we had a larger purpose that was far more important. We were saving mankind and didn't have a minute to spare. No distraction from that vital work could be tolerated, including time spent with you, our children.

Yet, to be honest, had I spent more time with you, had we spoken more, I would not have taught you any differently. I was as dedicated to the cause of scientology as anyone could ever be. At the time, I thought I was being the best parent I could be by being the best scientologist I could be.

I wrote this book for you. It may seem odd to write a book for an audience of two, but my hope is that at some point it will help you make that decision to find your own way out of the scientology bubble. Maybe not today or tomorrow, but someday. In the meantime, I believe there may be others who have had similar experiences and perhaps will find my story helpful.

If you are still in scientology as you are reading this, you are immersed in a carefully constructed cocoon that makes you believe, with all your heart, many things that are provably false. You will be certain this is a book of bigoted lies. I hope you come to see that scientology is a mind prison designed to be nearly impossible to escape.

Let me paint a picture that might be easier for you to understand. Imagine that from the first moment you could comprehend words being spoken, you were told that if you traveled outside the wall around the house in which you were born, a terrible fate would befall you. And that if anyone beyond that wall tried to tell you there was nothing to be afraid of on the other side, they were an agent of evil, simply trying to trick you into falling into their clutches, where you would die a horrible death and live in darkness for eternity. You were told how lucky and privileged you were to live in a beautiful house far from the cruelty and evil that run rampant outside that wall. Under those circumstances, it is unlikely you would risk walking out the door and jumping over that wall.

Like you, I grew up in that house and was afraid to venture beyond the wall. I didn't consider the possibility that there was anything of value in the non-scientology world. I had been taught that the wall was real and horrors outside the wall were waiting to engulf us all if we ventured beyond. That's what L. Ron Hubbard told us and so it was *true*. I passed this same message along to you. I believed with all my heart you were fortunate to be brought into the safe, happy, and ethical bubble of scientology.

Only when life within that world had become intolerable did I finally make the leap over the wall. It took me a long time, and I endured more hardships and abuse than one should to reach that point. I will try to explain in this book how I became immersed in a way of thinking that made the unthinkable perfectly rational and inured me to things "normal" people would never have tolerated.

When I did finally leave, I was astonished to discover that life beyond that wall—the non-scientology world—is not full of bogeymen, death, and destruction. It is a large, exciting, and vibrant place far less dangerous than we had been warned. It is in fact much healthier and more enjoyable than life inside the scientology mind prison. Since I escaped, I have been shouting back over the wall, throwing notes tied around stones, and skywriting to anyone who may look up—attempting to get the message through that there is a big, wide, beautiful world out here.

I hope you can discover the real world for yourselves, too. No matter what you may think, it is never too late to start over. I was fifty-two when I began afresh. An old dog can learn new tricks.

I owe it to you to try to tell you the truth, and I have to have faith that you, my own children, might eventually listen. Even the smallest crack in your conviction might lead to more questioning. And as soon as you begin questioning, the end of the nightmare is near.

I want you to know that I harbor no ill will toward you for the things you have said about me. In fact, the love I feel for you is greater today than at any previous time in our lives. Distance from the corrosive thought control of scientology has increased my capacity for compassion, empathy, and love—emotions not valued in scientology. That distance has also intensified my feelings of guilt for having put you in the circumstances you are in.

Today, I know what it means to raise a child. Your younger brother, Jack, has been brought up outside the confining walls of scientology. I take him to his soccer games; we eat out together; I help him with his homework and school projects. We go on vacations and spend holidays together as a family—things I never got to do with you. Helping Jack grow up is a beautiful and rewarding part of my life. But it is also a constant reminder of all the things you and I missed.

Maybe some of what I write will help you see through the propaganda that I am an evil person bent only on the destruction of mankind. Eventually, you may want to know about me, and I may not be around to tell you in person. Perhaps reading this book will help you understand the long path I took.

I love you.

—Dad

PROLOGUE

As I rushed out the front door of L. Ron Hubbard's former office at 37 Fitzroy Street in London and stepped into a beautiful June day in 2007, the only thing I was certain of was that I had to get away before anyone realized what I was doing. I left with only a briefcase containing my passport, a few papers, a thumb drive, and two cell phones. Had I attempted to take more, or had I tried to bring my wife and children with me, I knew it would make my escape impossible. I figured I would get them out once I was in a safe place.

I headed toward the nearby Warren Street Tube station, glancing over my shoulder to see if I had been followed. I knew if I ran, it might attract attention, so I resisted the urge until I rounded the first corner and ducked into a doorway to catch my breath. Although I had not physically exerted myself, my heart was racing as if I had just completed a hundred-meter sprint. I waited thirty seconds, saw no one, and stepped back onto the street, now walking faster, still acutely aware of my surroundings. I tried to maintain the appearance of a regular Londoner hurrying to the Tube, rather than a fugitive. I knew all the tricks they employed to track down someone like me— after all, I had done the tracking-down myself. I needed to get out of sight, remove the batteries from my phones, use only cash, and stay on the move.

The relief began to flood my body as I descended the long escalator.

I stopped at the bottom and surveyed the few people behind me. Still no familiar faces.

I stood on the platform, back against the tiled wall, and waited for the train to pull in. When it did, I stayed put until all the other passengers had boarded, jumping on at the last minute while glancing down the platform to see if there were any other last-minute riders. There were none. As I sat down and the train pulled out of the station, I breathed long and hard and tried to calm myself.

I had a couple of hundred dollars, but nowhere to stay, no clothes other than what I was wearing, no car or job, and no idea what I was going to do or where I was going to go. I knew only that I had to escape the madness my life had descended into. I hoped I could gather my thoughts and figure out a plan. I had no choice: my only other option was to return to the organization and lamely turn myself in.

That was unthinkable.

I had reached a point where anything was better than the life I was living. I could no longer tolerate the mental and physical stress that had been mounting after years inside the highest echelon of scientology's international hierarchy. The physical beatings. The malnourishment and lack of sleep. The constant humiliation. The scales had finally tipped for me. I had been taught since childhood that the "wog" (anything outside of scientology) world was dangerous, degraded, and dark, but now it seemed less so than the scientology world I was living in. I had reached the point where any fate would be better than the continued torture of life near the top of the self-proclaimed most ethical and enlightened group on earth.

From a scientology perspective, I was committing the ultimate act of betrayal that would damn me for eternity: deserting the only group that could save mankind from a hopeless future of ignorance, pain, and suffering. Stepping across that threshold meant that everyone I had known—including my family and all my friends and acquaintances—would be dead to me. To be accurate, once I took that step I would be dead to them. At least to all those who were scientologists. And that would be almost everyone I had known since the age of six.

I knew every good scientologist would do as they were required: not only refuse to communicate with me but also attempt to discredit and destroy me. I knew what was to come only too well, because I had done the same to others who had left. My years as the head of scientology's Office of Special Affairs dealing with "attackers" had prepared me for the inevitable assault that would be launched against me.

As I sat on the train, thoughts flooded in—*Have I made a huge mistake I'll regret once I've had a good night's sleep? Am I being selfish, thinking only of myself? Will I end up homeless, living under a bridge? Are my wife and children going to suffer as a result of my actions?*

My loyalties were torn, but like a prisoner who had walked into the sunshine for the first time in decades, I felt a sense of freedom that overwhelmed everything else at that moment. I would figure the rest out later.

That day in London, I broke out of the cocoon that had surrounded me for nearly half a century. It began a metamorphosis, slowly transitioning me from a fanatical follower of the cult I had been raised in to a dedicated whistleblower about the abuses I experienced, witnessed, and committed. I had taken the first steps on a journey to undo everything I had learned in a lifetime of scientology.

CHAPTER 1

THE BEGINNING

A civilization without insanity, without criminals and without war, where the able can prosper and honest beings can have rights, and where man is free to rise to greater heights are the aims of Scientology.

—L. RON HUBBARD

The first time my parents ever heard the name L. Ron Hubbard was in 1959, from our next-door neighbor on Victoria Terrace, a road that climbed the brown foothills in the easternmost suburbs of Adelaide, Australia. Back then, there was still so much undeveloped land that our Cape Cod–style house, only four miles from the city center, was across the street from two hundred acres of brushland, replete with wombats, kangaroos, and emus.

I was five at the time, so I don't have any recollection of my parents hearing the name, but it was a moment that would change our lives forever. The neighbor, Ian, had driven five hundred miles to Melbourne to attend Hubbard's lectures that expanded on ideas published in his 1950 breakout book *Dianetics: The Modern Science of Mental Health*, which promised to help people rid themselves of their fears and trauma as well as a host of physical ailments. The book was a worldwide phenomenon, making Hubbard a household name and giving him a global platform on which to tour and percolate ideas that would soon morph into scientology.

Ian had described Hubbard's incredible discoveries to my parents, and intrigued, my mother, Barbara, and father, also named Ian, bought one of Hubbard's dozen or so books. As they read they became increasingly convinced that this man had a lot to offer. They were attracted by the promise of eradicating unwanted emotions and insecurities, having better relationships, raising successful children, and maybe even saving the world. Neither of them was religious—they had never attended church—but the idea of being better people and helping the world become a brighter place appealed to them, as it did to many others. At the time, I doubt they even viewed scientology as a religion; to them it was more along the lines of a self-help practice. My father, who was a serial entrepreneur before the term existed, gravitated toward anything that could improve his ability to do business. My mother, a homemaker who sometimes helped out in my father's various business ventures, appreciated the self-improvement angle of Hubbard's philosophy. I think my father was also motivated to uncover the cause of his diabetes as well as an undiagnosed childhood disease (it might have been polio) that made his left arm weaker and slightly shorter than his right. Whatever the reasons, they immersed themselves in scientology, and like many other followers, once they were in, they were *all* in. Every part of their life was consumed by it. They signed up for and paid for—everything in scientology has a price, which must be paid in full before starting—as many courses that taught different aspects of Hubbard's writings as they could.

There was a lot to learn about this strange new "religion." Hubbard was prolific, writing book after book and delivering hundreds of lectures on his tenets of dianetics and scientology. He explained things with invented terms and acronyms, creating a jargon, really a secret code for only those inside the scientology bubble, that made it difficult for outsiders to comprehend. According to Hubbard, the term scientology means "knowing in the fullest sense of the word," derived from Latin *scio*, meaning "to know," and Greek *logos*, meaning "the study of," while dianetics is "the science of mind," from the Greek *dia*, "through," and *nous*, "mind or soul." There was little Hubbard did *not* offer his opinion on—from the origins of the universe to those he thought were trying to destroy planet Earth—but the fundamental concept behind it all was his theory of the "reactive mind." Hubbard claimed we store painful and traumatic memories, which he called "engrams," deep in our subconscious, and they have a negative effect on our physical and emotional health. Dianetics was the only way to get rid of the reactive mind. Virtually nothing escaped his self-proclaimed expertise, and he expounded on all possible subjects with unflinching certainty, from eliminating phobias to raising a child, from curing cancer to increasing your IQ to "treating" homosexuality. (Hubbard decreed in his early books that homosexuality was a perversion.)

Never one to understate his own genius, Hubbard proclaimed that his knowledge of life had surpassed that of everyone else in history. His certainty was (and still is) a mantle assumed by his followers, who believe that by studying his works and words, they too have the only true answers to every problem faced by anyone, anywhere, ever.

So, really, my life was preordained into scientology. Though I attended Burnside Primary School like all the other kids in our neighborhood, during school holidays starting when I was six, my mother would drop me off at the local scientology center (scientology calls these "organizations" or "orgs") in an old two-story office building near Adelaide's city center. It was an unimpressive facility with no outward indication that anything unusual occupied its linoleum-covered second floor, sparsely decorated with simple wooden tables and chairs and little else, other than the obligatory portraits of L. Ron Hubbard hanging on the walls.

The org was headed by two brothers, Jim and Wal Wilkinson, who had studied at scientology's "international headquarters" with Hubbard, who at this point had amassed a small fortune and bought a sprawling country estate near East Grinstead in the south of England. The Wilkinson brothers each had four sons, who, along with me; my younger brother, Andrew; my sister, Judith; and children from several other scientology families were the "scientology kids" in Adelaide. It was a small community, but like scientologists everywhere, we regularly attended study and counseling sessions (called "auditing") and were expected to participate in the routine events designed to keep the flock engaged.

During those school holidays my siblings and I—unlike our school counterparts who slept in and watched cartoons—were sent to do the Children's Communication Course. This was an introductory class designed to give new followers communication skills to improve their relationships, ability to sell, or whatever else they desired; adults took a similar course. Hubbard stressed that the way to get new people into scientology is to find their "ruin"—whether that be insecurities, anger management problems, or self-esteem issues—and tell them with absolute certainty that scientology can help them. The course was sold as a panacea for every problem anyone had, in order to get them in the door and participating, at which point other miracles of Hubbard's "technology" would be revealed.

Part of the Communication Course was a drill known as "bullbaiting." Its purpose was to help scientology counselors, called auditors, control their reactions to anything that came their way in counseling sessions, and also get rid of any impulse to flinch from attempted intimidation in life more broadly. Kids participated in these drill sessions too. We would do our best to get another person to react—laugh, crack a smile, something. If they did, it was considered a "flunk" and the session would continue until the person had no reaction at all. For us, it was an opportunity to swear, tell jokes, and act a little crazy with the full approval of the supervising adults. Each session was the same: We'd pair up, one "coach" and one student, both sitting upright in stiff wooden chairs facing each other, knees about a foot apart, looking into each other's eyes. The coach would start the session, then we were off to the races. Here is a typical play-by-play:

"Start."

"Your mom told me you wet your bed every night."

"Ha ha!"

"Flunk. You laughed."

"Start."

"Your mom told me you wet your bed every night."

A muffled laugh.

"Flunk. You laughed."

"Start."

"Your mom told me you wet your bed every night."

[Stone-cold, staring silence.]

Success.

Sometimes this would go on for what seemed like an eternity, until "the button was flat," meaning the student no longer reacted in any way to the provocation of the coach. Bullbaiting was something we all looked forward to dishing out, though not so much to being on the receiving end. This provocation, I now see, helped habituate us to verbal and even physical abuse, which is not a healthy lesson for anyone, let alone children.

My entire life became centered around the thinking of scientology, translated and passed on to me by my parents. The more scientology materials they read, the more time they spent in the org, and the more familiar they became with Hubbard's views, the more those ideas permeated into me. Like most young children whose parents are their guideposts, I never gave what they said a second thought or questioned its validity.

One of the things they taught me early on was the Contact Assist to heal bumps and injuries. It seemed very strange the first time my mother tried it on me. When I was about eight, I injured my hand on a stove burner. It was throbbing in pain, and my mother asked to see where exactly it hurt. Then she said, "Okay, so we're going to put your hand back where you burned it."

At first, I resisted. No way was I going to put my hand back on that burner, even though by then it had cooled. After much cajoling, I placed my hand very gingerly back on the burner, but quickly removed it out of fear. "Again," she said. This time I placed it back on the burner, giving it some more time before swiping it away. I did it again and again, until I didn't have any reaction. I experienced some relief and the pain in my hand had subsided—though perhaps only because my heart rate had settled back down after overcoming my initial fear. It seemed to be something that "produced results," which is the measuring stick often used in scientology, though the efficacy is almost entirely subjective. "Do you *feel* better?" is the question asked.

Another technique was the Touch Assist. This was Hubbard's version of the biblical laying on of hands, based on his theories about being "in communication" with your body. The spirit (or "thetan") is superior to the mind and body and has control over them. But unless the thetan addresses the body, it cannot heal it—being "in communication" is Hubbardese for "addressing." The same year that I burned my hand, I fell off my bicycle. I came home crying and my mother tried this technique on me. She had me lie down on my bed and stay still as she touched me continuously with her finger up and down my body, repeating, "Feel my finger." I never felt its power, but I wanted to believe it was helping and didn't want to disappoint my mother, so I went along and let her think it worked in making me feel better. Pretty soon I had convinced myself these methods produced small miracles.

Even more important was the theory of "overts and withholds" (O/Ws). If something bad happened to me, I must have done something bad first (an "overt"), and keeping a secret about such a discreditable action or thought (a "withhold") would cause me to be unhappy. This is a bedrock principle that, it turns out, has many practical benefits for scientology, though not so many for its followers. My parents explained the idea in simple terms—"Clean hands make a happy life"—and I agreed it made sense. Like so much in scientology, Hubbard took a widely universal platitude and bastardized it so much that it ended up bearing little or no resemblance to its original meaning.

In Hubbard's world, O/Ws are the *sole* reason for all bad conditions and experiences, which is both very convenient and very powerful. When life takes a turn for the worse or one begins to doubt or question Hubbard or scientology, the answer lies in uncovering *your* O/Ws. I started to believe I needed to be what scientology considered "responsible" and not blame others for my misfortunes. I needed to find out what *I* had done to cause whatever bad thing happened to me—in scientology-speak, to "pull it in." As a child, I would confess to being mean to a girl at school or playing with the neighbors at the "dump"— a vacant lot nearby that was off-limits because my mother thought it was dangerous. The nature of the O/W was not really important at that time, only that I felt guilt.

Like all good scientologists, my parents came to believe that the answers to all questions in life were to be found in the words of Ron. In fact, things were often explained to me in those terms: "Ron says . . ." and "What would Ron do?" Hubbard took on the mantle of a mortal god in my eyes; his words answered and explained everything. Soon, I too would wonder how Ron would deal with things I confronted in life.

We were in the tiny minority, though: The mid-1960s saw a backlash against scientology in Australia, so much so that it was outlawed in the state of Victoria in 1965 following a government inquiry that outlined the dangers of the self-proclaimed religion and its aggressive practices. The 175-page report pulled no punches; the bottom-line statement was that "Scientology is a delusional belief system, based on fiction and fallacies and propagated by falsehood and deception."

At this time, being known as a scientologist in Australia was tantamount to announcing yourself a witch. So we kept our involvement secret, and my parents' scientology materials and books were stashed in their bedroom closet. The Wilkinsons' home had been raided by the police, who were looking for "subversive materials," and so the local scientologists got into the habit of hiding their Hubbard books. The crackdown created a sense of fear of the government that I hadn't felt before—we had to hide who we were, what we did, what we believed. Hubbard claimed the Victoria inquiry was a massive conspiracy by the medical and psychiatric establishment to destroy scientology. And my parents told me that this assault was the result of people being resistant to new ideas, much like Galileo's claim that Earth circled the sun had been considered heresy by the Catholic Church. It made sense to me at the time and was the first inkling I got of the idea that scientology was in a valiant battle to save the world from its own ignorance. It gave the whole movement an us-versus-them mentality—the enlightened against the unenlightened, good versus evil—which only amplified everyone's resolve.

Though this ideology took hold inside our home, to the outside world I appeared almost boringly normal for a middle-class Australian kid in the 1960s. I had an active boyhood and the scabs and scars to prove it. I'd ride my homemade skateboard (built with a piece of wood from a jarrah tree with roller-skate wheels screwed onto it) on the road in front of our house, often falling and scraping my hands and knees.

Like a typical Aussie family, we went to the beach in Adelaide or south to Port Noarlunga in the summertime and took camping road trips to the Flinders Ranges, two hundred miles north of Adelaide.

In 1966, when I was eleven, we relocated to Sydney. My father was always looking for a new way to make money, mostly to support the scientology habit, as the further you advance in scientology, the more expensive the courses and auditing become. He turned a profit from a range of ventures, at various times owning restaurants, an Angora goat farm, a travel agency, and a wholesale grocery business, and from investing in real estate. In Sydney, his new job was managing an aerosol manufacturing plant—cans of hair spray and the like.

I quickly fell in love with Sydney, a bustling cultural city with a magnificent harbor and beaches, which was quite different from sleepy old Adelaide. I attended the exclusive Barker College in the class of Mr. Morris, a brilliant if somewhat eccentric fellow famous for winning *Pick-a-Box*, a game show that had a huge following in Australia. I rode the train to and from school, which was an exciting and different daily adventure, since I had walked to school in Adelaide. I joined dozens of other boys on the train platform each day in their Barker College uniform—gray suit, white shirt, red-and-blue tie, shined black shoes, and a straw boater hat. (Australia in general and its private schools in particular emulate life in Great Britain in many respects, and the boys of Barker College could have been transplanted en masse to Eton in England and not missed a step.)

After less than a year, in 1967, my father had saved enough money to take us to England so my parents could advance in scientology at the Hubbard estate outside East Grinstead. This was finally a real-world payoff for our involvement—up until then, scientology had been a secret way of life at home. This trip across the world was an adventure of a lifetime.

We sailed on an Italian cruise ship from Sydney Harbour alongside the still-under-construction Opera House, via Hong Kong, Singapore, and Aden, through the Suez Canal (shortly before it was closed by the Six-Day War in June) to Italy. We crossed Switzerland and France by train to Paris and then went on to London. It was my first taste of world travel, and I was fascinated by the throngs of people and exotic smells and food of the Far East; the Arab traders selling hand-beaten Nefertiti and Sphinx souvenirs in Egypt; the stunning, grandiose beauty of the Italian Alps; the architecture of Paris; and finally England, where, strangely, I immediately felt at home.

We proceeded to Haywards Heath, a town about forty miles from London and ten miles south of East Grinstead, where we would stay for the next eight months or so. As I was now twelve, I attended secondary school at Haywards Heath Grammar School. I donned a proper riding hat and jacket and took horse-riding lessons in the English countryside. There was such a difference from Australia: here I was surrounded by the stunning greenness of southern England's countryside and its magnificent shades of emerald, lime, and sage—a stark contrast to my country's dry and brown summertime landscape.

Shortly after we settled in, I got a chance to visit Saint Hill, Hubbard's home and the international headquarters of scientology. The estate encompassed a beautiful eighteenth-century sandstone manor house with various other buildings on sixty acres of rolling countryside. My parents went to the course room to attend their studies, while my brother, my sister, and I went off to the canteen—an old shed converted into a general store, coffee shop, and hangout for the students. As we walked in, I noticed two kids playing darts. They turned out to be Suzette and Arthur Hubbard, the two youngest Hubbard children. Suzette was my age, and three years older than Arthur. She had striking red wavy hair like her mother, Mary Sue. She was extroverted, while Arthur was quieter but somewhat cheeky. They were treated like royalty in the scientology world, so they pretty much did and said what they wanted.

Suzette must have noticed my brother and me watching them, because she eventually turned around and said, "Do you want to play a game? You're going to lose, but I'll let you play."

Though I was a good scientologist by this time, I didn't take any competition for granted and couldn't refuse the challenge.

"Sure," I responded with a nod as I picked up my set of darts.

I forget who won, but I remember how sassy Suzette was and that she was just as competitive as I was.

When we returned to Australia, we settled back in Adelaide, where my father began a wholesale grocery distribution business. We moved into what I consider my second childhood home, about a mile from the Cape Cod house on Victoria Terrace of my early years. This was in a more established neighborhood, no kangaroos or emus, though there was a huge gum tree in the middle of the road next to our house. It was so big and majestic that someone in years past had decided to build the road around it instead of destroying it. I attended another private all-boys school, King's College, two miles down the sloping foothills toward the city center.

It was an odd life in many respects. I lived a secret existence as a scientologist while attending an exclusive school where I acted like I was just the same as everyone else. Each morning we gathered in the school chapel to sing hymns and recite the Lord's Prayer. I don't know what the other boys were thinking as they sat in the pews, but I thought it was weird to be talking to and singing at a God who was supposed to be all-knowing and all-seeing. *If he is the creator of all, then why does he need us to say anything out loud to him or ask him for things?* But I maintained the appearance of a happy chapel-goer because I didn't want anyone to know that I was most definitely not a Christian believer.

Outside of school, my life seemed pretty normal. I did a lot of teenager stuff: went surfing, rode bikes, played football in the nearby park, went to dances and concerts, and met girls. Much of this I did with my best friend, Tom Pryor, who happened to be my next-door neighbor. Tom was the only person outside of the scientology bubble who knew my family's secret—I never spoke of it to my school friends. He didn't mention our being scientologists to anyone; I suspect he didn't want the stigma of association with anything scientology. Though my life had this ordinary-looking social veneer, I actually believed that the wog world was a malevolent trap designed to enslave mankind. Tom knew none of this; he was given the shallow PR rendition of what scientology is that makes it sound benign and misunderstood. The early exposure to the real world I gained through those teenage activities helped me in the end to escape scientology.

*   *   *

IN THE SECOND half of 1969, our family made a second trip by ship, this time across the Pacific and through the Panama Canal to England so my parents could do their OT levels to become Operating Thetans. The OT levels were the greatest accomplishment in the history of this or any other universe, according to Hubbard. He had discovered and overcome what he called the "Wall of Fire"—a secret, cataclysmic incident that had occurred seventy-five million years ago that had trapped every being on Earth in a dwindling spiral of pain and unhappiness—and had charted a path of exact, and expensive, steps that anyone could take to become an OT. OTs would have the powers and abilities promised in Hubbard's *Dianetics*—"cause over matter, energy, space, time and thought." We found a house to rent in Crowborough, another town in the East Sussex countryside, about ten miles southeast of East Grinstead.

Hubbard himself wasn't in England at the time. To accommodate the growing number of scientologists traveling to Saint Hill, he had built a replica of a Norman castle on the grounds in 1968 as a means of circumventing the local planning committee's refusal to approve building permits (apparently a man had the right to construct a castle on his own land). But the British government and press were hounding him, and from 1966 on, he mostly stayed away from England.

Despite Hubbard's troubles, the movement was flourishing in late 1969 with more followers than ever, particularly in England. They came from all over the world to be at Saint Hill, to be all in one place doing the same thing. It felt like a little world unto itself.

While my parents studied at Saint Hill, I attended Beacon Grammar School in the small town of Crowborough. Most of the kids had never met anyone from the Southern Hemisphere and so I became a minor celebrity with my Australian accent; they were entirely unaware of the nearby scientology headquarters or my involvement with it. A new school friend introduced me to many aspects of British life, including catching the train to London to attend Chelsea football matches at Stamford Bridge. I had never been to a live sporting event with such a huge, raucous crowd—and I loved every minute of it. Even getting to the stadium in West London was an adventure for me, having never traveled on the Tube before.

Once my parents completed their OT levels, which took the better part of a year, we moved back to Australia, to Leabrook, a suburb of Adelaide, where I returned to King's College. I was fifteen now, and as any good Aussie child does, I played football (Australian Rules football—a unique game played in the southern states of Australia, different from rugby or soccer) in the winter and cricket and tennis in the summer. I was no standout at any of them, but I enjoyed them, and was also pretty active swimming, skateboarding, surfing, and riding my bike when not in school or playing team sports. A benefit to attending a private school was the "boarders"—sons of farmers from the country who lived at the school during the term and returned home for holidays, often bringing along with them a "day boy" from the city like me to experience farm life. One September, I took a 250-mile bus trip with my friend Stanley from Adelaide to Mildura. His father picked us up and drove us another 90 miles due north on a dirt road to his home. Large properties that raise sheep or cattle are called "stations" in Australia. His was 130,000 acres for 40,000 sheep. The nearest living person to the homestead was about 30 miles away. We had to make a wood fire to heat water in the boiler to take a hot bath. The kitchen had a woodburning stove, though there was electricity. I loved every minute of my two weeks there. I learned to drive in an old Land Rover with no roof or windshield; there was nothing to run into except an occasional tree. I learned how to care for the sheep and shoot their predators. The peace of being in this quiet place, the brilliance of the stars at night with no other sources of light, the smell of the land and the camaraderie among the hardy folks that populated that remote outpost are memories that remain vivid today. The experience exposed me to so many different perspectives on life, and to people who were happy and fulfilled *without* scientology. Those memories remained in a deep recess of my consciousness for the rest of my life, even as I continued to live in the mind prison of scientology.

CHAPTER 2

JOINING THE SEA ORG

When I was seventeen, I was awarded a full scholarship to the University of Adelaide, but my future was preordained and it did not include college.

My parents had first told me about the Sea Organization (Sea Org) during our second trip to England. It was described to me as the elite corps of scientologists who lived and worked full-time with Hubbard aboard his ships in exchange for free auditing and advanced training. A couple of years earlier, a Sea Org "officer," Delwyn Sanderson, had come to Adelaide and made quite an impression on me. She was a commanding presence in her naval-style Sea Org uniform of dark blue jacket with two rows of gold buttons, white shirt, and black tie, and was treated almost with reverence by the local scientologists. Only a tiny percentage of the best and most devoted scientologists were part of the Sea Org, and children raised in scientology were perfect candidates. It was almost a foregone conclusion that their parents would proudly wave goodbye as they signed their contract to commit themselves to achieving the "Aims of Scientology" for eternity and headed off to become a part of the chosen few. The appeal of this idea was reinforced by Hubbard's very low opinion of formal education; he derided it as inferior and a waste of time. I knew I should devote my energies to studying scientology instead, as it provided a total understanding that transcended all non-scientology learning. There was nothing more important.

In early 1973, soon after I completed high school, two Sea Org members, John Parselle and Steve Stevens, came to our house. Without much ado, I signed my billion-year Sea Org contract at our kitchen table. That is billion with a "B."

L. Ron Hubbard had created the Sea Org in 1967, with uniforms and nomenclature drawn from his military service. Though his career in the US Navy during World War II had been less than illustrious, he painted the picture for all who would listen of himself as a ship captain and war hero. He viewed the Sea Org as his private navy, and claimed he created it to give him a safe place where he could continue his OT research in order to save mankind. The truth was that the Victoria inquiry in Australia had been a catalyst for renewed scrutiny by the US and UK governments, as well as by the media, in the mid-'60s. Seeing the storm clouds gathering, he had first left England in March 1966 for Rhodesia (now Zimbabwe), declaring that he was going to turn an entire country into a "safe base" for scientology.

Rhodesia may seem a strange choice, but Hubbard had his reasons. First and foremost, he believed he had been British imperialist Cecil Rhodes (after whom the country was named) in a previous life, and he was going to return to claim his rightful kingdom. (Hubbard did not announce this past life to those outside his inner circle, likely because Rhodes was a racist and often seen as the father of apartheid.) He also believed that the new government there, which had recently broken ties with Britain, would be sympathetic to his own problems with the establishment.

After a few months, not only had Hubbard failed to establish a safe base but he was denied a renewed visa to remain in the country. He attributed his fiasco to "suppressive influences" working against him— that is, those who wouldn't acquiesce to his way of thinking and were bent on his destruction, and thus the destruction of all mankind. He also asserted it was because he was "all alone" and "OTs do best with other OTs." He returned to England in mid-July 1966, claiming that he had made huge new advances in his research to save the world. Such was his power over scientologists; they stood cheering along the lengthy driveway of Saint Hill as he rode in triumphantly, waving from the back of a convertible like some returning Roman emperor. It was all a show. Hubbard was aware of the growing problems in England, where the government was working to deny him a visa extension to force him out of the country.

His days were numbered in England. He needed a new plan to escape government control and scrutiny. The best place to do that was in international waters. So, in 1967, he first bought an old fishing trawler, the *Avon River*, which he renamed *Athena*; then a ketch, *Enchanter*, renamed *Diana*; and finally a third ship, a larger former ferry called the *Royal Scotsman*, renamed *Apollo* and nicknamed Flag for flagship, on which Hubbard lived. Hubbard assumed the title of Commodore as the leader of his ragtag flotilla, and the Sea Org was officially founded on August 12, 1967.

In the Hubbard worldview, this new endeavor would be the means to accomplish the goal of creating a "cleared planet" to break the endless cycle of life and death and the "dwindling spiral" of mankind toward an infinity of darkness and pain. This task of saving humanity was a matter of enormous urgency. According to Hubbard in one of his most famous and often-repeated statements in scientology, "the whole agonized future of this planet, every Man, Woman and Child on it, and your own destiny for the next endless trillions of years depend on what you do here and now with and in Scientology. This is a deadly serious activity. And if we miss getting out of the trap now, we may never again have another chance. Remember, this is our first chance to do so in all the endless trillions of years of the past."

The Sea Org was the guarantee that we would all get out of the trap.

Hubbard, a master of manipulation, quickly made the Sea Org something that his followers would hold in almost mystical awe, and made sure scientologists knew he wanted the most dedicated to commit themselves to this prized group, often advertising in scientology magazines to recruit for it. One such advertisement in *The Auditor* magazine read:

> To join the Sea Org is the sensible thing to do. There is very little that could be more important to you than to add to this Power. If almost any person in the Sea Organization were to appear in a Scientology group or Org he would be lionized, red-carpeted and Very-Important-Person'ed beyond belief. For the Sea Org is composed of the "aristocracy" of Scientology.

> I pledged myself to an eternity in service of achieving Hubbard's aims, devoted to assisting him, in cooperation with the other Sea Org members, with the enormous and important job at hand.

WHEN I SIGNED on for the Sea Org in Adelaide in 1973, the recruiter promised I would train as a scientology executive under the direct tutelage of Hubbard on the *Apollo*. I was also told that after I learned all I needed to learn at the foot of the master, I would return to Australia to help expand scientology in my home country.

By that time, the Sea Org had extended into land-based outposts that gave us a presence in each part of the scientology world—New York, Los Angeles, and Toronto for North America; Saint Hill for the UK; Copenhagen for Europe; Johannesburg for South Africa; and Sydney for Australia, New Zealand, and Oceania (ANZO). So in mid-1973 I traveled from Sydney's Sea Org headquarters back to Saint Hill in England as the staging area before proceeding to the *Apollo*. There, I was required to undergo "security checks" by a "sec checker" on an E-Meter, the lie-detector-type instrument used in one-on-one auditing sessions. The meter is an integral part of scientology and is believed to measure thought. The person being audited holds on to two metal cans connected to the E-Meter, allowing a small current to pass through the body. The auditor watches the meter, noting what registers and using the results as a guide for questioning—Hubbard delineated how the reactions appearing on the E-Meter signified what was happening in the mind of the person being audited. This procedure was intended to ensure I was not a "security threat" or a reporter or a CIA agent seeking to infiltrate Hubbard's floating international headquarters. My sec checker was Denise Miscavige, who was doing scientology training at Saint Hill; she and her twin brother, David, were considered prodigies, engaged in advanced auditor training at age thirteen.

Deemed safe, I was ready to set off for the flagship *Apollo*. There was such secrecy surrounding where Hubbard was located that even as the "Flag liaison," a redheaded South African named Alan Voss, drove me to Heathrow Airport, I did not know my ultimate destination. Only at check-in was I finally told my flight was bound for Lisbon. My instructions were precise and exact. Questions didn't seem appropriate or wanted: "Chuck Adams will meet you when you arrive. Tell customs and immigration you are in transit to the *Apollo*." I had no idea who Chuck Adams was, or how I was supposed to recognize him, but I figured it would all be okay; after all, I was now operating as a member of the most accomplished, effective, and advanced organization on earth.

In the end, I didn't need any secret code or signal to meet up with Chuck. I was hard to miss. I arrived midafternoon through customs with twenty large brown boxes and one small blue suitcase. The boxes contained communications and reports from scientology outposts around the world, along with various supplies I was couriering to Flag. We loaded everything into the trunk, front seat, roof rack, and every other possible crevice of a waiting cab and proceeded to the dock on a typically sunny day in Lisbon.

As our cab drove through the Port of Lisbon's gates, I caught my first glimpse of the *Apollo*. She was not nearly as big as I had expected. I had seen photos of her, always taken from a low angle to make her look more impressive and imposing. My seafaring experience until then had been limited to the cruise liners on which we had sailed from Australia to Italy. Those were my idea of a ship; the *Apollo* was a utilitarian 1930s-era passenger and cattle ferry one-tenth their size.

The cab came to a stop. I got out nervously and was told to wait to be brought on board. I looked up and saw a couple of dozen people smoking cigarettes, leaning over the rail of the quarterdeck, peering down at me as the object of much curiosity.

I thought, *This is the first day of the rest of my life.* But it was more than just *this* life: this was a billion-year contract.

Many of the denizens of the quarterdeck who looked down as I stood on the dock were teenagers like me—including the Commodore's Messengers. These were the dozen or so, mostly American, girls (and a couple of boys) who ran messages for Hubbard so he didn't have to leave his office on the promenade deck. They were pretty, smart-mouthed, and dangerous to mess with.

Every scientologist believed Flag embodied the full application of the highest principles of scientology. It was home to L. Ron Hubbard, and his wisdom was the source of hope for all mankind and contained the technology to build a better world. Sanity surely reigned supreme in a sheltered and isolated environment headed by the wisest, sanest man on earth, populated by the elite of scientology. What could be better?

Frankly, almost anything.

I came aboard and saw the ship's interior, up close. The two upper decks, the promenade and A deck, consisted of small cabins decorated with knobby wood paneling and dark, worn linoleum floors (the open rear section of A deck was the quarterdeck). These decks were where Hubbard, his family, and his immediate staff lived and worked. Beneath the upper decks was B deck, containing the cramped galley and the dining room. Designed to feed fifty, it had to serve nearly three hundred crew four meals a day. ("Meals" was a polite word to describe the scrawny chicken, mystery meat, soggy vegetables, and watery soup that passed as food.) Below this were the tween decks—originally designed to carry the ferry's cattle and livestock, and now converted to a large open office space where the vast majority of the *Apollo* crew worked.

On the lowest deck, at the very aft of the ship, was where I was shown to my berthing. (Unsurprisingly, there is lots of nautical terminology in the Sea Org—"berthing" is where you sleep, the "head" is the bathroom, the floor is the "deck," walls are "bulkheads"; many more terms and acronyms are specialized to the Sea Org.) I had been led down a steep stairwell at the stern—at the bottom were two doors. The one on the right was the entrance to my new home, the Men's Dorm. On the left was the Women's Dorm.

Walking into the Men's Dorm was an onslaught to the senses: the overpowering odor of sweaty bodies and dirty clothes filled the pitch-dark, airless room. There was no porthole, view, or even a light. There was no air-conditioning. My room at home seemed like a prince's palace, a vision from a past life I wished I could teleport back to.

Guided by a flashlight, the "berthing in charge" suggested I hold on to the back of his shirt and follow him closely. As I looked around, I faintly made out a room about thirty feet wide and sixty feet long with several rows of triple-stacked bunks. With a ceiling height of six and a half feet at the most, the space crammed in about fifty men. My bed, sandwiched in the middle of a triple bunk, was at the very end of the room. Because the *Apollo* operated on both day and night shifts, there were always people sleeping, and thus, no lights. There were also no closets in the Men's Dorm, so people hung their dirty clothes on hooks next to their beds. Nor were there laundry facilities other than buckets to wash your clothes in saltwater (and then give a final rinse in precious fresh water). I felt like I had arrived in the Black Hole of Calcutta.

The showers were no better: Thirty seconds was all we could get, as there were only three or four showers available on the ship and always a line of men standing waiting for their turn. Fresh water was extremely limited, and it was not hot, so I couldn't bear much longer than thirty seconds anyway. I managed to be as efficient with my time as possible, following Hubbard's written directives on how to take the quickest shower: turn on the water to get wet; turn it off to soap up; turn it back on to rinse off.

I managed to get to bed that first evening, but I had to get out of the bunk to turn over, since my hips were too wide to roll over without hitting the metal frame of the bunk above. As I lay there struggling to breathe that night, I thought, *What the hell have I gotten myself into?* I also wondered what my parents would think. But I knew I had to maintain a "good roads, fair weather" veneer in my letters home, as saying anything even slightly negative about the world of Hubbard was forbidden in the bubble of scientology. They only ever heard that everything was great.

The old fable about the emperor having no clothes comes to mind, though in this case the emperor's clothes were in fact dirty rags everyone pretended were magnificent robes. It did not cross my mind at the time to wonder how it could be that none of the most competent executives on the planet thought the conditions we lived and worked in were incongruous with the concept of successfully guiding an organization to prosperity. The *Apollo* was considered the pinnacle of the use of what scientology touts as the most sophisticated and advanced "management technology" on earth.

The next day I went to see Maria Starkey, wife of Norman Starkey, captain of the *Apollo*. Maria was the Third Mate, in charge of the Hubbard Communications Office, which dealt with personnel. A South African with a short dark bob (which made her look strikingly like Barbara Feldon's character, Agent 99, on the '70s TV show *Get Smart*), she held herself in a distinctly *don't mess with me* posture and attitude. She curtly informed me in her clipped Afrikaner accent that my "post" (job) was to be a deckhand. This meant scrubbing the decks and chipping and painting over the rust on the outside of the ship—along with any other activity more senior people could not be expected to do, like loading food and supplies onto the ship when they were delivered to the dock.

"There must be some mistake—I thought I was here for executive training so I can return to Australia," I said as convincingly as I could. I was uncertain what this post meant for me and had a growing sense of dread that it was not going to be good.

She looked at me the same way a teacher might look at a kindergartner who had just used a bad swear word, slightly horrified but also bemused by my naivete. "Not anymore," she said. "You have been traded by ANZO." She added, "You are now Flag crew and will not be going back to Australia."

I was shocked. "What can I do about this?" I asked. Now the schoolteacher became annoyed by my impertinence. As a Sea Org officer in the top echelon of scientology, she was not to be questioned.

"Not a thing," she replied tartly. "You need to get to work. You are a Sea Org member and you perform whatever duty you are assigned." Her accent became even more pronounced as she spoke slowly and loudly as if to be sure I was not hard of hearing.

That was my first experience with promises made in the Sea Org that would not be kept, and the beginning of the systematic and intentional program of breaking down my critical thinking and eroding my free will. I started to feel confused and unsure of myself.

The reality was just as Maria had stated: There wasn't a thing I could do about it. The circumstances were beyond my control; I couldn't just walk off the ship. Despite the wealth of scientology, there was never money allocated to the crew. We weren't paid, other than a stipend of $17.20 a week and the honor of doing the good works of L. Ron Hubbard. There was a tiny amount made available for food for the crew, but not enough to provide one good meal a day per person, let alone three. Other things were always more important, like sending out promotional mailings to make more money for the organization.

Without money, I had no way to even get a cab to the airport, let alone a plane ticket. I didn't have my passport (I'd surrendered it to the Port Captain upon boarding the ship) and I didn't speak Portuguese. The internet and cell phones didn't exist yet. I was effectively a prisoner. As I lay awake in my tiny, smelly bunk and mulled over my new world, I tried to look at it from every angle. I feared being seen as a failure by the most important scientologists on earth and by my family; after all, everyone else in the Sea Org seemed to be doing okay. *Maybe I'm just weak? There must be things I don't know yet that everyone else does.* And finally, looming largest of all, the old scientology fallback for everything: *If I am unhappy or things are not going well, what overts and withholds do I have? What have I done to pull it in?* I convinced myself I just had to stick it out. This was my destiny, and if I wanted to be happy, I had to make myself happy despite whatever circumstances I was in, because I was, according to scientology, responsible for my own condition. And even if this wasn't what I'd been promised, at the end of the day all that mattered was that I was working with Ron to clear the planet.

Because I was with the Commodore, at the very highest level of scientology, life on the *Apollo* could not possibly be bad. This was the world of OT. This was the most important job on earth. That sort of hopeful thinking was psychologically protective in the short term, but it did not serve me well in the end. It kept me captive.

Concurrently resigned to my fate and reinvigorated by the Sea Org's mission, I got on with my day-to-day life as an *Apollo* deckhand. I wrote to my family back in Australia and told them I was staying to work with Ron—no details, just vague platitudes about how wonderful things were. I could not even hint at our location or the activities we were engaged in, not even that the weather was warm. My mother responded with news of the family at home and that they were all proud of what I was doing. No doubt my stature in the world of scientology was something they reveled in. Though I was a deckhand, I was still one of the elite, working directly with the Founder.

I settled into a routine of teaming up with my new friend Paul, a South African and fellow deckhand. Each morning by nine o'clock, the bosun (the officer in charge of equipment and the crew; in this case a bearded Dane named Peter Voegeding, who seemed to know a lot about boats and the ocean) would tell us our assignment. Most days, we would dutifully grab a wire brush, a can of paint, and a paintbrush from the bosun's locker in the prow of the ship and head out to scrape away at rust and paint from morning until night, when we were expected to go to the course room (the term used to describe where one studies scientology—distinct from a classroom, as there is no "instructor") and study the writings of L. Ron Hubbard. Sometimes there would be a different task, like caulking the teak deck with tar, or climbing over the side of the ship to re-paint where it had rubbed against the dock. Regular "stores parties" to carry supplies from the dock to the galley gave us plenty of exercise. We were allowed to go ashore once every two weeks for a day of "liberty" if our "stats were up" (meaning we had produced more than in the previous week—in the deckhands' case, measured in square feet of fresh paint). Back in those early times we actually had these biweekly liberties. Later they became rare and ultimately non-existent. On "libs" we would chip in to rent a hotel room and twenty or more of us would use it to take hot showers. The *Apollo* visited ports on the Atlantic coasts of Western Europe, so we enjoyed being outside in the fresh sea air, taking in the scenery when we could. Nobody paid us much attention and life settled down.

That is not to say life on board the *Apollo* ever became normal. Nothing was quite what it seemed, and there was an unseen menace and sense of danger at every turn. Take, for instance, the tween deck that housed the open-floor-plan "office" for the crew. It was really just a hodgepodge of secondhand desks, countertops, filing cabinets, and bookshelves. Everything in this makeshift office was tied to the bulkheads with whatever scavenged rope the desk residents could find to prevent it sliding around when at sea.

This was, I soon came to learn, an extremely dangerous way of doing things. In late 1973, Hubbard decided the *Apollo* should visit the Canary Islands, then make a trip back via Madeira to mainland Portugal, where we would spend Christmas that year. Departing the Canaries, the weather forecast was grim. A massive Atlantic storm was threatening, but we set off anyway, as the Sea Org is undaunted by anything. The *Apollo* hit the storm and was tossed around like a cork. It seemed as though we might capsize (I am sure there was little actual danger of this, though it sure felt that way), but things got real when I ventured into the tween decks. The system that had worked to keep the furniture steady in gently rolling sea swells did not hold up when it came to a storm that pitched the ship from side to side as if it were a toy. The ropes snapped, and as the ship tipped one way, the cabinets and desks slid and hit one side of the deck, and as the ship reared the other way, they all slid back to the other side. The force of a full filing cabinet smashing into a steel bulkhead sounded like a mortar round going off. Safety was ultimately found back in my bunk in the Men's Dorm, where everyone else had sought shelter, terribly seasick but out of harm's way. We eventually made it to Madeira, and I was never so happy to see an island come into view.

One might think that with the prison-like conditions endured by Sea Org members—the lack of a salary, the atrocious food, the unhealthy sleeping quarters, a dangerous working environment—there would be mutiny. But there was nothing of the kind. In the Sea Org, MEST (a Hubbard acronym for matter, energy, space, and time—or put another way, physical things, as opposed to spiritual ones) were considered relatively unimportant. "Purpose" was superior to everything, and the mission to save the world was the only thing that mattered. To Hubbard, the most successful groups in history were those that operated on purpose, like the Roman and later the French and British armies that had conquered the world. Hubbard pointed out that these great armies had been driven by purpose and had endured enormous deprivations. Sea Org members, with this in mind, were able to accept circumstances that a normal person would find intolerable. We "rose above" them and operated at a "higher level" beyond the wog concerns about comfort and personal possessions.

Our battle was to save all of mankind and this sector of the universe—so what did it really matter if we had no air-conditioning, ate only rice and beans, and slept four hours a night for weeks on end? It was a point of pride in the Sea Org to be tough and not complain about anything except someone else letting the team down and not doing their job. Another thing we certainly didn't complain about was the fact that Hubbard didn't personally submit to the life of hardship the rank-and-file Sea Org members lived. He had a chef who prepared meals, stewards to serve him, a large office, a real bedroom and bathroom (Mary Sue always had a separate bedroom, even at Saint Hill), and a dedicated "household unit" to do his cleaning and laundry.

Much of the control factor in scientology is based on peer pressure. The power of this method has been proven in studies where people go along with everyone else in making clearly erroneous decisions. Even in tasks as simple as picking which of two lines is longer, humans will invariably pick the shorter one if they observe that everyone else has done so. Being surrounded by dedicated, often fanatical scientologists created peer pressure that led me to believe I was part of an ethical group with a common purpose, nothing could be better than that, and any hardship they could take, I could too.

The other key contributing aspect of the pressure was the threat of punishment. It was well understood that if you didn't go along, you had better be prepared to pay the consequences. You were never, ever to challenge or question the teachings of L. Ron Hubbard or anyone higher on the chain of command than you. I learned this lesson early on when the ship's captain, Norman Starkey, either questioned or disobeyed something that Hubbard said and was summarily removed from his position. One moment he was at the right hand of Hubbard, the next he was scrubbing the decks. Nobody, no matter how high and mighty, had the right to question one's senior.

In January 1974, about five months after arriving, I was assigned a task nobody wanted: sitting every night from midnight to eight a.m. guarding a door behind which a ship electrician named Bruce Welch was in a full-blown psychotic episode. Hubbard claimed he was personally overseeing the matter as part of his ongoing research into ways of dealing with psychosis. He believed psychiatry was barbaric and had no solutions to man's problems, whereas he had all the answers, ones that would provide a solution for even the most deranged minds.

My job description was simple enough: I was in charge of making sure no one went in or made any noise to disrupt the patient, and that Bruce did not leave the cabin, no matter what. So for a few weeks I sat at the bottom of the stairs in the fo'c'sle, the forward deck of the ship where the anchor chains, paint supplies, and flammable items were stored, opposite the cabin that held Bruce. I was not sure how I was supposed to prevent him from escaping if he tried, as he was a large, beefy man who had previously torn apart the metal locker, bedframe, and mattress in the cabin with his bare hands and shoved the pieces out a tiny porthole. But I was told that was not for me to worry about— though I did constantly. The many ropes laced across the hallway tying his cabin door shut were a small comfort when it seemed Bruce was one yelling session away from ripping open the only barrier separating us. The only time anyone was allowed to undo the ropes was to bring him meals, and that would take the strength of three men, two to hold the ropes and one to carefully open the door enough to slide food in on the floor. Once the plate was inside, the door was slammed shut and the ropes secured again. Maintaining a silent environment was part of Hubbard's theory rooted in *Dianetics* of keeping the reactive mind from "restimulating" with words or environmental conditions, which could trigger earlier painful incidents that were causing the present psychosis. It seemed inhumane to not try to do anything to comfort someone clearly in such anguish, but I was certain the Commodore knew better than I what to do.

After a couple of weeks, Bruce calmed down and began auditing sessions. Eventually he was allowed out of the cabin and was sent home to the US. Hubbard announced to the world that his research (which was limited to this single guinea pig) had led him to discover the "cure" for psychosis and that the last reason for the existence of psychiatry on earth was now eliminated. He called this breakthrough the Introspection Rundown, and he detailed the steps to cure psychosis, the first of which is complete isolation of the person with nobody speaking within earshot.

Only eighteen and still naive in many respects, I was even more convinced by this episode with Bruce Welch that L. Ron Hubbard was intensively researching and solving the really ugly problems facing mankind, problems nobody else could tackle. To me, he truly was as close to a god as a man could be, and I was happy to be helping however I could with his wondrous new discoveries. I was eager to see what was next.

CHAPTER 3

THE *APOLLO* YEARS

In mid-February 1974, I went from scrubbing the decks and guarding the mentally unstable to a life of relative luxury as a driver for the team stationed in the tourist haven of Funchal, the capital of Madeira, a semitropical Portuguese island six hundred miles southwest of Lisbon. It was not due to any demonstration of competence that I was picked for this plum assignment: I was someone who was an "expendable," as the ship would still run fine with one less lowly deckhand. Hubbard's Personal Aide for Public Affairs, Kerry Gleeson, called me to his office and informed me to pack my clothes to move ashore.

I traded in my mop and paintbrush for a desk in an air-conditioned office, a regular bed in a small shared apartment with a kitchen, living room, balcony, bedroom, a real bathroom, and unlimited hot showers. I reveled in my new surroundings and soon had a favorite spot for my morning cup of coffee and pastry and discovered the best discos on Friday and Saturday nights. The crew of the "shore unit" (as we were known) were encouraged to "fit in" with the local population and try to be as "normal" as possible. The contrast in lifestyles could not have been starker, but the joy of the pleasures of a seemingly normal life would not last long.

Since its earliest days, the *Apollo* operated under a subterfuge Hubbard called a "shore story." Nobody in the local ports was supposed to know we were a scientology operation; rather, we went under the guise of an American business management consulting company called the Operation and Transport Corporation, or OTC. The nondescript name was intended to avoid drawing any suspicion from the wog world, and the acronym was also a play on words for us scientologists: "OT-C" for Operating Thetan Sea. Hubbard thought that keeping everything hush-hush would allow him to avoid the prying eyes of governments. Inevitably, though, the truth would be discovered, especially by the agencies that monitored Hubbard's travels. Host countries didn't take too kindly to being lied to, and providing false pretenses actually created more suspicion, because it raised questions. What were we hiding? What were we really doing? Were we smuggling drugs? Trafficking humans?

Such was the case in a number of ports that dotted the Mediterranean, and by the time I came aboard in 1973, the *Apollo* had already been thrown out of Corfu in Greece when officials got wind of the UK's and US's concerns about Hubbard's organization. She had also been escorted out of Morocco by its navy at the direct orders of the king, with whom Hubbard had sought to curry favor by peddling his security-checking technology (using the same E-Meter we used in auditing sessions), insisting it could ensure loyalty to the crown. An attempted coup d'état in 1972 made a mockery of the promises and the *Apollo* was ordered to leave the country immediately and never return. Hubbard fled to New York and lived incognito in Queens for a year until a safe base for the *Apollo* could be reestablished. That place was Portugal, and Hubbard had returned to the *Apollo* in September 1973, shortly before I arrived.

The new operation on Madeira was part of Hubbard's scheme to create what he called "safe points in society," which consisted of wooing government officials and dignitaries and providing what they "needed and wanted" so as to ultimately become indispensable to them, as he had tried to do with the king of Morocco. Had he delivered on his promise—discovering and rooting out those plotting the coup—the

Apollo crew would have been heroes and protected for as long as the royal family remained in power.

Madeira was a tourist hot spot for Europeans, with Brits, Germans, and Scandinavians flocking there for the beautiful weather, picturesque scenery, and relaxing seaside. Hubbard's scheme was to use his newly developed "survey tech" to provide the Portuguese government a plan to increase tourism revenues. A subsidiary company of OTC (which did actually exist as a corporate entity) was established, called Cindusta (an acronym from the Portuguese words for business consultants, *consultores industriais*).

I became part of Cindusta Madeira, a survey team that consisted of four multilingual women, who conducted the surveys, and two men—myself and Jim Dincalci. Jim had recently been deemed expendable, like me, but for a very different reason. Though not a doctor, Jim had been the *Apollo*'s Medical Liaison Officer (MLO), responsible for the well-being of the crew, including Hubbard. With Hubbard's dislike of the medical profession, the MLO was expected to deal with sickness while avoiding doctors as much as possible. So when, in December 1973, Hubbard was riding his Harley-Davidson on shore and got into an accident, Jim did his best to attend to him. Hubbard's pain—and the embarrassment of an accident when he proclaimed himself to be "cause over matter, energy, space, time and thought"—was taken out on those around him. Hubbard never believed his misfortunes were of his own making, despite his decree that this was true for everyone else. Jim was right in the line of fire for Hubbard's ire and was banished from the ship, put out of sight and mind.

Jim and I shared the apartment above a small rented office in Funchal, the main outpost of civilization on the island. We were right across from the high school, about half a mile from downtown, and about a mile from the quay where the *Apollo* was docked. The women lived in a separate apartment another half mile up the hill from us.

Jim was our cook and I was the driver, communications director, and receptionist, though I spoke virtually no Portuguese at first, and learned only a bit over time. The women—who were fluent in German, Dutch, English, French, and Spanish—set about doing the surveys. I coded and sent telexes to the *Apollo* each day reporting on our progress. Hubbard was a big fan of telex technology; he viewed it as the state-of-the-art upgrade from telegrams and had telex machines installed at Saint Hill in the 1960s to stay in touch with scientology organizations around the world. I also picked up mail from the airport that had been shipped from the liaison unit in Lisbon. Hubbard's wife, Mary Sue, had a red Mini estate wagon that was kept on the rear deck of the *Apollo*, but she rarely used it, so it was loaned to us, which was an indication of the importance of the survey project to Hubbard. The red Mini was the only one on the island and was well known by the locals as the *Apollo* car. It was another perk of my new assignment—I could go anywhere I wanted to—and though the car was not especially cool, it was definitely noticed wherever I went. By non–Sea Org measures, ours was a frugal life, yet compared to existence on board the *Apollo*, we lived like kings. The cost of food was very low and the exchange rate for US currency was excellent, so even the meager few dollars we were allocated went a long way.

This relatively idyllic existence would be short-lived. In April 1974, the Portuguese government was overthrown by the armed forces in a popular uprising sparked by long-festering and terribly unpopular wars in Portuguese Angola and Mozambique. Soon after the revolution, rumors began to spread that the *Apollo* was run by the CIA—by now a hated symbol of American imperialism in Portugal that had worked to keep the country's dictator in power. The ship had always attracted plenty of attention and gossip: a mysterious yacht with many good-looking young Americans who kept to themselves and, when asked, offered up an obviously fake story about being a management consulting company that nobody had ever heard of. There were enough oddities that the CIA rumor was believable.

To me, the idea of the *Apollo* having anything to do with the CIA was absurd. Hubbard hated the US government and its spies. It was as crazy as the other charges being whispered about the *Apollo*. Drugs were not tolerated in scientology and there were certainly none on the ship. And there were a lot of young, attractive female crew members, true, but we were the furthest thing from being engaged in trafficking or slave trade—after all, we were freeing mankind from the slavery of the reactive mind and the causes of human misery. These sorts of allegations and rumors only made me, along with everyone else in the Sea Org and in scientology as a whole, believe even more fervently that the world was in a sorry state and that what Hubbard said about governments and others trying to destroy us because we threatened their evil empires must be true.

Unfortunately, the lies of governments were met with lies from scientology. And our lies created an environment that fed the suspicion. Whispers grew, and graffiti with messages like APOLLO = CIA started popping up on walls around the ports where the ship docked. Local papers began publishing pieces based on the rumors, which only fueled Hubbard's hatred for the media.

Hubbard didn't want any trouble, so while the Cindusta team carried on with our surveys in Madeira, the *Apollo* left the mainland ports and sailed to the Canary Islands and then returned to Madeira on October 2, 1974. The idea was to be out of sight and out of mind for a few months and thus quell the CIA rumors.

Madeira is a tiny, isolated island without much for the locals to do. It was pretty common for fights to break out at the sidewalk cafes and bars that proliferated along the harbor front as the local "sport." The day after the *Apollo* docked, youths and men hanging out at the bars decided they were going to confront the imperialist lackeys tied up in their harbor.

Spoiling for a fight, they grabbed cobblestones and bricks and loaded the trunks of a small fleet of taxis, then headed for the ship. On the dock the crowd grew to about three hundred people, who chanted, "*Apollo* is CIA!" and pelted the *Apollo* with rocks. Alarmed, Hubbard called a "repel boarders" drill and had the crew begin to shower the crowd with firehoses. The angry mob retaliated by pushing a number of crew-owned motorcycles parked on the dock into the harbor. Mary Sue's red Mini, which had been driven to the ship by Jim and the other surveyors, met the same fate. The crowd began pulling the mooring lines off the bollards. Hubbard hurriedly ordered the engines started and the *Apollo* headed to the safety of anchor at sea.

At the time, I didn't know such an uproar was going on down at the harbor. I was, in fact, the only person from the shore unit who had not gone to the ship that evening. I had been put in charge of keeping an eye on things at the office in Funchal, oblivious to the revolt happening a mile away.

Around ten o'clock that night, our neighbor—a captain in the Portuguese army whom Jim and I had befriended—frantically banged at our apartment door. I opened it to his very animated announcement in broken English, "There's trouble at ship. I am going to find out and let you know. DO NOT leave apartment. DO NOT open door for anyone other than me. Be quiet, turn out all light, and draw blinds."

He left as quickly as he'd come, and I stood there in a state of confusion.

I had no idea what was going on, but I was sure this was not a prank. From what I knew of him, he was very nice and friendly, but not given to joking around.

I did as the captain instructed and stood at the door waiting for his return, thinking he had probably gone downstairs to make a phone call and would be back quickly. I peered out the peephole, which offered a narrow view of the entrance to Funchal harbor. I saw the *Apollo* steam by. *What the fuck is happening?* I asked myself. I was scared, confused, and my heart felt like it was exploding in my chest.

The captain was back at my door ten minutes later with an update. He explained about the mob. "It is not good. They pushed your red car into the harbor. People threw rocks at the ship. She sailed away. They are now coming here. Do NOT leave apartment for any reason. I will get some help. I try to get a helicopter to get you from the roof. Don't do anything, I will be back."

With that, he left again.

We had a bottle of Johnnie Walker whiskey in a cupboard. I grabbed it and began drinking straight from the bottle and chain-smoking Portuguese cigarettes. The alcohol had absolutely no impact; the adrenaline coursing through my system was overpowering whatever effect it might have had.

I couldn't see anything, but I began to hear chanting, faintly at first, gradually getting louder, and eventually becoming discernible as it grew close: "*Apollo* is CIA! Down with USA!"

Everyone in Funchal knew where the "*Apollo* office" was—two floors down from where I was sitting in the dark. I was stuck. I had nowhere to go. And I had no idea what to do other than try to be invisible.

Then I heard the rumbling of large trucks. I went over to the glass doors of the balcony that overlooked the square in front of the high school. As I peeked through the slats of the venetian blinds, I saw four army transports drive around the square and pull up in front of the building. About fifty armed soldiers jumped out and surrounded the structure in a cordon facing outward. My captain friend had come through with protection. I felt some comfort in knowing there were soldiers now stationed to keep the troublemakers at bay, but I was not entirely certain yet they were on my side.

The mob arrived, shouting and banging drums. And there they would stay for four hours, yelling, arms in the air, looking for blood.

I am not sure how I got through it, except to say the alcohol eventually helped calm my nerves. Around five a.m., the captain was back at my door, asking me to go down to our office. Some of the demonstrators were still there and had demanded entry to search the premises for evidence of CIA activities and weapons. I did what the captain asked of me and let them in; a dozen people from the mob rushed past me and systematically trashed the place. When they found nothing, the captain said I was free to leave, but he and his men had to return to military HQ and that the local Guarda Fiscal would replace them. He had a soldier summon a taxi to come pick me up, and I loaded a few things into the cab that I thought were most important.

Immediately after he left, the Guarda Fiscal claimed I did *not* have permission to leave, and the demonstrators hastily unloaded the taxi and sent it away. Luckily, *Apollo*'s Port Captain, Peter Warren, had been sent to retrieve me. We tried to plead, argue, and beg the officer in charge to allow us to go, but it was futile. The crowd had thinned out, and it was almost daylight by this time, still the officer seemed worried that if he let us go he might be seen as a CIA sympathizer. So there we stayed, unable to do anything for another hour or so, until around six a.m., when the captain returned. He scolded the Guarda Fiscal for disobeying his orders and reiterated that I had been granted permission to leave.

The captain's men escorted me in a taxi down to the pier.

The ship, which had anchored outside the harbor, sent a lifeboat. As soon as it came, I jumped in with the few things I had grabbed, mostly clothes, relieved to finally be off Portuguese soil. I was never happier to get back on board the *Apollo*, cramped quarters, crappy food, cold showers, and all.

The mob encounter made me more convinced than ever that the wog world was not a good place. Its comforts—a nice bed and a hot shower, coffee, pastries, and discos—did not make up for its darker forces. The abstract ideas of violence and the degradation of society had been replaced with up-close-and-personal experience. It reconfirmed everything Hubbard said about the decline of civilization. I was determined to work harder and longer and accept the living conditions on the *Apollo*. We had a planet to clear. And fast.

After that harrowing night in Madeira, which became jokingly known within the Sea Org as the Madeira Rock Festival, the shore unit was no more, and Portugal was added to the list of no-go countries in the Mediterranean. We loaded up on provisions and fuel, and Hubbard ordered the *Apollo* to cross the Atlantic, charting a course for Charleston, South Carolina. We were thrilled to be returning to a place where everyone spoke English and McDonald's and supermarkets were readily accessible.

With my survey job eliminated, I wasn't sure where I'd be placed next, but the former supervisor of the Madeira Shore Unit, Kerry Gleeson, had plans for me. Kerry was a native New Yorker who was charming, smart, driven, and a bit of a bad boy. His job had also become obsolete when we abandoned Madeira, so he was appointed Commanding Officer Flag Bureau, responsible for managing all the scientology operations internationally. In his late twenties (which seemed old to nineteen-year-old me), he was already an experienced hand at

navigating the world of scientology, and I was appointed his communicator, scientology lingo for a personal assistant.

This was my first experience in the higher echelons of scientology
management, though I had little actual responsibility other than to run
errands and help control the flow of communications from Kerry and
his staff on board to scientology organizations around the world. I was
now a vital cog in the organization's machine, no longer an expendable.

My life as a communicator followed a fairly standard routine. I
had a small desk right next to Kerry's and I was his gatekeeper. Anyone
who wanted to speak to him had to get my permission. Kerry would
shout, "Mike! I need coffee!" or "There's no paper here; how am I
supposed to do my job without paper?" or "Take this to the Treasury
Aide." I was all over the place, never a dull moment. This new position
gave me some authority, or at least the protection of Kerry's authority,
which was considerable. Only Hubbard's Messengers and aides were
senior to Kerry. While Hubbard ultimately ran the scientology empire,
he had created a hierarchy to carry out his orders. When it came to
expanding the scientology outposts around the world, that was the job
of the Flag Bureau (FB), which consisted of about 150 people. Because
of my proximity and gatekeeping role, members of the FB knew they
needed to be nice to me. It also meant I would interact with Hubbard's
inner circle.

When I had first arrived on the *Apollo*, Hubbard had been a presence in his office on the promenade deck, but as a deckhand I had no
reason to be in direct contact with him. He ate in his own private salon
with his family members—Mary Sue and their four children: Diana,
Quentin, Suzette, and Arthur (the latter two I had met playing darts at
Saint Hill). When he was in his office, nobody was allowed to walk on
the decks outside for fear of disturbing him from a moment of genius.
There was a palpable fear among the crew of ever doing anything that
might "piss the Old Man off." His Messengers were his eyes and ears all
over the ship—snitching, rephrased as "reporting," on others is inher-
ent to scientology culture. We were in fact required to write reports on
anyone who violated Hubbard's codes. If a person was found guilty and
punished whom you knew had been breaking rules but had failed to

report on, you got the same punishment they did. So while Hubbard rarely ventured from his upper deck, it seemed as though he was always watching, much like Big Brother in Orwell's *1984*.

One morning around four o'clock (with scientology organizations all over the world, we were a 24/7 operation), I was on my way to deliver a dispatch from the tween decks to the promenade deck. In a hurry, I darted up the red linoleum stairs and as I reached the landing at the top, I came face-to-face with Hubbard. The Commodore was holding court over members of his personal staff right outside his office. I stopped short, horrified at my lack of awareness and dumbfounded by being in his presence, as some of his staff gasped at my indecorous arrival. He, on the other hand, smiled, waved me on, and said, "Don't want to get in the way of a busy man." At once, I was relieved that this brief interaction passed successfully, bursting with pride knowing my parents would think this a great moment for our family, but also hit by a wave of fear that I would somehow prove inadequate.

We had been sailing across the Atlantic for about ten days, with a layover in Bermuda for fuel, water, and provisions, and were twenty miles off the coast of Charleston when we received an urgent radio message. The FBI and IRS knew of Hubbard's imminent arrival, and federal agents were waiting on the dock to board the *Apollo*. Hubbard ordered a 180-degree turn and we headed instead to Freeport, Bahamas, the closest non-US port. Freeport became the first of many Caribbean ports we would visit over the next year—from there we went to the Dominican Republic, Jamaica, Saint Lucia, Barbados, and Trinidad. Ultimately, a lot of time was spent in the Dutch island of Curaçao. While none of these countries were "friends" of Hubbard and scientology, the Dutch were at least neutral. So the "ABCs" (the Dutch protectorates of Aruba, Bonaire, and Curaçao) became favorites. They were also south of the usual track of hurricanes between June and October.

As we cruised the Caribbean, my work routine deepened. The Flag Bureau operated on a night shift, as a lot of our work involved communicating with scientology organizations around the world in various time zones, and unlike those who tended to the operations of the ship, we didn't need daylight to do our duties. Splitting the schedules also helped ease the load on the galley.

I had a circle of friends whom I had come to know through hanging out on the quarterdeck at mealtimes, smoking cigarettes and talking. Almost everyone on the *Apollo* smoked—it was the only permitted vice in the Sea Org other than alcohol for special parties, and Hubbard himself was a heavy smoker right up until his final days. Duty-free cigarettes were also cheap. Apart from the other Messengers, who were mostly about my age, my closest friend was Elizabeth "Bitty" Blythe, who worked in personnel. She was, and had been, on the *Apollo* since she was fourteen. Bitty was strong-willed and independent. I was infatuated with her, though she not so much with me. We had a short-lived period of chaste dating, until she decided she was more interested in Foster Tompkins, who had become my "minor's mate" (my legal guardian, as I was still under twenty-one) even though he was only three years older than me. Bitty, Foster, and I, along with Hubbard's daughter Suzette, all became close. Suzette joked that she was my mom and Foster was my dad, and she took to calling me "son," something I became accustomed to, as did everyone else.

Every two weeks, providing we were not in trouble, we had a day off. And as we were all over the Caribbean, I saw a lot of the islands, usually at a hotel by the pool and beach during the day (we didn't rent a room, just showed up and used the facilities and nobody ever took offense—things were more relaxed in the Caribbean). We would then go find a local discotheque and dance until four in the morning, when we would return aboard and collapse on our bunks.

During the time in the Caribbean, Hubbard devoted a great deal of effort to furthering his public relations technology (he designated everything he invented a "technology" in an attempt to give it gravitas, as if it were heavily researched and science-based). This work, in particular, laid out how to establish goodwill and "PR area control." Whenever Hubbard made a new "breakthrough," he would write a "policy letter" or a "bulletin" detailing his discovery. These were most often written longhand and sent down to the bowels of the ship, where a typist would type them up and run them through a mimeograph machine.

Copies would be sent out around the world as well as distributed to each crew member on board. Everyone had to stop what we were doing to read these missives at once, as they were considered the word of God being delivered from the mountain, and we were the fortunate ones to be first on the planet to be privy to his latest wisdom.

Part of his new PR control strategy involved photography. Hubbard had dabbled in photography earlier in life and while hiding out in New York in 1973 after fleeing Morocco, and thus claimed he was a professional photographer. So he passed time in the Caribbean shooting photo essays for scientology books and promotional flyers. Asserting that education levels were declining in society, he felt people needed pictures to get them to understand and accept scientology. Unfortunately, the photos were terribly amateurish. Sets consisted of some old plywood sheets nailed together to make "rooms" populated with bookshelves stocked with a few random books against backdrops of flat, monochrome paint. The models wore clothes scavenged from thrift shops, and the shots were taken in bright daylight with its harsh shadows. (I was fortunate never to have appeared in any of his photo shoots.) Of course, in the eyes of scientologists, they were hailed as photographic masterpieces. It was impolitic to find fault with anything Hubbard did. The emperor not only wore beautiful clothes, he took award-winning photographs as well.

Hubbard also turned his hand to composing and directing music. He formed a musical group from the crew on board—he dubbed them the Apollo Stars. Once again, based on his claimed experience (this time from past lives and space societies he had been part of), he researched and discovered "new breakthroughs" in music. He claimed these groups would take the world by storm and that by performing for free in local ports, the Apollo Stars would be welcomed everywhere with open arms. As absurd as this sounds to me now, I was a true believer at the time. North Koreans are told their Dear Leaders ride horses faster than anyone, hit holes-in-one eighteen times in each round of golf, and are always right. They buy it, because everyone else in the country buys it (or they are shot or sent to a prison camp). They know no other reality. We knew of no other reality than the mythology of Hubbard.

None of Hubbard's self-described discoveries or photography or musical talent resulted in a very welcoming attitude in the Caribbean nations, and soon we would find ourselves sailing away from ports on this side of the Atlantic too. At one point, the authorities in Curaçao claimed that because of a water shortage on the island they could provide no fresh water to the *Apollo*. The commercial cruise ships didn't have a problem, it seemed, only us. So thirty-second showers became no showers at all. Water was used only for cooking. This was only further proof that scientology was the victim of an international conspiracy. That scientology is unfairly persecuted is an article of faith among adherents. Hubbard expounded on it often through the years; he never forgot nor forgave. In fact, one of his edicts states: "People attack Scientology; I never forget it, always even the score."

Initially, the primary targets of his conspiracy theories were psychiatrists and the medical profession, because they had rejected *Dianetics* as quackery in 1950. But Hubbard saw threats everywhere, and he would eventually add the World Bank, the Rockefellers, the CIA, FBI, IRS, and most government agencies, along with the media, to his list of enemies. He believed there were internal enemies too, often those who worked most closely with him. He repeated over and over that there was a high-level conspiracy to keep mankind enslaved and that he and his dedicated followers were the only hope to save every man, woman, and child from a fate worse than death. He consistently wrote about "destroying" these enemies, relying on his purported experience as a skilled US Navy intelligence officer. (I would later learn that his "intelligence" experience consisted of a few months screening personal letters during a rather undistinguished time in the navy cipher department. This was like much of Hubbard's history—he was a master of embellishment and teller of tall tales to make himself seem important, experienced, or special.) He also expounded on a corollary: attacks on scientology are proof that it works and is succeeding magnificently; otherwise, why would the forces of evil bother? It is childish logic built on a faulty premise that scientology is doing good. But it sounded perfectly rational to me and every other scientologist I knew.

So important was our mission that failing to perform any duty was tantamount to letting mankind down. Such failures were, according to Hubbard, attributed to the reactive mind. Because not everyone had been cleared, the only way to control those terrible impulses was to provide enough external pressure and threat to keep the reactive mind at bay. That is the ethics and justice system of scientology, and its many punishments for straying from the path of righteousness were its primary tools of enforcement.

It was part of my job to mete out punishment to those who were not doing their jobs or had displeased Kerry in some way—from failing to complete an assignment on time to having "downstats," a term that is used a great deal in scientology to describe both the condition of less production and someone who is performing poorly. A favorite penalty was to send the perpetrators to climb the crow's nest. This was a small, partly enclosed platform high on the forward mast. The higher you are on a ship, the larger the arc of the ship rolling on the ocean swells. I had to make sure the guilty—commonly someone who failed to complete a task properly or quickly enough—who had been sentenced to thirty minutes or an hour in the crow's nest got there and stayed the required time.

The crow's nest as a punishment was mild stuff compared to being sent to the Rehabilitation Project Force (RPF). In early 1974, Hubbard had decided there were certain crew members who were incorrigible deadweights, holding him and everyone else down with their laziness and evil incompetence. He felt there was a need for a more severe program for those who had failed him, so he created the infamous RPF. Being assigned to the RPF was a terrible disgrace. It was for those who were downstats, "overt product makers" (those who messed up assignments), or those with "evil purposes" (bad intentions toward scientology or Hubbard). Like most things in scientology, there was a lot of wiggle room in the definitions, so assignment to the RPF was quite arbitrary. At the outset it was mainly restricted to those Hubbard designated, but soon it became a more widely used tool by Sea Org executives. RPFers were sent to the dark depths of the lower hold and were not allowed out until they had been rehabilitated. They slept, ate, worked, and studied

in this tiny, cramped space out of sight of any other crew, and were forbidden from communicating with anyone outside the RPF, including
their spouses. They had to wear black boilersuits, and somehow they
were supposed to "redeem" themselves by confessing their crimes and
evil intentions in order to rejoin the regular crew. Staying out of the
RPF became a primary objective of everyone on the *Apollo*.

As strict as Hubbard was, he did allow us to let our proverbial hair
down at times. Scientologists don't believe in Jesus Christ, so Christmas
was not a time for decorated trees, gift exchanges, and singing carols,
but still the world around scientology shut down over Christmas, so
every year by tradition on the *Apollo* it was time for a two-day reprieve
when everyone took hard-won time off and enjoyed the holiday season.
Hubbard would arrange for cases of spirits to be provided for the crew,
and the revelry began at six p.m. on Christmas Eve with the pirate-
themed Bosun's Party. From that time through Christmas Day and into
the afternoon of December 26, all activity on board was overtaken by
an alcohol-fueled party. Alcohol was not prevalent at other times of
the year—you could not get auditing or even do study if you had consumed alcohol within the previous twenty-four hours—but the rules
went out the window for these two days. The dining room became a
dance floor. A round-the-clock poker game with serious money changing hands (a few had funds outside their Sea Org allowance) was established in the aft lounge (not a lounge, in fact, but a small canteen that
sold cigarettes and coffee for a couple of hours a day). A lot of people
slept wherever they ended up and with whomever they ended up with.
It was the ultimate release of pent-up stress, long hours, seriousness of
purpose, and deprivation of comfort. For two days the world of scientology ceased to exist.

Outside the Christmas bacchanalia, entertainment on board was
limited. There were no TVs or radios. But many people had cassette
players, including Kerry. Elton John was a big favorite, and I learned
the words to every song from his first six albums verbatim—it seemed
there was an Elton John song playing throughout the tween decks
all the time.

Though there wasn't a TV, there was an old projector that was used to show Hubbard's filmed lectures to students, which led to an idea hatched between Foster, Suzette, and me. We could fly in rented movies from New York and show them to the crew. We mentioned our idea to Kerry, who immediately got behind the plan, demanding we rent his favorite movie, *Patton*. He thought it would be a great motivation for the crew to see what real toughness and determination looked like. We printed up some tickets on the mimeograph machine and began selling them for one dollar apiece for a showing of *Patton* on the aft well deck two weeks hence. We figured if we sold 150 tickets, we would have enough to rent the movie. Unfortunately, we had not anticipated that we would need a special lens to show *Patton*, as it had been shot in wide-screen format. We had neither the lens nor the money to buy one. We decided to show *The Thomas Crown Affair* instead, and sent courtesy tickets to Hubbard and Mary Sue, but when Hubbard caught wind about why *Patton* was not being screened, he gave us one hundred dollars for season tickets for himself and Mary Sue so we could buy the lens we needed.

After that, Friday movie nights became a weekly event, and Hubbard would sit in his seat of honor with his family front and center. It was the only time I ever saw the Commodore doing something with the entire crew where he was not barking out orders and everyone around him was not walking on eggshells. This gesture once again proved, in our eyes, what a great, kind, and generous man he was.

He was, however, not so healthy. While we were in Curaçao, in 1974, Hubbard had his first heart attack—although no one outside his innermost circle knew this at the time. Only a few trusted aides and Messengers were aware that he was even in the hospital. It would have shattered the world of scientology if the man who had cause over life and death, who had developed the technology to cure every imaginable ill of mankind, had suffered a debilitating heart attack. Given that he was chronically overweight and a two-pack-a-day (at least) smoker of unfiltered Kool cigarettes, it was hardly surprising. But in the world of scientology, Hubbard's spiritual enlightenment and belief that the spirit was senior to and controlled the body trumped everything, including the laws of physics and sound medical thinking. He even expounded on his theories one time with a now infamous statement that it wasn't smoking that caused lung cancer, it was not smoking *enough*.

At the time I knew nothing about this incident. Hubbard vanishing for days was not something I or anyone else dared question, but the heart attack had a significant fallout. Hubbard decided in 1975 that we had to get to the United States and covertly find a base there where we would transfer the functions performed aboard the *Apollo* to land. As far as the crew knew, this was being done because the ship was now just too small to accommodate the nearly three hundred people who lived and worked on it. It was so crowded that some slept in the lifeboats (which could be viewed as an improvement over the dark, dingy dorm rooms). In fact, it was so we could relocate to a place where good hospitals existed.

CHAPTER 4

WE COME ASHORE

When Hubbard decided to give up the sea for land in mid-1975, an operation akin to a World War II invasion was initiated. Hubbard covertly dispatched several teams of Sea Org members to scour the Eastern Seaboard of the United States, specifying that a suitable location for our new base must have a warm climate, an international airport, and facilities large enough to accommodate not only all the staff but also the scientology public who would visit for auditing and training services.

By the early '70s, scientology was at its peak of popularity, appealing to the counterculture as a trendy anti-establishment organization. A lot of the attraction was *because* governments and the media appeared to dislike it so much. There were now more than a hundred scientology organizations around the world, and each was taking in money from its paying customers who wanted to go up the Bridge—the sequential levels one must achieve to attain spiritual freedom. All scientology courses and services are paid in advance, in full, with discounts offered for buying large amounts of services at once—which are deducted from the total as they are taken, in the case of auditing as each hour is used. These services are expensive, ranging from hundreds to tens of thousands of dollars, which meant the organization was raking in hundreds of thousands of dollars every week.

Clearwater, Florida, seemed the perfect choice for the new location: the climate was warm, and the city's Fort Harrison Hotel was being sold at a fire-sale price, along with the nearby Bank of Clearwater building, which would house the administrative offices. Unfortunately, Tampa International Airport turned out to be international in name only—one or two flights a week to the Bahamas qualified it for that title—but that was only realized after the sale went through. However, there were plenty of flights from all over the US and connecting through New York and Miami from other parts of the world. Good enough.

Once Clearwater was decided on, plans were set in motion to move all three-hundred-plus people and functions from the *Apollo* to the new facilities. It required months of detailed preparation and precise execution, because it had to be done without alerting the US government and putting Hubbard at risk.

First, those who were not US citizens needed to get visas to enter the country. There were about a hundred of us, and if we all showed up at once at a US embassy asking for work visas, it would have rung alarm bells at the State Department. Not only was it unlikely they would have granted so many visas, it certainly would have tipped them off that Hubbard was planning to return to US soil. Secrecy about Hubbard was always of paramount importance, and he was to be protected at all costs. So we applied for tourist visas at a number of American embassies in the Caribbean, spread out over a few months.

Once we all had the stamps in our passports, we flew to different airports—Miami, Fort Lauderdale, West Palm Beach, and Daytona—in small groups so as not to attract the attention of US immigration officials. We were drilled beforehand on what to say if challenged: "I'm just taking a short vacation with friends to Florida." We also had return tickets to the Bahamas ready to show as evidence we would be leaving again. I was relieved when nary an eyebrow was raised by the guy who stamped my passport, who gave me a cheery "Welcome to the United States; enjoy your stay." All of us made it in without a hitch.

We met up with our US-citizen counterparts at a staging area in Daytona Beach. I assume the reason we met there rather than heading straight to Clearwater was to be sure everything was in order a few weeks before the final closing on the properties. Our temporary home in Daytona was a seaside motel called the Neptune Inn, a classic '60s two-story, pale yellow building that backed onto the wide, hard sand of the Atlantic shoreline. As we pulled into the parking lot, I thought, *We have landed on the beach*. Phase one of our D-Day had been accomplished.

Hubbard took up residence in a condo a few hundred yards down from the motel with a few Messengers and personal staff. He remained out of sight, fearing the attention of government agencies.

The Neptune Inn was no five-star hotel, but it was a big improvement from the tiny, hot, cramped spaces of the *Apollo*. We lived two to a room so as not to attract unnecessary attention with too many people crammed together. For the first time since Madeira, I slept on a real bed, had closet space to spare, and showered with endless hot water. There were even TVs, and radios tuned to Top 40 stations to replace the well-worn Elton John cassettes. Daytona Beach was a pleasant culture shock for us all. Stores like Sears and J. C. Penney and fast-food chains like McDonald's and Denny's were all easily accessible. We indulged ourselves on white bread, whole milk, orange juice, and bacon for breakfast, and chicken with meat on its bones and burgers for dinner. It was a whole new world. My impression of America was that bigger and more was always better.

Not that we had much time for watching TV or shopping. Everyone had been given special assignments for the transition to Clearwater. One group, including Kerry, had been sent to New York to run the international scientology network from a house in Queens near JFK airport. This was dubbed the Relay Office New York (RONY), as it had been the location where airfreight had been shipped to and from the *Apollo* in the Caribbean. The rest of us in Daytona were to prepare for the move and set up operations. My role was to establish the telex and other communication lines. For the first week, I drove daily to the Daytona International Speedway to send and receive telexes and pick up and deliver airfreight at the Daytona airport. I drove a gold Chevy Nova that was the height of luxury compared to the red Mini: air-conditioning, a radio, power windows, and way more than 50 horse-power. I loved driving back and forth every day listening to KC and the Sunshine Band and other pop hits, as well as hearing news of the world for the first time since I had left Australia.

I was only in Daytona for about a week before heading off to Clearwater to set up the telex and airfreight lines. I arrived at the old Fort Harrison as one of the last guests of the hotel in late November 1975, eating breakfast in its Lemon Tree Restaurant with a few die-hard elderly patrons and some even more elderly waitresses. The hotel had been a landmark and the center of social life in Clearwater for many years. Its demise had come with the advent of new hotels built on the beach, a mile across the Intracoastal Waterway. The downtown core, just half a block away, had become a sleepy, neglected small town whose heyday was decades in the past.

While the once-grand Fort Harrison was reduced to a shell of its former self, the excitement of the future burned bright in my imagina-tion. This was to become the international headquarters of scientology. No more old ferry boat; the *Apollo* sat abandoned with a skeleton crew in Freeport, awaiting a buyer. Now we had an eleven-story building with a swimming pool, an auditorium, elevators, and kitchens large enough to cook for the crew and the scientologists who would soon arrive for their auditing and training. Everyone had plenty of space to live in—married couples had their own rooms with private bathrooms. As a single person, I was assigned to a room with three other men. The Fort Harrison seemed to be proof that the upward curve of scientology we had fervently believed to be inevitable was now becoming reality.

The move from Daytona to Clearwater occurred in early December 1975 under the banner of a vaguely Christian-sounding front group created for the purpose: United Churches of Florida. Like the Opera-tion and Transport Corporation, this was another shore story to shield our real intentions: Hubbard apparently thought Floridians would be more receptive to a Christian-sounding religious group and less likely to question us, out of politeness. As with the OTC and the disaster it had led to in Madeira, he should have known better. An unheard-of "church" in the Bible Belt of the United States? Locals were quick to ask, "Who are these people? I know my churches and I've never heard of them before." Typical Christian churches didn't require that many people to conduct their Sunday services. This new "church" didn't even congregate on Sundays, and when the buildings were bought, there were no parishioners to speak of. In a small place like Clearwater, the fear of outsiders was heightened.

So, once again, the whispers grew. It didn't take long for the local media to track down the names and scientology connections of those on the incorporation papers of the Southern Land Development and Leasing Corporation, the entity created to purchase the properties and "lease" them to United Churches of Florida.

Clearwater mayor Gabriel Cazares began making public statements expressing his concerns about how a shady organization had snuck into town under false pretenses with unclear motives. Cazares then became a target of the program to ruin his political career, pursuant to Hubbard's "Fair Game" doctrine, which detailed specific steps to investigate, harass, and destroy anyone deemed an enemy or critic of scientology. (In Hubbard's words, those designated as enemies of scientology, or Fair Game, "may be tricked, sued, or lied to or destroyed.") To that end, scientology operatives planted false documents in government files, spread rumors that Mayor Cazares was an adulterer and a bigamist, framed him for a hit-and-run accident, and managed to inveigle an insider as his lawyer. (Cazares resigned as mayor in 1978 and sued scientology for $1.5 million. The case was settled for undisclosed terms in 1986. He died in Clearwater in 2006.)

The mayor was not the first target of such harassment: In 1969, journalist Paulette Cooper had run afoul of scientology by infiltrating the New York org and writing a disparaging article in *Queen* magazine. She was subsequently spied on, set up in a phony bomb threat, sued, physically threatened, and ultimately made to fear for her life as scientology operatives tried to get her imprisoned or institutionalized, even to commit suicide. She became the poster child for scientology's efforts to destroy its perceived enemies, those it deemed Suppressive

Persons (SPs). Suppressive Persons—those who oppose scientology or its objectives—according to Hubbard, are focused on destroying scientology because they want mankind to remain enslaved.

Our PR spokespeople spun the Cazares story so well that we believed he and his cohorts were SPs attacking scientology because we had cut across their scheme to depress and then corner the local real estate market, which they would then develop at a large profit. The absurdity of the real estate story never dawned on me—why hadn't these SPs snapped up the fire-sale properties themselves if this was their scheme? Of course, nothing need make sense when it's attributed to Suppressive Persons. They are considered insane and maleficent, and therefore sane people cannot understand them. I bought the explanation and carried on with my job—Kerry had now arrived in Clearwater with the RONY team, and I was reassigned once again as his communicator.

The war against SPs was fought behind the locked doors of the secretive Guardian's Office (GO). Established by Hubbard in 1966 to protect scientology from outside threats, the GO was under the control of Hubbard's wife, Mary Sue. It had several branches, including Public Relations, Legal and Social Reform, and the top-secret department euphemistically named the Information Bureau, which was scientology's intelligence agency. They recruited and trained spies, had lock-picking and bugging equipment, and manufactured their own false government IDs. Like the rest of the GO, they believed they were above wog rules, answerable only to Hubbard's law, and adhered to the directives Hubbard had codified in the GO operating manual based on his "expertise" as a self-proclaimed authority on espionage and military strategy.

The rank-and-file Sea Org members like myself were mostly oblivious at the time to the battle against SPs waged in the name of scientology. In our insular surroundings, it was business as usual, and our first Christmas at the Fort Harrison meant another wild and crazy Bosun's Party. In the *Apollo* days premarital sex was not, strictly speaking, allowed but was rarely the subject of discipline as long as there was some discretion employed. Cramped quarters had also made such rendezvous challenging. Now that there were dozens of sparsely populated hotel rooms, however, many of us seized the opportunity and, with the addition of alcohol, the holiday was a two-day free-for-all that became the first and only Sea Org orgy.

When Hubbard found out, he was furious. Everyone ordered to report on anyone suspected of having extramarital sex. That included me and Cathy Rubio.

Cathy had arrived as a new member of the Flag Bureau while we were still sailing in the Caribbean. Originally from Queens, New York, she was feisty, worldly, and beautiful. Cathy and I got drunk and slept together the night of the Bosun's Party. We made it onto the long list of offenders as the investigation unfolded over some weeks, and were called into Kerry's office in the Bank of Clearwater building and given an ultimatum. No small talk or chitchat, just a matter-of-fact declaration: "You are both going to be assigned to the RPF unless you get married. You have an hour to get back to me with your decision." We were lucky: Many were not offered this option and were just dispatched to the RPF, which had been relocated from the lower hold of the *Apollo* and set up in the parking structure of the Fort Harrison. I believe Kerry interceded on our behalf because he did not want to lose his communicator or replace Cathy, who was in charge of ensuring new people were starting on the Bridge in scientology organizations around the world.

Cathy and I talked over our options. It was a no-brainer. A huge upside was that if we were married, we would be assigned our own room. We had been a "couple" within the Victorian norms of the Sea Org prior to the Bosun's Party: we ate together at mealtimes and walked home together at night and maybe shared a cigarette on the roof of the Fort Harrison before going to bed. That was "dating" in the Sea Org. You could not engage in sexual activity or live together unless married. Nothing else would really change in our lives. We informed Kerry of our decision, and he congratulated us. I wrote to my parents to let them know, and though they had no idea who Cathy was, they wished us the best. We were married "after post hours" in the Fort Harrison auditorium. Foster Tompkins was my best man. Suzette Hubbard and

Bitty Tompkins, née Blythe—she had recently married Foster—were bridesmaids.

And just like that we were man and wife. I left my three room-mates behind, as Cathy did hers, and we moved into room 766 of the Fort Harrison, next to Foster and Bitty in room 764. We had a beauti-ful view of the Intracoastal Waterway and Clearwater Beach out our window, but we didn't get to admire it much, as we got up early in the morning to head to work in the Bank of Clearwater building a block away. Working from nine a.m. until at least midnight each day was a typical Sea Org schedule back then—in later years it got worse, and four or five hours of sleep a night was considered normal.

Cathy and I got to know each other, though married life in the Sea Org is nothing like a normal marriage. We loved each other, mostly because of our shared dedication to the cause, but shared none of the normal marital responsibilities: We didn't have bills to pay. We didn't have a mortgage or rent to worry about. No groceries to buy and cook. It was a marriage of convenience more than anything. And this was typ-ical for the Sea Org. Our responsibilities to the organization trumped our obligations to each other. We often spent months or even years in different cities when our positions required it. We never questioned it.

The sanctity of marriage and the importance of family are threaded throughout Hubbard's writings. Yet, again, his own behavior did not align with what he preached. He had abandoned his first wife, Polly, and their two eldest children to begin an affair with another woman, Sara. He then abandoned her and their daughter, Alexis, to marry Mary Sue. In fact, in one of Hubbard's only TV interviews, he denied that he ever married Sara and that he was Alexis's father, though he had dedi-cated his second book, *Science of Survival*, to Alexis. (One look at Alexis leaves no doubt who her father is.) Hubbard was a proponent of *do as I say, not as I do*. I was too blind to recognize it, and to be fair, a lot of the information about his life was hidden or embellished to make him seem like a perfect man. Scientology claims to be all about family and maintaining successful marriages—it even offers introductory courses designed to attract new people based on these themes. But scientology's approach to marriage and family, as with everything else, is conditioned

upon what is best for the organization. If a spouse is no longer committed and cannot be brought back on board, the remaining scientologist
is expected to divorce that partner.

While we were operating in Clearwater, Hubbard had installed
himself at the King Arthur's Court apartment complex in the next
town north, Dunedin. This was a well-kept secret: I was aware he was
nearby but not of his specific location. As always, he did not want the
government to know where he was, so limiting the number of people
privy to that information reduced the likelihood of a leak. Nevertheless,
things heated up in Clearwater in early 1976. Our arrival continued to
be the subject of endless discussion around town, with stories on the
front pages of the local papers. Other community leaders began speaking out in addition to the mayor. Hubbard decided the climate was too
hostile and fled Dunedin for Washington, DC.

Around this time, I was sent on a "Sea Org Mission" to Chicago's
scientology organization to select some staff members and send them
to Clearwater for special executive training. Missions were always done
in pairs, and for this trip, my partner was a woman named Julie. Our
mission went well, so we were told to go to Buffalo and do the same
there. Hubbard required the Sea Org to operate on a shoestring budget,
so expenses were always limited. There were no company credit cards
or expense accounts, and cash was handed out sparingly. We had been
told funds would be waiting for us in Buffalo. One problem: a blinding blizzard delayed our flight, and by the time we landed at ten p.m.,
nobody was there waiting for us with any money. We scraped together
fifty dollars between us and took a cab to find a hotel.

We arrived at a Holiday Inn out in the suburbs somewhere, which,
according to the cabdriver, was the closest lodging to the address of the
scientology org. The cab dropped us off, and with thirty dollars left, I
told Julie I would go in and find out how much a room cost.

I came back shortly. "Julie, one room is twenty-five dollars a night.
We don't have enough for two rooms. I'll get a room for you and I'll
sleep in a chair in the lobby."

Julie replied, "No way. You're in charge of the mission, so you
should take the room."

We haggled back and forth, but in the end, though we were worried about the appearance of impropriety, we decided the best course was to take one room and sleep in separate beds. She waited outside while I paid for the room and went up in the elevator. Then she came up separately. The front desk clerk probably thought we were sneaking around having an affair.

The next morning, without money for another cab, we walked twenty blocks in the snow to the storefront that served as the Church of Scientology of Buffalo. Being used to warm Caribbean weather, neither of us had clothes suitable for a snowy Buffalo winter. We didn't have hats or gloves, and our light raincoats were no match for the frigid air, but Julie had it worse, as she wore open-toed shoes. We saw it as part and parcel of being tough as Sea Org members. We would "make it go right," the unofficial motto of the Sea Org, no matter what, even if our fingers and toes didn't agree.

When we got back to Florida, we were debriefed by John Gilliam, the "Debriefer" in the Action Bureau of the Flag Bureau, which was now headquartered in the Bank of Clearwater building. This is standard procedure after every mission. Both of us were forthcoming and explained our predicament at the hotel in Buffalo. Instead of being lauded for our hard work and resourcefulness, we were in trouble. Big trouble. We were called before a Committee of Evidence (Comm Ev), which is the scientology version of a court-martial. Being called before a Comm Ev is considered a black mark no matter the outcome—which was virtually a preordained guilty verdict. The crime? We had been charged with having sex outside of marriage. The mere fact of our sleeping in the same room was considered enough evidence to condemn us, though Cathy knew it was not true—laughable, in fact—and Julie had no spouse or boyfriend.

Because we had carried out our orders and extracted trainees from Chicago and Buffalo, our punishments were mitigated from being sent to the RPF to being assigned "lower conditions." Hubbard delineated various states of unacceptable operation in a descending list of conditions, below "Normal Operation." They descended from "Emergency," to "Danger" and "Non-Existence," and then the "lower conditions" of "Liability," "Doubt," "Enemy," and "Treason." (He would later add "Confusion.") There were also "high" conditions up to "Affluence" and "Power." There is a series of steps one is supposed to follow to rise up the conditions. One of the steps to get out of lower conditions required us to do amends and make up for the "damage" caused. To finally be restored to normalcy we had to get the approval of every person in our organization or group (in this case, the FB) after presenting a petition detailing what we had done to make good.

At the time, I wrote off this entire incident in my mind as unimportant in the overall scheme of things. I knew I had done nothing wrong. What was some unfairly meted-out discipline when the very future of every man, woman, and child on earth was at stake? Hubbard told us that as Sea Org members we had all "run planets" before, so we should not be worried about small inconveniences, injustices, or hardships, as they were mere trifles compared to hundreds of millions of years of experiences. As usual, this sounded great in principle, while in reality our mess-ups or foibles were treated as major catastrophes preventing mankind from going free.

When I had first arrived in Clearwater, my job had been to oversee communication lines for External Comm, the department responsible for the incoming and outgoing communications from Flag. After I left, it had turned into a mess. On the one hand, failing to properly "turn over your hat," as it is known, is a Comm Ev–worthy offense, and Hubbard, who was aware of what was happening, was of the opinion that I had neglected to ensure those who took over from me knew how to do their jobs. On the other hand, Hubbard placed enormous importance on the speed of communication—"speed of particle flow alone determines power" is one of his often-quoted pieces of wisdom. So he ordered that I return to External Comm to fix it. Though Kerry was upset that he was losing his communicator, when Hubbard issued an edict such as this, Kerry had no say. Nor did I, though it was a daunting task, and I was worried I couldn't pull it off.

External Comm sent and received the mail from the scientology outposts around the world by airfreighted packages. The post office was too slow and, more importantly, could not be trusted. More immediate communications were sent by telex. Every organization was expected to report in constantly about its activities, detail how much money it was making, and respond to orders that had been telexed out to it from "management."

Because of Hubbard's paranoia, all of our telexes were encrypted by hand, using a code. There were pages and pages of code words and dictionaries for special words not on the code sheet. If the word "extension" needed to be coded and was not in the existing list, you looked it up in a specific dictionary and used the page number and counted how many entries down the page it was: the thirty-seventh entry on page 143 became 143037. It was a tedious and massively time-consuming exercise to encrypt and decrypt hundreds of telexes a day. Hubbard's system of how to run an organization is a study in inefficient micro-management. (As Hubbard's directives remain in force forever without revision, scientology still calls its communications telexes today, and probably uses the same convoluted numbering system, even for messages sent over the internet.)

In my absence, External Comm had accumulated a backlog of many days' worth of telexes. I waded into the mess and sorted it out, mostly by insisting the Telex Operators get a good night's sleep. They had been staying up day and night trying to catch up, but as each hour passed they became slower and more incompetent, to the point of achieving almost nothing. I got the telex lines flowing again and cleaned up all the backlog. In doing so, I cleared my name in the eyes of Hubbard, who was very pleased and wrote a commendation. Overnight I was sitting pretty, with the Commodore anointing me an "upstat" (high producer).

While in External Comm I ran across David Miscavige. This was my first interaction with the boy who would become king. He had recently joined the Sea Org at Flag, following his older brother, Ronald Jr., known to everyone as Ronnie. Dave had been assigned to the LRH External Comm (LEC) unit, which handled all of Hubbard's communication. He was a perfect candidate, as Hubbard preferred lifelong scientologists in his inner circle since they were low security risks. LEC was an important link to ensure Hubbard's whereabouts remained unknown. It was a "cutout" to insulate contact with him. Part of Miscavige's job was to pack up the communications for the Commodore and seal them in envelopes with special tape that was then baked in an oven so it was impossible to steam open or tamper with. The paranoia was high. Even as a new kid on the block, Dave instantly assumed an air of superiority; though small in stature, he was confrontational at any opportunity, right down to the condescending and dismissive way he answered the door when I handed him mail or telexes to be forwarded to Hubbard. From day one, he seemed to be determined to kick, scratch, or claw his way up the ladder.

Soon after the commendation from Hubbard, I started full-time executive training to study the Organization Executive Course (OEC) and Flag Executive Briefing Course (FEBC)—the very training program I had originally gone to the *Apollo* to do three years earlier. The courses would cover most of the hundreds of "policies" that Hubbard had written, laying out how scientology organizations are to function—everything from how the files are to be kept, to how to assign personnel, to how to make money. All Sea Org members were expected to study all of these writings, though few did. Sea Org members are supposed to study for two and a half hours each day, but study time and sleep were always the first casualties of dealing with emergencies. And everything always seemed to be an emergency that had to be dealt with now, now, now. I considered myself lucky to be given this opportunity. I was excited and felt privileged and honored to have no other responsibilities outside of reading and absorbing the words of Hubbard. My indoctrination into the mindset and worldview of scientology continued at a fast pace.

I studied in the tenth-floor ballroom of the Fort Harrison, which had been converted into the executive training program course room. We began at nine in the morning and ended at ten thirty at night with short breaks for lunch and dinner. It was the first time I had experienced "full-time study" and it was mentally exhausting. I longed to be outside, get some exercise, and do something other than read all day.

But I was well aware that if I expressed any of those thoughts, I would spend many more hours finding "misunderstood words" (MUs).

Study is done with a supervisor who monitors you to ensure you don't go past a word you don't understand, and wandering attention or desire to be somewhere else were considered symptoms of having gone by a misunderstood word. Hubbard had his own "technology" of study, centered around the idea that people failed to comprehend because they did not understand the definitions of words they read. He never considered his words hard to understand, false, or confusing. If there was something you failed to comprehend, or disagreed with, it was your own fault, and there were steps you took to find the word you didn't understand. (This, I now know, is a form of self-indoctrination—or if there is such a thing, self-brainwashing.)

MUs or not, I often wondered how long I could last. The days turned into weeks and months, until Kerry decided he needed me back in the Flag Bureau urgently enough to take me out of the executive training program. I had completed seven of the nine courses. I was relieved to no longer have to sit reading all day.

Hubbard didn't tolerate mistakes any more than he did MUs. Around the time I returned to the FB, a fire broke out in the Bank of Clearwater building. Nothing like a fire happens in scientology without an extensive investigation to find who's to blame. That turned out to be my wife, Cathy—she had apparently stored something in the top of a closet in her office too close to a light, and the papers had caught fire, which soon spread to adjoining offices and the roof. In the Sea Org a mistake is not accepted as an explanation for something bad happening. Hubbard's theory of an individual being responsible for everything that happens to them is magnified when it comes to SO members. I was certain that underlying such a catastrophe were overts and withholds and what Hubbard called evil purposes (Ev Purps). The RPF is where O/Ws and Ev Purps are uncovered—thus the root cause is resolved and the situation will not recur.

Once Cathy was identified as the person responsible for the fire, everyone understood she had something undisclosed that caused her to "pull it in," so of course she needed to do the RPF. She was distraught—not about going to the RPF but about having caused such a huge flap. Like any good Sea Org member, she accepted her punishment, determined to get to the bottom of her failings and correct them—not that she was even aware of what terrible things festered inside her, she just knew that they must exist because Hubbard said they did. She had faith the tech would resolve them. I at the time agreed it was the best thing for her, even if it seemed like the end of her world at that moment. So she dutifully went off to her punishment, donned a black boilersuit, and found her spot on a mattress on the concrete floor of the parking garage of the Fort Harrison, where she ate scraps along with eighty or so other RPFers. She was forbidden to talk to anyone outside the RPF except when I was allowed to visit during her thirty-minute dinner break. There she stayed for eight months. During this period my parents had no idea of Cathy's confinement. Internal Sea Org matters were not for those outside our immediate world to know—not even dedicated scientologist family members. I suspect that even if they had discovered the truth, they would have accepted the party line that this was for her own good and the tech would resolve everything.

Severe punishment of members is a hallmark of scientology, just as much as is severe retribution against enemies. This was the era when the Guardian's Office reached the zenith of its activities. Not only did its members actively work to destroy Mayor Cazares and others in Clearwater, they infiltrated US government agencies, law firms, elected officials' offices, and any other institution that was considered an enemy of scientology. Many US government agencies were considered enemies, especially the IRS. I was aware of the massive conspiracies against scientology, as Hubbard railed against them often, but I was not aware until much later of what he had ordered be done about them.

The Guardian's Office sent dozens of spies into government agencies around the world to gather information about their plans and to steal files that contained negative information about Hubbard or scientology. It was the GO, in fact, that carried out the largest infiltration of the US government in history. Given the scope, it was inevitable that one of its agents would eventually be caught. In June 1976, that is just what happened. GO operative Michael Meisner was discovered inside IRS headquarters in Washington, DC, with a fake ID. The Guardian's Office whisked him away to Los Angeles to prevent him being questioned by the FBI, but he eventually got tired of hiding. When he insisted that he wanted to turn himself in, his handlers tied him up, put a tennis ball in his mouth, and moved him from safe house to safe house to keep him out of the hands of the government. He eventually escaped, went straight to the FBI, and informed them of the extent of the bugging of government offices, the break-ins, the impersonation of government officials, and the fact the GO had kidnapped him. He became the key witness that resulted in the FBI getting search warrants and raiding scientology offices in Los Angeles and DC.

Neither I nor anyone who was not in the highest echelons of the Guardian's Office knew of this. I was busy working in Clearwater, focused on matters in the scientology world and moving up the ranks.

Hubbard always stayed a step ahead of efforts to bring him before a judge or jury. All the while he railed against the justice system, courts, police, and FBI and claimed they were intent only on persecuting "good citizens" like him. After all, he was the sole individual in history who had risen above the vicious traps implanted by psychiatry and discovered a pathway to save humankind from a bleak future worse than death itself.

Just before Meisner's arrest, Hubbard moved to California, where he took up residence in a nondescript apartment in Culver City codenamed Astra. He had a few trusted Messengers with him but otherwise remained in hiding there for a couple of months. In July 1976 he moved to a property he had purchased in the town of La Quinta, near Palm Springs, California. This was highly secretive. He explained to us he was going to make movies to promote scientology and train scientology auditors. It was an extension of his idea that photos would help people understand scientology. Now he could show auditors precisely how he expected them to conduct an auditing session and operate an E-Meter. Like his photo essays and the music of the Apollo Stars the actual movies he directed did not bear out his claims of artistic expertise and skill.

The establishment of this new headquarters in California also marked a significant change in the structure of the Commodore's Messengers. It had always been the case that the Messengers were with

Hubbard in his immediate vicinity. Now a unit of the group was left behind in Clearwater to be his remote eyes and ears. The Commodore's Messenger Org Clearwater (CMO CW) was established. The unit of Messengers that was with Hubbard now became known as CMO International (CMO Int). Bitty had joined CMO CW, and so had Ronnie Miscavige, David's older brother. Bitty divorced Foster and married Ronnie, remaining in Clearwater, while David moved on to La Quinta to be part of CMO Int with Hubbard.

In July 1977, based on the information from Meisner, the FBI executed search warrants and seizure orders on the scientology Guardian's Offices in LA and DC. It was the largest raid in FBI history—they seized tens of thousands of extremely incriminating documents. When word reached Hubbard, he jumped in a getaway car that was on standby at all times and fled La Quinta in the middle of the night, this time to a motel in Sparks, Nevada, with a few trusted Messengers and his scientologist doctor, Gene Denk.

When news of the FBI raids broke, I bought the story the GO peddled that scientology was being singled out for persecution by the US government because their operatives had "stolen Xerox paper." One of the charges against the organization was theft of government property—the spin was that these people were being harassed for taking photocopy paper from an IRS copier, while the government was ignoring the wholly justified attempt to correct the false information that had been placed in government files by the psychiatrists and their minions. This explanation rang entirely true in the well-conditioned echo chamber of my mind, and I was totally convinced this was further proof that governments were trying to stop scientology because it alone could free mankind. In some ways it was very comfortable to not have to observe the facts too closely and to merely retreat into the agreed-upon mindset shared by everyone around me. We were right, and evidence to the contrary was just further proof of the conspiracy. We were *always* right, and absolutely certain about it: L. Ron Hubbard proclaimed it was so.

Because Mary Sue was in charge of the Guardian's Office, the wrongs of the GO were squarely on her head. Just like Cathy and the fire, she was responsible and fell on her sword for her husband—protecting him at all costs, claiming he knew nothing about the activities of the spies and government infiltration. She eventually pleaded guilty and went to federal prison, along with ten other GO officials. Mastermind Hubbard remained an unindicted co-conspirator, because all the underlings from Mary Sue down insisted Ron was unaware of their actions, and his name never appeared on any incriminating evidence, so the DOJ could not bring a case against him.

In return for her loyalty, Hubbard banished Mary Sue from their home in La Quinta and never lived with her again, as she was now a "threat." It was a sad end for her. On the *Apollo* she had always been a protector of staff well-being. When those around Hubbard were working hours that were running them into the ground, she interceded and told Ron to ease up and let people sleep. He did, making an announcement, apparently out of the blue, about the importance of the crew being rested. She'd had a lot of influence over her husband, but he was always the boss. Mary Sue was compassionate and motherly, especially to the Messengers, though she was a snarling, saber-toothed attack dog if anyone threatened scientology or her husband.

In what many Sea Org members regarded as a distraction from the vital job of Clearing the planet, Cathy became pregnant in 1977. We relocated to the QI, a former Quality Inn motel about seven miles from the Fort Harrison, off the main highway through Pinellas County. Scientology had purchased the property specifically for parents who had children, and it was so run-down that it emphatically belied its previous name. We weren't the only parents-to-be: there had been a rash of births after we arrived in Clearwater. It had not been permissible to have children on the *Apollo*—there was no room for crying babies, nor was it a safe environment for kids. Any pregnancy there had been terminated with a trip ashore or even abroad to a doctor, or the woman was sent off the ship to be reposted elsewhere. Now, with many couples wanting children, the shackles were off.

My daughter Taryn Kelly Rinder was born on January 22, 1978.

Cathy and I were joyful, and a bit anxious at the prospect of having a baby, as any new parents are. We welcomed my mother and father, who flew in from Australia to meet Cathy and visit their first grandchild, but that is where the parallel with conventional parenting stopped. At the time, I only knew what parenting as a Sea Org member was like, and that meant Taryn was to be raised from infancy by the Sea Org, not by Cathy and me. That seemed normal and superior to the wog way of doing things.

Taryn was placed in the Sea Org nursery within a few days of her birth so her mother could get back to her more important job of saving the world. The nursery sounds far more legitimate than the reality of the actual facility. It was a few motel rooms at the back of the QI where a handful of untrained Sea Org members "oversaw" the children. These so-called nannies were staff who could be spared, expendables— the equivalent of deckhands on the *Apollo*. They tried their best under enormously difficult circumstances. The children were all fed Hubbard's barley formula, based on what Hubbard said he knew from past lives was fed to Roman legionnaires: barley boiled in water sweetened with Karo syrup. (I wonder how there were not more dental issues among the children.) Of course, there was no time for breastfeeding, and in any case, Hubbard's formula was "better." There were no disposable diapers and the place smelled accordingly.

Every morning before we went to work, we delivered Taryn to the nursery, thinking how lucky we were to have a safe and pure scientology environment available for our child. Hubbard had written extensively about the care of children and so, as in every other segment of scientology, his dictums were followed verbatim. Assists—Touch and Contact Assists and others designed to calm a crying baby—were used, along with all the technology of dianetics. The overpowering smell of dirty diapers, the lack of child-appropriate furniture with cushioned surfaces or locked cupboards, and even the inexperienced and untrained nannies were unimportant—just as these sort of wog concerns always were in the Sea Org. Taryn was there seven days a week, from morning until we collected her each night around midnight. Parents who lived at the QI had the added burden of travel time to and from downtown Clearwater—no special consideration was given in the schedule for this.

This was "family life" in the Sea Org. We shared little time and few activities with our daughter. Though we loved her, we both understood that we could not be distracted from our mission to save the world. More importantly, we wholeheartedly believed in the scientology concept that we are spiritual beings merely occupying a temporal body. Taryn, like all children, was an old thetan occupying a young body, who may well have been my mother in an earlier life, or no relation at all. What your body is in this lifetime and who your parents and children are is temporary, and will change from lifetime to lifetime, while scientology will go on forever. In our view, Taryn was a fortunate thetan who had chosen to be born to Sea Org parents, and she would be a future asset to the Sea Org.

Like all the other kids, as soon as she could read and write she began being inculcated into the world of the Cadet Org—the prep school of the Sea Org. She never attended normal wog school. When Taryn signed a billion-year contract at age ten, Cathy and I were proud of her, just as my parents had been proud of me. And with good reason: Taryn was a perfect scientology specimen being raised in the isolated and protected laboratory of the Sea Org.

The same year that Taryn was born, Hubbard believed things were safe enough for him to return from Sparks to La Quinta, as the government seemed to have lost its interest in prosecuting him. But the stress had caused him to suffer another heart attack. David Mayo, the most senior auditor in scientology at the time, was summoned to provide Hubbard auditing to help him recover and supposedly prevent any further heart problems. This resulted in the invention of a new advance, what Hubbard called the Second Wall of Fire, or New Era Dianetics for OTs (NOTs)—another secret level that was and still is to this day promoted as the cure for all bodily ills, including cancer. In this case, Hubbard used himself as the sole guinea pig for this "breakthrough," widely announced as the next big thing. In the scientology world, the carrot of ultimate spiritual enlightenment and happiness keeps the donkeys moving up the Bridge and, of course, paying more money. Nothing is free in scientology. Every level of the Bridge has an exact cost, with prices growing steeper the higher one ascends. NOTs also became a huge moneymaker.

It's a recurring theme of scientology—the hope that tomorrow, next week, or next year, things that have been promised will be realized. The British writer G. K. Chesterton said: "Hope is the power of being cheerful in circumstances which we know to be desperate." This is a perfect encapsulation of scientology in so many ways. And it kept me, and many others, on the hook for far too many years.

CHAPTER 5

COMMODORE'S MESSENGER

I sat on a chair in the tiled hallway alongside a plain wood door, waiting to be summoned. Inside, L. Ron Hubbard slept alone in a modest bedroom in his house in La Quinta, California.

"Messenger!" his voice boomed. I jumped up and went inside as fast as I could. "Turn down the A/C by two degrees, it's hot in here."

"Yes, sir!" I responded. I hurried to the thermostat and adjusted it, then reported back, "I turned down the thermostat two degrees, sir."

I returned to my post, ready for the next command, question, or whim. And I did this on rotating six-hour shifts each day, from the time I handed him his slippers as he got out of bed in the morning to when I delivered a late-night snack prepared by his chef before he retired.

I couldn't believe my luck to get this prized opportunity. My old friend Bitty had become one of the Commodore's Messengers, and in turn had engineered my being transferred into the CMO CW in April 1978. This was the pinnacle of achievement in the Sea Org—I had been selected to become one of the elite. I was thrilled. Since the day I arrived on the *Apollo*, I had been envious of peers who had been in the CMO and so it was as if I were finally being invited to sit at the cool kids' table. Hubbard had written a directive for all Sea Org members, which stated in part: "A Commodore's Messenger is an emissary of the Commodore. What is said or done to that Messenger by staff or persons receiving the Messenger's orders is being said or done to the Commodore." This meant I was answerable only to those senior to me in the CMO and Hubbard himself. Instantly, Kerry and all those I had worked with previously, even my wife, were required to address me as "sir," in keeping with Sea Org rules. Then, in late 1978, I was sent to train at the feet of the Commodore at his compound in La Quinta.

With the formation of CMO CW (and subsequently other remote CMO units in different parts of the world away from Hubbard's immediate location) there were now Messengers who had never interacted with Hubbard personally. While it was impossible for all the people in the CMO to have face-to-face experience with Hubbard, it was considered a necessity that the heads of those remote units have familiarity with being a Messenger for Hubbard in person. This created another special class within the CMO: Watch Messengers, those who had served him personally. Given the paranoia about Hubbard's security, only a tiny handful ever had the opportunity to be brought in to learn the ropes as Watch Messengers in training with Hubbard at his home in La Quinta, California.

I think it was November 1978 when I left Cathy and Taryn in Clearwater and flew to Los Angeles. I was driven to a mall parking garage in the Eagle Rock neighborhood, where I was picked up, put in a vehicle, blindfolded, and driven to Hubbard's secret location twenty miles southeast of Palm Springs. A sprawling property that had at one time been a date farm, it was across a dusty road from the exclusive La Quinta Country Club, a luxurious enclave in what at the time was a very undeveloped region (now it's the home of the PGA West golf courses). Nestled at the base of the San Jacinto Mountains, it was well off the beaten path in a dead-end valley that felt a long way from the desert resort of Palm Springs. It was intensely hot. On the property there were a number of houses scattered around, as well as old buildings that had been used for packing dates and storing farm equipment.

Hubbard lived and worked in a modest house a few hundred yards distant from any of the other buildings. Security was high. The home was code-named Rifle. Nobody was allowed to say Hubbard's name or make any reference to him. All windows had to be covered, going outside was kept to a minimum, and contact with friends or relatives was strictly forbidden.

Rifle was built in Southwest Spanish style with red tile floors and dark wood doors. Hubbard's office and the adjoining anteroom where the Messengers worked and waited to be summoned were detached from the kitchen, dining room, and living room.

There was always at least one Messenger in the room with him, but he would often shout "Messenger!" and whoever was the next in line sitting in the anteroom would enter the office with a yellow legal pad and pen in hand. It meant he had sent the person who had been with him off to deliver a message to someone, or that he wanted them to carry on with what they were doing and for an additional person to take down a note and type it up at once while the others continued with whatever tasks he had assigned them (searching for a reference or document or rearranging his cushions or lighting his cigarette). We had all spent hours practicing how to write longhand dictation and would at once return to the anteroom to type up what we had written down. There was a recording being made at all times wherever Hubbard was so not a word of Ron's wisdom would be lost; if we could not read our own writing, we had to wait for the next cassette to be filled and then check the tape. His dictation was always signed "*" when typed, which was the code for "LRH."

There would be times when I opened the door and before I could even look up, he would issue an order. "Messenger, tell the cook I want steak for dinner and that the last time he made it, he used too much salt."

"Yes, sir," I'd respond, already heading for the door. I would then report back: "Sir, the cook is preparing steak for your dinner and he will use less salt than last time."

Hubbard micromanaged everything. One minute I would be sent off to tell the person who did his laundry that they needed to rinse his clothes seven times to ensure they didn't smell; another I'd be told to go to the "Sets in Charge" to change the background color for a scene

Hubbard planned to shoot, and other times to the car mechanic to ask him at what pressure he was running the tires on the white Cadillac stretch limo with curtained windows. There was neither rhyme nor reason to the inquiries, and in the orbit of the Commodore, nobody was allowed to just do their job without meddling from the very top.

As long as I got his order right, Hubbard would respond with a "very good" or "thank you" and I would stand easy, ready for the next one. If I messed it up, he would send another Messenger to do it right, and I would be sent to "cramming" for correction. Cramming is supposed to uncover the underlying reason for your mistakes or incompetence, whether it's misunderstood words, overts, or another of scientology's maladies.

As awestruck as I was at being in the presence of such greatness, working close to Hubbard was not easy. He fluctuated between moments of extreme anger and lighthearted humor. He was completely unpredictable, which kept everyone walking on eggshells. If he got a report about something in a scientology org that displeased him, he would go red in the face and utter a stream of expletives, usually directed at some individual who had failed to "do what Ron said." I believed the mercurial mood swings were due to the fact that he was a thetan able to "move easily on the Tone Scale." This scale is Hubbard's classification of emotions, which measures one's survival potential. Being fixed at a particular tone level, like always angry or perpetually in fear, is considered very bad, so, his crazy ups and downs were thought of as a good thing.

Though his moods were inconsistent, one thing always remained constant: Hubbard was first and foremost a storyteller. He was proud of his history as a writer—churning out pulp and science fiction was his professional claim to fame. His ability to spin yarns and come up with anecdotes is apparent throughout his scientology writings and even more so in the thousands of recorded lectures he delivered. While reading or listening to his lectures and his rambling anecdotal discourses could be engaging, witnessing them in person was mesmerizing.

Throughout the day and night he regaled us with endless stories demonstrating his knowledge and expertise, from his ability to stay focused as learned in a previous life driving atomic-powered race cars on some distant planet orbiting the star Arcturus to how to properly prepare a steak in a cast-iron skillet: with salt, cooked on one side, and then turned once when the blood showed on the cool side, a skill he learned from an authentic cowboy in the Wild West. There was not a subject that he did not have an opinion about, and he always spoke as if he were not just the leading expert on every subject on earth but the *only* person who understood its full meaning.

I was captivated, and believed every one of his stories to be absolute fact. When I was with Hubbard, I was more committed and dedicated as a scientologist than at any other point in my life. It was truly the apex of achievement in scientology, to be one of the chosen few who served Hubbard personally as a Commodore's Watch Messenger.

At La Quinta I became reacquainted with David Miscavige, who had moved from LEC in Clearwater to CMO International. His assertiveness and aggressive tactics had worked for him as he climbed the ranks to become a Watch Messenger and the "Action Chief CMO International," an important executive position in the CMO. Hubbard liked his approach and referred to him as "Misc"—even in written communications.

Dave had become fast friends with Pat Broeker, who was also in the CMO. I knew Pat from the *Apollo*. He was the sort of person who made you wonder what he did all day. He was more inclined to be explaining things than doing them. He had been in the Finance Department on the ship, going ashore to "do banking." But how he spent his time was always vague. Pat had somehow made it into the CMO, probably due to the influence of his wife, Annie, who was a Senior Watch Messenger and one of the handful who were the original Messengers on the *Apollo*.

While at La Quinta I was assigned to sleep in the same Men's Dorm with Dave and Pat, the four other male Messengers, and a couple of others I don't recall. It was a far cry from the ship: a large room with windows, five or six bunk beds, plush carpet, and its own bathroom. There were now about half a dozen male Messengers, though we were still a distinct minority compared to the women within the CMO, in both number and status.

After about six weeks working alongside Hubbard daily, I was deemed ready to return to Clearwater, having satisfied the Commodore and the Senior Watch Messengers that I could do things the way he expected. I was now qualified to assume the position of the head of the Commodore's Messenger Org Clearwater, making me the most senior person at scientology's "spiritual headquarters." I was the "emissary" of Hubbard at the Flag Land Base, which was, and still is, the single most important scientology organization on earth because it is the source of the greatest revenue—more than all other scientology orgs combined. Hubbard's edict about the Commodore's Messengers being his personal representatives and their actions being his actions meant that whatever I said was unchallengeable by anyone in the local area; I was answerable only to those in California with Hubbard.

Heading up CMO CW gave me my first taste of the incredible power that a position of authority brings in scientology. It is unlike anything else imaginable except perhaps being a member of the royal family in an absolute monarchy. I had been next to the power of Kerry—albeit in an environment where Hubbard was located. Now I was the emperor of my own kingdom. It was intoxicating. It gave me a sense of invincibility.

Luckily, I had someone senior to me who reminded me that I was neither all-important nor invincible: Dede (Diana) Reisdorf was my boss. She was the child of founding scientologists from the Midwest and had been on the *Apollo* as an original Messenger. Though she was stationed at La Quinta, she communicated with me every day, and her guidance and direction kept my head from growing too big. It helped that I had known Dede since our days on the quarterdeck and that she was (and is) one of the nicest, kindest, and most down-to-earth people I have ever known. I learned to appreciate and respect her more than anyone else I ever met in the Sea Org.

During this time, as the senior executive in the largest scientology facility in the world, I was given priority and progressed through my lower auditing steps to the Operating Thetan (OT) levels. These are the confidential levels of the scientology Bridge to Total Freedom where Hubbard claimed one would attain enormous powers and control over one's life and infinite future. The most infamous of these is the third, or OT III, dubbed the Wall of Fire. Hubbard saw this level as an enormous breakthrough in the history of this planet and the final step needed to free mankind (until he invented the next "final step"). He announced that he had nearly died researching this "cataclysmic event," but had somehow been able to fight his way through and forge a path for others to follow. It was confirmation of what he said in what is considered his most important edict, a policy letter titled "Keeping Scientology Working," which is required reading at the start of every course in scientology—that only he in all the eons had managed to rise above all others and solve the mysteries of the universe.

When I first read the OT III materials I was stunned. Almost speechless. And confused. Very confused.

There in Hubbard's own handwriting was his explanation of the cataclysm that made planet Earth a living hell from that point forward. Seventy-five million years ago, Xenu, the head of the Galactic Confederacy, consisting of seventy-six planets, solved the problem of overpopulation by rounding the citizenry up, freezing them in glycol, shipping them to Earth, placing them in volcanoes, and dropping hydrogen bombs on them. Humans now have uncounted numbers of these disembodied spirits stuck to their bodies, and these spirits (called body thetans) must be removed from the body in order for people to be able to think and act for themselves rather than being influenced by all these other "voices."

I know how crazy this sounds, especially coming from a self-professed author of cheap science fiction. It's not that it didn't seem incredible at the time. It did. But I viewed it through the eyes of a true believer. As much as I questioned it—specifically whether disembodied "dead" thetans were all over my body, affecting my thoughts, feelings, and even physical state—I wanted it to be true. I had been told by so many people beforehand that OT III "will change your life." I was afraid to say anything even the slightest bit negative for fear of being summarily labeled a "No Case Gain," a highly derogatory term in scientology that means you do not respond to scientology counseling. This is a label tantamount to "leper"—something you can never recover from. On top of that, in scientology, it is forbidden to discuss anything about this subject—you must be extremely careful even uttering the word "Xenu." So it was impossible to compare notes with anyone else to get their opinion. I was isolated with my thoughts and wondered whether my perspective was correct.

In addition, I, like all scientologists, had been indoctrinated into blind faith in the E-Meter lie detector machine. So, following in the footsteps of many before me, I decided to see what the meter said by reading parts of the OT III materials while connected to the E-Meter, and lo and behold, I got reads on the meter that "confirmed" everything in Hubbard's elaborate story. I was absolutely certain the E-Meter never lied.

The E-Meter is a stroke of genius by Hubbard. I don't understand the entire construct of it and how it works, but here are a few things I believe to be true.

Hubbard claims the E-Meter reacts to emotions and upsets—these cause physical changes in the body in some way that then show up on the meter. How and why this happens I don't know, though I came across something interesting in Tom Shadyac's 2010 documentary *I Am*. In it, a scientist connected a bowl of yogurt (with two electrodes like those that are used in auditing) to a device that measures electrical currents (similar to an E-Meter) to demonstrate the yogurt bacteria's reaction to Tom's emotions about his agent and recent divorce. When he thinks about these subjects, the meter needle moves without any direct physical stimuli, apparently just from the emotional charge of his feelings. If you have ever had someone who is very upset or very angry walk into a room, you can feel it. The E-Meter is akin to how a lie detector works, measuring physiological changes caused by an electrical current passing through the body. But the mechanics of the E-Meter are really not important to scientologists: its accuracy and effectiveness are a matter of unshakable certainty.

Hubbard said, in one of his many important but ignored contradictions, that the E-Meter reacts and that is *all* you know. You don't know what it is reacting to or why. But he also went on at great length to describe in minute detail what every sort of reaction on the E-Meter signifies. One reaction means you have evil purposes, another means you are "trying to exteriorize from the body," another means you have undisclosed withholds. And on and on. This is what all scientologists come to believe.

In scientology, the E-Meter functions not only as a lie detector but as an emotion detector that tells when you are happy or upset or sad. Hubbard claimed it "reads" just a little below your conscious level. So you may not yet understand that you have hidden thoughts or intentions, but with some prodding and guidance from the auditor, these can be uncovered just below your level of awareness. The success of the E-Meter relies on a great deal of positive reinforcement and confirmation bias, which brings it a mythical, almost godlike, status in scientology.

Here is what a typical auditing session looks like.

The auditor sits in a small room with her back to the door, while I, the person being audited, always sit farthest from the door (so I cannot escape). My auditor welcomes me, asks if I have had enough sleep and eaten well, ensures I am comfortable in the chair, and then says, "Is it okay if we begin the session?"

There are a few preparatory questions at the start of each session, called "rudiments," to ensure I'm not distracted, and then the session begins in earnest.

"What problem have you had with your father?"

I respond and she notes what I say while watching the E-Meter for reactions and using it to guide me to give details. Once I have exhausted those, if the E-Meter has not given the appropriate reaction (called a "floating needle") she asks:

"Is there an earlier similar problem?"

I cannot think of anything that seems to answer her question, so she prompts me, "Take a look and tell me what you see, no matter how foggy or dim it may be."

A moment later, the E-Meter reacts.

"What was that you just thought of?"

"My father is yelling at me, I think."

"Okay, what else do you see?"

I wonder to myself if I "see" anything but try hard to come up with some details: "I think I spilled milk on the floor."

"Very good, when was that?"

This session continues until I have described a full scene.

"Your needle is floating," she finally says, which means we can move on to the next question.

These auditing sessions are also used to prompt the recall of supposed past lives and experiences from millions of years ago. One is asked to find "earlier incidents" based on the theory that if you can remember the first incident of a trauma, you can erase it. Often, the earliest incident you can think of in this life does not result in the appropriate reaction on the E-Meter, so you're encouraged to look "earlier" by contacting past lives.

The E-meter is an integral part of convincing the subject that the things they're "seeing" are not just the imagination running wild. If I doubted that a thought that popped into my mind—say, an image of a soldier holding a musket in 1792—was a real memory, the auditor would kindly inform me, "That is reading." In this fashion, things that may have seemed incredible become plausible, and with confirmation from the E-Meter and the auditor, they are suddenly reality.

I was so convinced that the E-Meter was infallible that when the needle moved as I read the list of volcanoes where people were supposedly blown up with hydrogen bombs seventy-five million years ago, I took it as confirmation that the story must be true. It was simply buried below my ability to perceive, and by using the E-Meter I could plumb the depths of my horrific experiences at the hands of "implanters" who had enslaved me and every person on this planet with electric shocks and other assorted tortures. It is a wild story torn straight from the pages of a science fiction novel, but every good scientologist who reaches the level of OT III believes it wholeheartedly. There is one final piece of this that Hubbard included to prevent it being exposed and ridiculed. He claimed these events had been deliberately hidden and "booby-trapped" so if anyone who was not ready for OT III or had ulterior motives did uncover them, they would become sick and die.

When I made it to OT III, I joined the privileged few in this universe who had been freed from this terrible trap. Those who had walked through the Wall of Fire before me apparently found it credible—including my parents and others I worked with and respected in the Sea Org. I wanted to believe it.

In truth, the reactions I saw on the E-Meter may have been caused by my fond memories of a trip to Hawaii (one of the main locations of the volcanoes in OT III), or simply by the insane idea that hydrogen bombs would be dropped in volcanoes. Why volcanoes? I allowed myself to be convinced that this magical device, the E-Meter, could confirm things that are scientifically untrue. (The list of volcanoes Hubbard offers as the locations of the bombings did not exist on Earth seventy-five million years ago—let alone spaceships that looked exactly like DC-8 airplanes. . . .)

You arrive there on a slow voyage of self-delusion. In the early stages of scientology indoctrination, you need to accept only one small thing you can easily agree with, like the idea that "the truth will set you free." Step by step, you make your way until you fully buy into even the most absurd space opera fantasies. As the delusion grows, you convince yourself you are the truly aware person and the poor wogs are wallowing in ignorance.

It is one of the many paradoxes of scientology that the vast majority of Sea Org members never make it to the OT levels, even though scientologists are told every person on planet Earth is in mortal peril until they traverse the Wall of Fire. The contradiction is even more startling given that one of the stated purposes of the Sea Org is to "protect the top of the Bridge" and *only* Sea Org members are allowed to deliver the OT levels to scientologists. The reason most scientology parishioners do not make it to their OT levels is they simply don't have the means to travel to one of the seven Sea Org bases and pay the hundreds of thousands of dollars required to ascend to the top of the Bridge. But Sea Org members don't pay for any services and are already at the bases where the OT levels are available. (Sea Org members don't pay with money, that is: I did pay with my time and life. And if you leave the Sea Org, they put together a bill—called a Freeloader Bill—for all the services you participated in that they expect you to now pay for, as if your time and life were a meaningless contribution.)

So there is no excuse for SO members *not* making it through the OT levels, especially when it is claimed they make you able to think and act rationally and be "cause over life." If scientology leadership really believed in the power of the OT levels, they would ensure those at the top of the food chain on planet Earth had those abilities. But that doesn't happen. Most Sea Org members make little or no advance up the Bridge because they don't pay for services and thus don't generate revenue and more importantly: nothing comes before their obligations to do their job, including their own spiritual progress, relationships with their family, or physical well-being. This dedication to the job drives every aspect of life in the Sea Org.

While I was busy delving into the fantasies of Xenu and the volcanoes, Hubbard bought another property on the other side of the San Jacinto Mountains from La Quinta. It was a derelict resort where he had shot some scenes for one of his scientology training films. It had in earlier, better years been a spa and golf course centered around the Gilman Hot Springs. The hot springs had dried up when an aqueduct had been drilled through the mountain to bring water from the Colorado River to Los Angeles, and the place had sunk into a permanent state of decline. The five-hundred-plus-acre property, bought at a bargain price, was intended to become the summer headquarters or "SHQ" because it was just too hot in La Quinta in the summer months. I guess Hubbard wasn't aware of how hot it was at Gilman. Though it's not strictly in the desert—it's often incorrectly described as such, when in fact Gilman is in an agricultural community with a large dairy farm across the riverbed, turkey farms down the road, and crops in the fields—the heat in summertime is stifling, the area being far removed from the cooling influence of the Pacific Ocean.

In early 1979, when the location of La Quinta was blown because two Sea Org members had escaped and threatened legal action, year-round operations were relocated to Gilman Hot Springs, which became the home of Golden Era Productions film studio. Today this property is known as Gold, Gold Base, or the Int Base. It is about eighty-five miles east of Los Angeles in Riverside County, a few miles from the city of Hemet and about three miles from the smaller town of San Jacinto.

Gilman Hot Springs was a ragtag collection of structures, including an old golf clubhouse, several rows of motel units, assorted odd buildings, garages and sheds, and a one-room USPS post office. Hubbard devised a new shore story for the Int Base. He declared that the mountains behind the property looked like the highlands of Scotland (he saw them when they had tufts of grass for a few weeks in winter; the rest of the time they looked more like New Mexico), so the property would be renovated with a Scottish motif and would be known for the wogs as SHQ, which stood for Scottish Highland Quietude. He dictated that the buildings should all be painted white and the roofs blue and that stonework should be used extensively to decorate them and the property. This is why it looks like a sort of Disney fantasy village plopped between the sandy dry wash of the San Jacinto River and the steep, scrubby foothills of the San Jacinto Mountains. Since the mid-1990s, it has been dominated by the massive $10 million mansion that was built overlooking the property from high on the hillside and "the Castle"—a huge soundstage dressed up to look like one of those Medieval Times dinner-and-jousting places you see alongside the freeway. I guess it's supposed to resemble a Scottish castle. Whoever designed it has never been to Scotland.

Gold is split by highway 79. The north side perches on the lower slopes of the mountains and is where the majority of the senior scientology hierarchy is located. The south side borders the dry wash of the San Jacinto River, which flows every few years for a couple of days after a storm. This was the location of the lower-level Gold crew who made scientology films, reproduced cassette tapes (later CDs) of Hubbard lectures, and assembled E-Meters. Hubbard's house was the highest building on the property—hence named Bonnie View, as it commanded an impressive view of the San Jacinto Valley. (The original Bonnie View was bulldozed to make way for the subsequent mansion constructed after his death.)

When everyone else who had been at La Quinta relocated to Gold, Hubbard took up residence about five miles away in an apartment complex in Hemet code-named X. He did not believe it was safe to live at Gilman Springs. A few staff lived there with him, and Commodore's Messengers came and went from Gold, most notably every Friday morning with the weekly stats.

Every organization in scientology reports its statistics each week. These measure "production"—that is, how much money each organization made, how many books it sold, how many people it managed to get in on a scientology service, and so on. There were (and likely still are) more than 150 reports telexed in by every scientology organization on Thursday. They are a matter of life and death to scientology executives, whose fates rest in large part on whether they are "upstat" (doing better than last week) or "downstat" (failing). The stats are aggregated continentally and then internationally. Each week a report and graphs of these stats were delivered to the Commodore so he could issue orders about what should be done to expand scientology and make more money.

After reviewing the stats, Hubbard dictated extremely detailed orders that were then transcribed from tapes and distributed Friday morning, sometimes up to fifty pages of single-spaced commentary, conclusions, and orders that would then become the marching orders for scientology around the world for the week.

When stats were flat or down, Hubbard would routinely come up with a scapegoat to explain the failure. It is a fundamental truth in scientology that if Hubbard's tech is applied exactly as he wrote it and administered precisely as he dictated in his thousands of policy letters, scientology will grow exponentially. In 1979, Hubbard claimed the lack of growth was because of widespread incompetence of the staff. He believed they were unable to comprehend what he had written because literacy levels around the world were dropping because schools failed to teach proper English grammar. So he created a lengthy course to define every small, common English word ("is," "at," "the," etc.), because he was sure people did not actually understand their meanings but only thought they did, and thus these were deemed hidden "misunderstood words."

To test this "breakthrough," I was brought to Gilman Hot Springs along with Ronnie and Bitty Miscavige and the head of the CMO in Los Angeles, Barbara Saecker. We were to be the guinea pigs to pilot Hubbard's new Key to Life (KTL) course. It was seen as his latest genius that would finally make it possible to clear the planet.

Yes, defining small words and grammar would save the world, along with a bit of scientology counseling using modeling clay. So-called clay table processing was to help those who were under the influence of Suppressive Persons and thus were PTS, or Potential Trouble Sources. The clay was used to create depictions of problems in your life, with the idea that if you could represent them in clay, you could overcome them, and instead of being mired in problems you would be free and clear to expand scientology.

After I completed the Key to Life Course, I felt I was ready to take on the world. This was the new gift from Hubbard, and I was fortunate to have gotten it so soon and now had to live up to the expectations that came with that status. I did not return to Clearwater immediately; instead I stayed at Gilman to oversee exporting KTL to Flag and Los Angeles. Hubbard had decreed that only a KTL grad could administer or export it to anyone else—because of course anyone who had *not* done KTL would mess it up due to their inability to understand what was to be done. Nobody else in CMO International had completed KTL—Bitty and Ronnie were needed back in Clearwater and I was already a trained "Mission Ops," which was needed to carry out the export. My being chosen was a foregone conclusion.

This was my first experience working directly for David Miscavige. As the Action Chief, he had the function of sending and running Sea Org Missions, and so I came under his purview even though he could not himself direct the missions I was running. He was brash and hard-core, intent on having things go his way no matter what. Everyone around him felt it, even his superiors, and they were all a little (or a lot) afraid of getting on his bad side. He had not yet ascended to the top of the tree, but he had a bullet by his name and was rising up the Billboard chart fast. He was dedicated to being the best at everything, including defeating anyone he saw as a competitor, although he was careful with me, as he could not touch someone who had done KTL and was thus irreplaceable. Others did not fare so well, often being on the receiving end of his bullying on a daily basis. It was cringe-inducing to witness him constantly belittle and berate his subordinates.

I eventually completed the project of exporting KTL and returned to Clearwater.

Soon after I arrived home, two of Hubbard's most trusted associates, Mike and Kima Douglas, escaped from X in the middle of the night (what's known as "blowing" in Sea Org parlance). This was a catastrophic breach of security; for all Hubbard knew, they had gone right to the FBI and IRS to report on his whereabouts. So once again, in early 1980, he took off in the middle of the night, this time with Pat and Annie Broeker. They happened to be at X at the time and as a married couple could leave together. From that moment on, Hubbard disappeared from the scientology world. With Pat, Annie, and the handyman Steve "Sarge" Pfauth as his "security," Hubbard headed first to Newport Beach and then traveled around California in a Blue Bird bus motor home, eventually settling near San Luis Obispo on a ranch purchased with cash under an assumed name.

Back in Clearwater, I was oblivious to the fact that Hubbard was on the lam. He was still sending orders, including to me. Hubbard assigned me a code name and addressed me in his communications as "Duke."

I was fully dedicated to carrying out Hubbard's grand scheme for saving mankind and firmly believed the forces of evil were seeking to destroy him because they wanted to keep men ignorant and enslaved as he sought to free them. This is scientology dogma. It was my dogma.

CHAPTER 6

THE GO TAKEOVER

After the FBI busted Guardian's Office operative Michael Meisner for breaking into the IRS, it was not clear what the fallout would be. When it became evident that the documents recovered in the 1977 raid would make it impossible for Mary Sue and her lieutenants to avoid being prosecuted, Hubbard's fear of being implicated in the investigation escalated to anger. He raged that the GO had not only put him in danger, they had also done irreparable harm to his and scientology's reputation. Despite her many years of unblinking loyalty, Mary Sue was banished from his life entirely. Those who orbited close to the star of L. Ron Hubbard were always in flux. The man who claimed to have solved the mysteries of human behavior routinely "discovered" that his closest and most trusted associates, whom he had lauded for years, were in fact enemies of himself and, by extension, mankind.

While he had privately dispensed with Mary Sue, he had yet to come out with it publicly, for good reason. She had wielded enormous power over the GO—the people in it were intensely loyal to her, and any rumblings of dissatisfaction could have catastrophic consequences. In their eyes, she was the closest thing to a perfect example of an OT after Ron. Not only that, the GO controlled all of scientology's international bank accounts and held all official corporate positions registered with the government.

No doubt in addition to being concerned about Mary Sue's power, Hubbard also realized avoiding any statement about her or the GO was his best strategy to evade prosecution. He had to appear unaware of the GO's actions so as not to open himself up to additional legal exposure. He had already been designated an unindicted co-conspirator and certainly didn't want to be exerting his personal authority over GO members while they were being prosecuted. The last thing he desired was to be indicted. However, this made gaining control of the GO more difficult.

With Mary Sue still formally at the helm of the GO even though under prosecution, the Commodore directed his Messengers to find proof that the GO had gone wayward, and use that information to take control. The move would be tricky, and Miscavige, as Action Chief, was responsible for pulling it off. To get a foot in the door, he persuaded Mary Sue to allow the CMO to send four Messengers to GO headquarters at Saint Hill Manor in England to observe what was going on. She could hardly object, given the catastrophe the GO had brought down upon scientology.

I was chosen as one of the Messengers. In April 1981, I was summoned by Miscavige to the Int Base for briefing on the plan and from there traveled with the three other Messengers to the Guardian's Office World Wide (GOWW). Even though this trip was designated a fact-finding mission, Miscavige knew that once we got in the door, we would be able to get the necessary information to justify bringing the GO under our control. None of the four of us had any experience dealing with scientology's external affairs—which covered everything from public relations to ongoing legal cases, corporate regulations, and the gathering of intelligence on perceived enemies—yet it was expected that we would "make it go right" and figure it out as we went along. This trip began my descent down the rabbit hole into an entirely new world.

We stayed in a bed and breakfast in the nearby town of East Grinstead and rented a white van, which I drove because I was the only member of the group who had experience navigating on the "wrong side" of the road. Pulling through the gates at Saint Hill was familiar to me, but none of the other three Messengers had been there before. The GO offices were located in Hubbard's manor house itself, which reflected the status the branch had had in his eyes. Nobody but GO personnel were allowed inside the building. But there we stood, dressed in full Sea Org naval-style uniform at the designated GO side entrance to the Manor, next to the kitchen. The grand front doors were reserved for the lord of the Manor himself. We had no idea what to expect. The GO had generally looked down their noses at Sea Org members. Although a few of them had come to the *Apollo*, they hadn't intermingled with the crew and had operated behind closed doors. I always felt they viewed us as kids playing soldiers while they were dealing with real life, taking out the world's Suppressive Persons. As we buzzed the doorbell, thoughts flashed through my mind. Were they expecting us? Would the reception be hostile? Would they even let us in?

Eventually a woman answered the door, and we announced we needed to meet with Acting Guardian World Wide David Gaiman. (Jane Kember, the Guardian WW, was busy fighting criminal charges that had been filed against her in the US.) She closed the door and went off to get someone more senior to deal with us aliens on their doorstep. They eventually allowed us to enter and, as we walked up to Gaiman's office, people in the halls quietly whispered to one another, wondering what was going down.

Gaiman, a tall, somewhat gangly but charming and quick-witted Englishman, was standoffish but cordial—he was not quite sure what to make of us. With reassurances that this was simply an observation, he cooperated. We did our job thoroughly, spending ten days "observing"—looking through hundreds of files, interviewing dozens of people and putting them on the E-Meter, and particularly noting instances where the Guardian's Office was not following Hubbard policy.

The four of us had worked as Messengers, so our perspectives on the inner sanctum of the GO were virtually identical—we were uniformly horrified by how "Off-Source" it was. (As Hubbard is often referred to simply as "Source" in scientology, things that are not done in accordance with his writings are deemed "Off-Source.") We were used to a world where everyone was in lockstep with Hubbard's administrative policies as dictated in his letters, which were known as Green on White because they were printed in green ink on white paper (to distinguish them from Red on White, which described auditing procedures). Policy letters are the inviolable laws of scientology organizations and it is a high crime to fail to follow them. The GO was an Off-Source twilight zone unlike anything we had experienced in scientology. Even a minor infraction was considered a huge and indelible black mark. Theirs ranged from a failure to follow the standard procedure of routing communications laid out by Hubbard to violating personnel assignment policies. We found the evidence we needed to justify further action.

We returned to Gilman, where Miscavige debriefed us. The information was digested and analyzed, and a strategy was formulated to get the GO under our control. We knew that what we had unearthed gave us authority from Hubbard to take more drastic action. To us, the GO's refusal to comply with policy explained all its failures, though in fact, doing precisely what Hubbard ordered in his intelligence directives was what had brought down the US government's wrath. But in scientology, history is written by those who have the ear of Hubbard, and that no longer described Mary Sue—it was now Miscavige. The Off-Source GO had become fair game.

I traveled back to GOWW a few weeks later with one other Messenger, who had never been to Saint Hill before, to officially begin the process of bringing the GO to heel. We stayed at the same bed and breakfast as on the earlier visit, and the owner, Martin, greeted me like a long-lost son. We drove to Saint Hill on a beautiful late-spring day, the green English countryside as our backdrop as we pulled up and parked right in front of the Manor and walked into GOWW without any trepidation. We proceeded to inform David Gaiman and the leadership of GOWW that they were now officially under the control of the Sea Org, Mary Sue was no longer their boss, and we were there to get them back "On Source." Even the GO personnel understood this rebuke and had to accept the consequences—they were first and foremost scientologists. Their world was rocked. It took a while for it to sink in, but they soon came to understand that things were now different. We proceeded to dismiss those who had been involved in the FBI debacle or had knowledge of it. It was important to be able to publicly position these people as "wayward" and "misguided," and they had to go. Mary Sue's closest allies and the leaders of the Guardian's Office were also removed from their positions, including Gaiman. Everyone who remained at GOWW was required to join the Sea Org or be dismissed. In the end, about two-thirds remained.

We repeated the same takeover at the Guardian's Office in Los Angeles. It was the largest GO in the world, with more than one hundred staff members. It was also where much of the criminal activity had been directed from. We dismissed the main people responsible for actions that did or could result in criminal prosecutions and, as with GOWW, required the rest to join the Sea Org or be dismissed. About two-thirds signed up and remained as part of the "new" GO, now under the control of the Sea Org.

While Hubbard's view was that everyone in the Guardian's Office was part of a conspiracy against him, my dealings with these people face-to-face, day in and day out, left me less certain. The vast majority were simply run-of-the-mill scientologists, doing what they thought was the "greatest good." Truthfully, they hadn't done anything I would not have done had I gone into the GO rather than the Sea Org, but I had a righteous job to do to protect Hubbard (and scientology) and was not going to waver from that task by demonstrating any sympathy for them.

Taking control of the GO also involved removing GO members from their positions within the international corporate and finance structure of scientology. In the '60s the IRS had revoked the tax-exempt status of scientology organizations— including the Church of Scientology of California, then the "Mother Church"—for illegally funneling money to Hubbard. The tangled web of scientology corporations that had grown up willy-nilly around the world—from individual churches in different states and countries to entities formed in tax havens like Liberia and Panama—continued to operate, with GO members in leadership positions. This mess of entities and financial transactions between them created a potential pathway to Hubbard's doorstep. So, along with getting rid of the "bad hats," as Hubbard liked to call the wayward GO members, he deemed it a priority to create a corporate structure that could pass muster with the IRS. This necessitated creating dozens of new organizations (yes, more entities and acronyms) that had articles of incorporation, board members, bank accounts, and financial records that could hold up under IRS scrutiny. The reorganization would not guarantee exemption, but it would remove fundamental barriers to even discussing the possibility of qualifying for exemption.

This corporate reorganization was a massive undertaking, but apart from removing the GO from control, it didn't change the internal operations of scientology at all. Everything on paper was superseded by the authority of the Sea Organization. None of the corporations really had any autonomy, though if challenged in court as mere window-dressing (which is exactly what they were), the answer was simple: "The Sea Org is not incorporated, has no bank accounts, has no location, and cannot be proven to do anything. It is merely a 'fraternal religious order.'" Scientology's new corporate front was like replacing an inmate's orange jumpsuit with a jacket and tie. It didn't change the man, but it made it more likely he would get in the door for an interview.

The timing of this restructuring also coincided with Hubbard doing his estate planning. Hubbard's personal fortune was worth hundreds of millions of dollars, a fact very few scientologists were aware of, though had they been it would not have mattered to them: he deserved everything he had. Since the organization always took precedence in scientology, even over Hubbard's family, he intended to bequeath the majority of this fortune to a newly created entity called the Church of Spiritual Technology (CST), while providing a pittance to Mary Sue and the three children he had not completely disowned. For CST to qualify to receive his money, he stipulated it must have tax-exempt status. He did not want the government getting any of his inheritance in taxes.

CST's job was paramount in Hubbard's eyes. It was tasked with preserving his writings and lectures for eternity for the good of mankind and all life forms in the universe. *Everything* he had ever written or said, the millions of words and thousands of hours of lectures, needed to be safe from the nuclear holocaust he predicted would soon engulf Earth. Cost was no object. He had *very* specific directives for this plan, which were explained in confidential briefings given to the "most dedicated" (and wealthy) scientologists in fundraising pitches to finance the activities until Hubbard's own money had passed through probate. His words were to be etched onto stainless steel plates and his lectures recorded on gold CDs and nickel LPs. These were then to be stored in argon-filled titanium containers, protected by heat shields of the same material used on the outside of a space shuttle, and secured away in secret nuclear-bomb-proof underground bunkers. CST, though little known to the outside world, became the single most important scientology entity on the planet, for it was the guarantee that Hubbard's genius would be available for all future generations. Nothing was more crucial.

To carry out Hubbard's wishes, CST had to gain tax-exempt status. Only then would it have the hundreds of millions from his estate needed to complete the vaults designed to preserve his legacy forever. CST would be at the top of the scientology hierarchy—it would also own all the rights to Hubbard's works after his death once his estate had transferred, meaning every scientology organization would have to get permission from CST to use the copyrighted material and trademarks.

The entire scientology corporate hierarchy had to be regularized to pass muster with the IRS as an exempt religious organization. The task of gaining that exemption seemed almost impossible. Not only had the IRS determined that earlier organizations of scientology were not tax exempt, but the GO had appealed these rulings in court and lost. The judicial decisions were even more negative than the IRS determinations. In addition, there had been an earlier failed attempt to straighten out the corporate and financial mess under the direction of Mary Sue. It was called Mission Corporate Category Sort Out (MCCS). The MCCS personnel recorded their planning meetings, and though the plans were never implemented, the recordings would be focused on in a decision from the US Court of Appeals for the Ninth Circuit in June 1990. Having studied the transcripts, the court concluded that scientology not only intended to cover up past criminal wrongdoing but planned future fraud against the IRS. There was nothing positive on our side of the ledger; the IRS held all the cards. The only thing we had was an almost insane conviction that if Hubbard said something, it had to be done—there was no option but to forge ahead, no matter the apparent impossibility.

A secondary objective of the restructuring was to make it as difficult as possible to bring Hubbard into litigation. Licenses and agreements were executed and corporate niceties were put into effect that formed barriers to litigants or law enforcement seeking to drag Hubbard or senior scientology organizations into court.

Even with the corporate reorganization in place, the odds of winning the battle with the IRS were bleak. The agency had court decisions in its favor, mountains of evidence of earlier financial and corporate wrongdoing, and the prosecution of prominent scientology leaders, including Hubbard's wife. Additionally, the list of criteria the IRS required to grant religious tax exemption included many hurdles, such as proving scientology's religious beliefs and practices and compliance with "public policy" (generally meaning activities for the good of society). It seemed there was no way we could overcome the past.

Yet as bad as this was, the IRS was not the only problem. Someone in the Guardian's Office in Los Angeles had accepted a subpoena for Hubbard in a civil case. This was a catastrophic mistake. It could well require Hubbard to appear in court, even if just to contest the validity of the subpoena—the thing he most feared. Hubbard became even more convinced the GO was out to destroy him from within and more desperate to avoid being dragged into court. He ordered Miscavige to get an all-clear—meaning removing any legal impediment, civil or criminal—to Hubbard coming out of hiding. Hubbard expected whatever was required to make that happen to be done. To this end, Miscavige hired a small law firm located in the San Fernando Valley consisting of two brothers, Steve and Sherman Lenske, and their partner, Larry Heller. They were, of course, given a code name: the X attorneys. Only a limited number of people even knew the name of their firm, such was the paranoia about Hubbard's security.

While there were ongoing shakeups in scientology, my family had been going through its own bit of restructuring. Cathy had become pregnant again in early 1982. I was excited, but even more than before, I was completely preoccupied with saving the world. I had been in Clearwater forming the Flag Service Organization Inc., the corporation to house the Flag operations that are the largest source of revenue in scientology—millions of dollars a week paid for auditing and training, accommodations, Hubbard's books, and numerous and varied donation demands from related scientology money-making entities, from building funds to educational programs. During the latter half of her pregnancy I was ordered back to California. Miscavige had purged the leadership of CMO International, including Dede Reisdorf, her sister, and her sister-in-law, all of whom had been with Hubbard on the *Apollo*. He had informed Hubbard that they had been sympathizing with Mary Sue; Hubbard then banished them to become permanent public room cleaners at the Fort Harrison. Since Hubbard was traveling around California incognito in a motor home writing fiction books while the CMO was supposed to be running scientology for him, there was an urgent need to fill the now vacant positions there. I headed back to Gilman to assume an executive position in CMO International.

In October 1982, I flew back to Clearwater to see our daughter Kimberley born. She was perfect, and Taryn was excited when we told her she now had a baby sister. But my visit was short-lived. I left just three days later. I had very important work that could not wait on a new child coming into the world. There was no question in my mind, nor in Cathy's, that getting back to CMO Int was paramount. My family would be fine, as Kimberley would be turned over to the Sea Org nursery, joining Taryn. *My daughters are in good hands*, I thought. So I kissed my wife, Taryn, and our new daughter goodbye, and I went back to work.

Two days after my return to Gilman, David's wife, Shelly Miscavige, knocked on my door in the middle of the night. I had been friends with Shelly since I first walked onto the *Apollo*. The *Apollo* old-timers shared a bond—an unspoken mutual respect no matter our positions in the present.

"Mike, you need to get up and get dressed to fly back to Clearwater," she told me.

I was used to being woken up in the middle of the night for various emergencies, but not by Shelly Miscavige. I knew this was not something normal.

"What's happening?" I asked.

"Your baby suddenly became ill and dropped her body," she replied, using the scientologese phrase for died.

I was already sleep-deprived, and being awoken after only a few hours in bed left me dazed and numb. I got dressed and sat quietly as I was driven to LAX. I was like a zombie; I couldn't even think straight.

Back in Clearwater, I met Cathy at a suite in the Sandcastle hotel (part of the Flag operation), where she had been temporarily located, along with an auditor and some other people ordered by Shelly to take care of us. The hospital said the baby had succumbed to sudden infant death syndrome, commonly known as SIDS. Cathy was shaken and extremely upset. I tried to comfort her, but there was little I could do or say to help. And in my mind, the best thing for her was to get in session. Though we were both devastated, we also believed the thetan who had briefly occupied that infant body would move on to another body, as had happened countless times before. In some ways that was a comfort. In scientology, death was not something to fear, because while the physical body may come and go, we believed we lived on forever. Grief could not be allowed to consume too much of my time and energy. Things of greater significance to the future of the world were more pressing.

Besides, in scientology, and especially in the Sea Org, sadness and grief over a loss are considered "misemotion," which scientologists believe stems from the reactive mind and is "counter-survival" (similar to the word "counterproductive," this was a label for things that do not enhance your well-being). In the Sea Org it is especially undesirable, as according to Hubbard, misemotion, also called "human emotion and reaction" or HE&R, prevents you from doing your job.

The auditor was ready and waiting to take me in session to "run out the loss," eradicating the negative emotions associated with the death of our child. In dianetics this is a "secondary" (a loss) on a chain of "engrams" (described in *Dianetics* as moments of pain and unconsciousness that affect your decisions and emotions), and if you isolate the first engram on the chain, whether in this life or millions of years ago, you will no longer grieve. The session followed the standard pattern of all scientology auditing. I sat in a room with an auditor on the other side of a desk who operated an E-Meter—he could see the dial of the meter and what reactions were occurring. I held the two metal cans connected by leads to the E-Meter. He made sure I was comfortable in the chair and then asked me to "Recall the moment of the loss," and guided me using the E-Meter reactions as he asked questions, stopping me at times to say, "Tell me about that thought you just had." After about forty-five minutes I got beyond any feeling of grief. Cathy underwent the same process. In a few days, I left Cathy in Clearwater and returned to Gold. It was what a good Sea Org member was supposed to do—and I was a very good Sea Org member.

EN ROUTE TO Clearwater, I had run into David Miscavige and his entourage at LAX. They were returning from what became known as the "Night of the Long Knives" West Coast Mission Holder convention in San Francisco. Mission holders owned lower-level outposts around the world to recruit new people to scientology. (These "missions" were formerly known as "franchises," but that sounded too commercial, so the name was scrapped.) Anyone could set up a mission with permission and remain open as long as they paid a 10 percent tithe on their weekly income. There were hundreds across the globe, but the US missions were the ones that brought in tens of thousands of dollars a week.

The Mission Network originally had been under the wing of the Guardian's Office, which was supported by their tithes. There was little oversight—as long as missions sent their money, nobody from the GO paid much attention to them. With the GO now in disgrace, Hubbard's continued paranoia had him believe the missions were ripping off "his" organizations and that unscrupulous scientology businessmen

connected to the GO were stealing his mailing lists and profits. They
too had to be brought under the control of the CMO. He dismantled
the formerly successful Mission Network and implemented the World
Institute of Scientology Enterprises, yet another oversight department
to corral, control, and collect percentages from scientologists' busi-
nesses and "keep them off the backs of orgs," a phrase Hubbard coined
for those he thought were taking advantage of his organizations for
their own profit.

Miscavige used this West Coast Mission Holder convention to
establish himself and show the mission holders who was boss. Those
present at the meeting weren't willing to just lie down and cede their
autonomy to Miscavige and his men—at first. But Miscavige did something that had never been done before. He verbally declared the first
people to protest as Suppressive Persons right in the hotel conference
room. This was shocking in itself—until that moment, Suppressive Person declares had always been formally issued in writing in an HCO
Ethics Order.

They were then physically escorted out of the room after being
forced to resign from their missions and sign over their bank accounts.
There was a new sheriff in town, and he announced himself loudly.

Miscavige sent a report of this meeting to Hubbard, who was
thrilled with the "effective action" and "advised" the transcript of
events be published to the world. The word "advised" was always used
to make it seem like Hubbard was merely offering helpful suggestions
when everyone knew his words were law no matter what label they
were given. It was a way to insulate him from accusations that he was
running scientology and thus could be held liable. Of course, he *was*
running scientology. Hubbard thought the publication of the transcript
would establish "Ethics Presence" (his term for authority or command
value) for his henchmen.

A subsequent convention of other mission holders in Clearwater
a few months later turned ugly in protest of the imperious treatment
of the West Coast mission holders in San Francisco. They demanded
justice and formed what Miscavige later described as a "mutiny,"
demanding action be taken against church leadership for their mis-

treatment of the missions. They insisted one of their own be installed to "run the church." Miscavige flew in from California to squelch the uprising—declaring a bunch more of the prominent names of scientology Suppressive Persons in the process. It was drastic, but he achieved his objective. He proved who was in charge and that he was not to be messed with.

Squelching resistance was a theme of the early '80s, as the decade continued to see an increase in threats internally and externally. Dozens of civil lawsuits were filed against scientology organizations all over the US by people claiming they had been damaged and defrauded by Hubbard's technology. Of these, perhaps the most problematic was a probate case by L. Ron Hubbard's estranged eldest son, L. Ron Hubbard Jr., known to everyone as "Nibs."

Nibs was the son Hubbard had in 1934 with his first wife, Margaret, known as Polly. For a time in the 1950s, Nibs had been his father's right-hand man, often seen at Hubbard's side. But Nibs became disillusioned with his father, and in 1959 cut off all association and changed his name, claiming in subsequent media interviews his father had used him as an enforcer to collect debts, had abused drugs, and had simply made up a lot of his discoveries without conducting any of his claimed research. As he did to anyone else who didn't follow the party line, Hubbard had set the GO on his firstborn son to discredit and destroy him. He had also disowned him.

Nibs retracted his earlier statements about his father after a great deal of pressure by the GO, although he would later recant the retraction. What is undeniable is that Nibs was another casualty of orbiting too close to L. Ron Hubbard. Once a lauded figure in the scientology world, Nibs ultimately was deemed, like so many others, a traitor, liar, and all-around rotten person intent on the destruction of mankind.

The upheavals sometimes created opportunities. So while Nibs's 1982 probate case caused huge problems, it opened the door to a golden opportunity for Miscavige. Nibs claimed that either Hubbard was dead and scientology was concealing this fact, or he was being held prisoner against his will. (In fact, Hubbard was hiding in his motor home in a secret location.) Nibs sought to claim his inheritance as

Hubbard's eldest son. Nibs's lawyer, who also represented numerous plaintiffs seeking to win judgments from Hubbard and scientology, had formulated this strategy to force Hubbard to appear in court to prove he was alive and not a captive. The easy thing would have been for Hubbard to come before the judge and tell him he was okay and that he had disinherited Nibs. But if he did so, he would have been served in numerous civil cases and probably by the IRS and other government agencies as well. That would have been catastrophic.

Miscavige and the X attorneys formulated an alternate strategy. They hired experts to manufacture a special batch of ink that could be dated with certainty by them and composed a declaration they forwarded to Hubbard to sign in February 1983. With this, there could be no doubt, based on the testimony of the expert, that the declaration had been signed within a day of its being presented in court—thus proving Hubbard was alive and didn't need to appear. Miscavige and the attorneys drafted a declaration for Hubbard stating his affairs were being properly taken care of by his "good friend" David Miscavige. His sole focus was to get the court to buy into the idea that he did not need to appear in person and that his affairs were being properly managed.

This was a stroke of genius on Miscavige's part. Though Hubbard trusted Annie and Pat Broeker, he could not say his affairs were being competently cared for by them, as they were in hiding with him. It would have been just as catastrophic for the court to then ask for Pat or Annie to appear, as they *did* know where Hubbard was located. Miscavige was the public face for the court, yet he did not know Hubbard's whereabouts. Hubbard's declaration was filed and he was not required to make a personal appearance. His declaration subsequently became a linchpin Miscavige used to convince scientologists he was Hubbard's nominated successor and best friend. Few know the circumstances under which the declaration was signed. Miscavige only began using it as leverage with scientologists after Hubbard and the Broekers were out of the picture.

In late 1981, Miscavige had assumed the role of Chairman of the Board (COB) of Author Services Inc. (ASI), a for-profit company that was described as Hubbard's literary agency. ASI was yet another shield for Hubbard—a nonreligious business was his only contact point with the outside world. It was an ostensibly legitimate agency for Hubbard, the fiction author who was getting on with his life unrelated to scientology. He was, in fact, writing his bestseller *Battlefield Earth* at this time, and subsequently his awful sex-, torture-, and drug-infested "satire" series *Mission Earth*. Yet every member of Author Services was a long-term Sea Org officer and executive, so nobody questioned their authority over scientology despite the pretense that they were completely unrelated and only serving Hubbard's fiction-writing needs. Thus ASI, manned and run exclusively by Sea Org members and controlling the only line of communication to Hubbard, became the top of the scientology worldwide pile, supplanting CMO International. It also became the new conduit for funneling money to Hubbard. As COB of Author Services, Miscavige was now top dog. The only people between him and Hubbard were Pat and Annie Broeker.

Miscavige was consolidating his power at every opportunity, removing those he saw as current or future potential rivals. David Mayo, the person who had been brought in to save Hubbard's life at La Quinta in 1978, became a target of Miscavige's after he refused to kowtow to him in 1982. Mayo had been around since the early days of scientology and had risen to the most senior "technical" position (which is the scientology term encompassing the activities of auditing and training), Senior Case Supervisor International. He was also a typical New Zealander, and tended to dislike those with overblown opinions of themselves. Mayo's lack of subservience signaled he was a threat to Miscavige's power, especially as Mayo was a very well-known and much-loved figure in scientology. Miscavige would have none of that and informed the Commodore that Mayo had been stealing money from the organization. There was nobody to say otherwise, as the only communication to the Old Man in his motor home was through Miscavige's old friend Pat Broeker.

Broeker was the go-between and cutout (the intermediary in a clandestine operation that shields the principal from exposure) for communication to and from Hubbard. When Hubbard had orders he wished to relay to the scientology world, Miscavige would be paged to a pay phone where Broeker would tell him the time and location of the meetup. When Miscavige had "traffic" (any communication in written form) to go to Hubbard, he would page Broeker and wait to be notified as above. The pager/pay phone setup served as another valuable cutout—if Miscavige ever had to testify under oath, he could truthfully say he had no way of contacting Hubbard and that he had no idea of Hubbard's whereabouts.

Controlling the information to and from Hubbard served Miscavige well, as he was now able to take out any potential competitors as heir to the throne of scientology. After Miscavige presented the information about Mayo, Hubbard was sure he had yet another traitor in his camp and directed what he considered an appropriate penalty, which he dictated onto his ever-present Dictaphone. The tape was relayed through Broeker and Miscavige to the super-secret transcription unit at the Gold base. Once typed (and signed "*"), his instructions were hand-delivered to the recipients, often the Messengers who would then carry out Hubbard's wishes. Hubbard ordered Mayo to run in circles around a tree. Literally. Mayo was sent out into the sweltering heat at Gilman from morning to night to run and keep running. He ran all day long, only taking short breaks for food and water. He wore a path in the dirt around a large oak tree behind the old golf clubhouse as he circled endlessly in a pair of shorts, a T-shirt, and a baseball cap. Of course, nobody questioned this absurdity—the order came from Hubbard directly, and obviously he knew what he was doing.

This in fact became a popular form of punishment: the "Running Program." Over subsequent years I and many others at Gilman were sent to "run around the pole." The oak was replaced with a palm tree and a graded gravel track was constructed around it. It was a nasty, physically exhausting experience that was supposed to be another Hubbard cure for recalcitrant Sea Org members. Remarkably, this punishment has been remarketed into a program called the Cause Resurgence Rundown, based on Hubbard's claim that circling around a fixed object "aligns your energy flows" and "restores your power as a thetan." People pay $5,000 to run in circles around a pole in the center of a large room at the Flag Land Base—a testament to how scientologists will accept anything if they are told it comes from Hubbard.

As a result of his unfair punishment, Mayo became convinced Miscavige and company were destroying Hubbard's legacy, and eventually he and his wife, Julie, escaped from the Int Base. He gathered a few other former international scientology executives who had run afoul of Miscavige, including Dede Reisdorf, and formed a splinter organization in Santa Barbara in early 1983 called the Advanced Ability Center (AAC). It was a who's-who of big names from the old school of scientology. This was the first real challenge to scientology's "new breed" leadership, and it would not be the last we would hear from Mayo.

CHAPTER 7

THE OFFICE OF SPECIAL AFFAIRS

Scientology saw massive upheaval in 1983. That year also marked a challenging period for me personally, as I was really struggling with my role in the Sea Org for the first time since I had arrived on the *Apollo*.

Following Kimberley's death, Cathy was desperate to get pregnant again. She did not take the loss as "well" as I did—understandable for a mother who carried and delivered the baby, but perhaps at that point she was also a more compassionate person than I was. She insisted the only way she felt she could put the loss behind her was to have another baby. Our son, Benjamin, was born on September 13, 1983, and Cathy, who had been relocated to Los Angeles with the rest of the Flag Bureau (the management body from the *Apollo*; the public delivery organization remained in Clearwater), stayed in LA with Taryn and the baby, while I went back to my post at Gilman Hot Springs when he was just a few days old.

Unlike most fathers of two young children, I was not stressed by my parental duties—the kids were not even in the same city as I was. But as a senior Sea Org member, I found my life more stressful than ever. I was trying to cope with the enormous load of my assigned responsibilities.

I was no longer an expendable; in fact, as a trained Watch Messenger I was a rare commodity. Three years earlier, Hubbard had created the Watchdog Committee (WDC) to oversee every sector of scientology. It was a "secret" body within the framework of CMO International— a committee of Senior Messengers tasked with ensuring scientology operated in an On-Source manner and thus continued to expand, as Hubbard was avoiding the government and process servers and no longer physically present. By early 1984, on top of being in charge of five divisions at CMO International, I had been handed five WDC sectors. Everything of significance in these sectors had to be cleared by me: executive assignments, major purchases, implementation of new programs, advertising campaigns, even justice matters. I had become one of the most senior scientologists on earth at the pinnacle of the scientology organizational hierarchy, and it was a huge honor. It was also an enormous burden. I was sleep-deprived and overwhelmed.

The jobs were too much for one person, but I was one of the only people eligible to do them. Because it follows Hubbard's policies, scientology has a top-heavy structure that requires myriad reports and little autonomy. Every executive appointment or removal in every scientology organization—whether Los Angeles or Bulawayo—required approval from WDC. The same went for promotional campaigns, purchases of property or major equipment, new proselytization programs, and much more. Every day there were hundreds of pages of reports, proposals, statistics, telexes, and dispatches, each and every one considered vitally important and requiring my direct approval or response. I could not physically accomplish the task, so I resorted to skimming. I knew I was failing.

Though I tried to find others to share the load, due to the stringent qualifications required to work in CMO International, it was impossible. The only solution was to work longer hours, but that was ultimately self-defeating, as the speed with which I could focus and handle things diminished in direct proportion to my lack of sleep. In my mind, the consequences of my failings were immense—I truly believed the future of the planet hung in the balance. I was convinced failure on my part might well be what tipped the scales against mankind. The stress was intense.

It didn't help matters when, after a weekly stats report, the Commodore himself got the impression that I had lied to him. While my report showed rising numbers, he received a separate report from the "computer banks" (called INCOMM—another scientology acronym for our internal computer system, or International Network of Computer Organized Management) that the numbers were falling. Never mind that INCOMM had screwed up—they had provided me with a different set of numbers than those that went to Hubbard. To him I had "false reported" because I had Evil Purposes. This was another breakthrough that explained the failures of those working for Hubbard—people like me were messing up because we had evil intentions toward him and scientology. These inhibited our ability to do good. I was immediately and unceremoniously sent to Los Angeles to do the Rehabilitation Project Force program.

My demise was as inevitable as it was a relief. Had it not been that, I would have messed up something for real and that would have been my undoing. Physically and emotionally, I was at the lowest point in my Sea Org career, even though I was at the very top of the scientology hierarchy. Yet my downfall did not shake my certainty. Instead, it gave me renewed hope. I was convinced Hubbard understood things about me that I did not know about myself; I had to look into my heart and with scientology auditing, uncover the evil that lurked within, and eradicate it. The fact that I had not false reported didn't matter—to me or anyone else. A pronouncement such as this from Hubbard was never questioned. Knowing that my misery was of my own making, according to fundamental scientology principles, I felt like a lightbulb went off in my head. *The reason I am not doing well and am so unhappy is that I have unhandled False and Evil Purposes.* It all made sense: Hubbard may have been mistaken about my report, but he surely knew why I had been doing so poorly, and I needed to be rehabilitated.

I left all my belongings other than the clothes I was wearing and my toiletries behind and was escorted onto the van that traveled twice a day between CMO Int in Gilman and LA. I was escorted to the RPF space in the basement of the old Cedars of Lebanon hospital complex on Sunset Boulevard we had purchased in 1977, known within the scientology world as PAC (Pacific Area Command) or PAC Base, and turned over to the RPF Bosun. What a fall from grace: from the top of CMO International to the bottom of the ladder in PAC. I donned the black boilersuit that all RPFers were required to wear so their status would be clear to everyone and began operating under the stringent rules of the lowliest category of Sea Org member: I was not allowed to walk; RPFers had to run everywhere. I could not speak to anyone unless spoken to. I slept on an old mattress on the floor. We ate the leftovers in the mess hall during our fifteen-minute mealtimes and were assigned the dirtiest, most unpleasant jobs, like cleaning the kitchen floor or garbage area. But we got seven hours of sleep most of the time and there was a comparatively low level of stress. I was unhappy to have failed the Commodore, but not unhappy to be relieved of the burden of trying to do the impossible at CMO Int. The RPF wasn't always rainbows and butterflies, though. There were times when the pressure to complete specific assignments was over-the-top insane and the punishments were quite grotesque.

For example, the RPF was made responsible for renovating certain sections of "Big Blue"—another nickname given to the complex, as Hubbard had ordered it painted sky blue so it would be a standout, visible reminder of scientology's presence. Typical of Sea Org renovation projects everywhere, and especially those employing RPF labor, there were no proper tools and equipment to do the job. We did demolition work with absolutely no protective glasses, gloves, or helmets. We used rollers to paint thousands of square feet of walls when it could have been done in a fraction of the time with a sprayer. We cracked cement blocks with sledgehammers rather than jackhammers. It was intended to be hard manual labor, and power tools would have defeated that objective. Nobody was actually trained in the skills necessary to do any of the tasks we were assigned. It was learn-as-you-go—according to Hubbard, Sea Org members are supposed to be able to do any job assigned, whether they've been trained or not. Every member of the RPF became somewhat proficient at hanging drywall, basic electrical installation, painting, and rudimentary carpentry as a result of trial and error. Because of these factors, and the ridiculously optimistic promises that were made to keep bosses happy, these projects invariably ran way behind the targets for completion. The solution was never to get better equipment, give more realistic targets, or add more manpower. The answer was invariably "work longer." During these renovation stints, we went days on end with no sleep at all. When we were told we could sleep for an hour or ninety minutes, we would lie down on the bare concrete floor right there—not wanting to waste the precious seconds or energy to negotiate a flight of stairs to rest on a mattress. I was not the only RPFer who fell asleep standing up. Painting a wall, it was easy to doze off leaning against the roller. Someone would eventually notice the roller wasn't moving and kick me awake again.

One of the punishments for those who messed up in the RPF was assignment to the RPF's RPF. You slept and ate separately from and were not allowed to even talk to other RPFers. When I hit the RPF's RPF for some infraction I don't recall, I was assigned to clean Rat's Alley. This was the crawl space beneath the main galley where the grease and slime ended up as the ovens and meal prep stations were cleaned up. It was a space about two feet high, inhabited by numerous rats who lived on the food waste that accumulated there. To clean Rat's Alley I had to lie on a furniture dolly on my stomach and wheel myself around with a flashlight to scrape grease into a bucket for two days until I graduated back to the regular RPF.

After about six months in the RPF, I was put on a special assignment by my old friend Vicki Aznaran. I had long been her boss in Clearwater, and she had now become the head of the new Religious Technology Center (RTC), which had been created in the corporate reorganization to perform an "inspector general" function for scientology. Though technically still in the RPF, I was no longer assigned to do manual labor. Vicki put me in charge of a project to computerize legal case files. It was highly unusual for anyone to use RPFers for any sort of skilled job, and using a computer and inputting legal files was certainly not something to be entrusted to anyone with evil purposes. But I had done well on the False Purpose Rundown auditing in the RPF, and since Vicki had been presented with an emergency situation that she needed to solve, she took a gamble on me.

The legal case in question had been filed by the Church of Scientology of California (CSC) against Gerry Armstrong, a member of the Sea Org and longtime research assistant to Hubbard's official biographer, Omar Garrison. During his research, Gerry had dug up incriminating documents that revealed inconsistencies and lies about Hubbard's exploits, credentials, accomplishments, and even his marriages and family. Gerry subsequently spoke up to the person in charge of Hubbard's biography at Author Services and said the truth should be told about Hubbard's life. This made him instantly and enormously unpopular. Nobody wanted to hear it, and he became public enemy number one. Gerry left the Sea Org and was subsequently declared an SP. Before he departed, however, he made copies of the evidence he had uncovered and delivered it to his attorney as an insurance policy against future harassment. Following Hubbard's directive to always attack, never defend, CSC sued him for theft in 1982, a suit that eventually came to trial in 1984. It did not go well. Judge Paul Breckenridge, who presided over the case, stated, among other things, "The organization clearly is schizophrenic and paranoid, and this bizarre combination seems to be a reflection of its founder LRH." The case was a blow to the reputation of Hubbard and scientology.

I performed well on my file computerization project and was officially reprieved from the RPF to work in the legal department of the newly established Office of Special Affairs (OSA), the department that superseded the Guardian's Office. OSA had just assumed the functions of the old GO with a new name. It was a public relations move: "We got rid of the rogue Guardian's Office." What was not said was that many of the people who had remained in the GO now simply changed their titles and carried on as before in OSA.

I was thrilled to be out of the RPF and finally get back to working on something more significant in achieving a cleared planet than painting walls or slopping grease into a bucket. And once again, I was in the realm of David Miscavige, who was still working to gain the all-clear for Hubbard to come out of hiding, as he'd been ordered. I knew I had to be careful around Miscavige, as with Hubbard. But if I wanted to be doing the most to accomplish the goals of scientology,

I also needed to be close to the man in charge, and accept the risks that came with it.

Working for the legal department of OSA, I was first assigned to oversee a lawsuit that had been filed in the late '70s by the GO and was only now coming to trial against the Portuguese government over the Madeira Rock Festival. Since most of the higher-ups were tied up trying to extinguish the bigger legal fires in the US, they needed someone to assume responsibility for this matter. I flew to Lisbon, briefed the lawyers, and appeared as a witness at the trial, which was conducted in an empty classroom. It was a most bizarre "courtroom": black-robed judges sat at a table at the head of the room, while the wide-open windows along one side wall let air in but, since we were on the first floor, also granted easy access to the chickens that wandered the grounds and would occasionally pop in to check on the proceedings. We prevailed; the court ruled that the Madeira riot had been a direct result of the false rumor circulated that the *Apollo* was CIA and the government had not acted appropriately. The judges awarded us a token amount in damages. Though this didn't change anything in the larger scheme of things in the US, a victory indicated a job well done and enhanced my status.

When I returned to Los Angeles, I was appointed the head of the Office of Special Affairs United States (OSA US), now located in one of the wings of Big Blue. I was happy to be given a more important role—I was on my way back to being a trusted member of the A-Team again. As the Commanding Officer (CO), I was now responsible for the external affairs activities across the entire United States. My role encompassed Investigations (intelligence), Public Relations (dealing with media), Legal (litigation and compliance with laws; though there were certain legal cases that were under the control of a "Special Unit" run by David Miscavige), and Social Reform (the front groups intended to position scientology as a positive human rights organization), as well as eradicating attackers and threats to scientology. I had much to learn, which meant a lot of reading to do; as with everything in scientology, there was an enormous amount of Hubbard material on exactly how to go about everything.

Soon after I assumed my new position, I got a call from Marty

Rathbun, who worked for Miscavige directly in the Special Unit dealing with the most sensitive matters relating to Hubbard. I had encoun-
tered Marty previously in passing, as he had been pressed into duty
working on the US legal cases under Miscavige. Intense, serious, and
short-tempered, he was good at his job, but not someone I wanted to
spend time with if I could help it.

He ordered me to report at once to the extra-secure Intelligence
Files wing of OSA US. I ran up a flight of stairs, negotiated the lock on
the heavy steel doors that protected the most sensitive files, and walked
into one of the offices down the corridor. Both Marty and David Miscavige were waiting. Neither was prone to lighthearted chitchat, but
this was extra serious. They proceeded to brief me on a highly confidential plan to carry out an undercover operation to set up Gerry
Armstrong. Though he had prevailed in the initial case in front of Judge
Breckenridge, Armstrong had not gone away. He was still public enemy
number one, and intelligence reports indicated he was working with
the IRS Criminal Investigation Division to take down scientology.

Matters with the IRS were extremely tense already. Miscavige was
in the crosshairs of its LA Criminal Investigation Division. Massive tax
assessments were being issued against different churches. Bank accounts
were being frozen. In addition, the civil litigation front had heated up.
The fight for the very survival of scientology became even more real and
urgent. And I believed it was my duty to mankind to take that fight to
the mat and sacrifice whatever was needed to ensure we prevailed.

My briefing went along these lines: "You have demonstrated your
loyalty to Hubbard and the cause. Because you knew Gerry on the
Apollo, he will likely believe you. You are going to be the leading voice
of a fictional internal group named the Loyalists who want to bring
down the 'new breed' of scientology management [meaning Miscavige
and his supporters]."

I nodded in agreement. I was up for anything to prove myself once
again and help the vital cause of protecting scientology. "Why does
Armstrong think there is such a group?" I asked.

"We have another agent who has laid the groundwork."

That agent was Dan Sherman (code-named Sheepskin), an LA-area scientologist who was a published though not distinguished author of espionage novels. He fancied himself a superspy and had cultivated a relationship with Armstrong, who had bragged to him that he was working with the IRS and that they were willing to assist in bringing down the people who were protecting the lies of Hubbard. Sheepskin set up a meeting between me and Armstrong.

Rathbun went on: "You need to get him talking about how he could help the Loyalists accomplish getting rid of the 'new breed' and presenting the honest story of the life of Hubbard. We will record the conversations to get evidence that the IRS is improperly colluding with civil litigants . . ."

To carry out this plan, Gene Ingram, a prototypical sleazy private investigator right out of Central Casting, arranged for a covert taping of our meeting from the back of a motor home parked near a picnic table in Griffith Park. At the time, none of us had any idea how to set up a secret recording, and Ingram was the go-to PI for scientology. He couldn't have been more brazen. A disgraced former LAPD cop, he drove a red Lotus Esprit (the car of James Bond at the time) and sported white suits with red shirts and black ties.

I took up my position at a secluded wooden table in the park on a typically sunny LA day. Armstrong approached somewhat cautiously, shook my hand, and sat down. Ingram's motor home was parked nearby to pick up the signal from the hidden microphone in my shirt, and he snapped photos of us as we talked.

"So you're one of the Loyalists, eh? Happy to know there are some people who are smart enough to realize things need to change." Gerry wasn't one for social pleasantries.

"Yes, there are a bunch of us," I replied, hoping I sounded convincing. We got right into the details, and he talked about his relationships with the IRS.

The "Armstrong Tapes" were meant to be evidence of the IRS's collusion with civil litigants, and when they were exposed, we believed they would end the IRS "harassment" of scientology. The details were published in *Freedom*, the scientology propaganda magazine, in May 1985, and filed in court cases. Nobody in the government, courts, or media seemed to care at all. It was a massive disappointment, and in our minds, it added yet another piece to the puzzle of the conspiracy we faced that was intent on destroying scientology. The IRS, media, other government agencies, civil litigants, and who knows who else were working together. The only silver lining from my personal perspective was the fact that I had done my job again.

With the hope of getting the IRS to back off dashed, Miscavige was rightly worried that the agency could bankrupt scientology by freezing, or worse, seizing, all the organization's bank accounts. In response, we created the International Association of Scientologists (IAS). It was a "membership organization"—a uniquely European entity—designed to keep all money made by scientology outside the US so that it could not be touched by the IRS. Bank accounts were set up in Cyprus, and all funds that had formerly been sent to the US by scientology organizations around the world were diverted to this new entity.

The IRS was not the only problem, though. Scientology lost a massive civil case judgment in Portland, Oregon, to a former scientologist named Julie Christofferson. The five-year-old case was originally a dispute over a refund of $3,000 she had paid for scientology courses she said did not provide what was promised. When it eventually came to trial in May 1985, the jury awarded her $39,000,000. This was the first time there had ever been such a large award against scientology. With dozens of other cases already filed and attorneys around the country looking to line up more, the precedent represented a potentially devastating threat. The future of scientology had never looked so hopeless.

Miscavige flew to Portland and commanded scientologists from around the world to travel there with him to hold vigils and protest the verdict in the streets. Behind the scenes, one of the lawyers representing scientology managed to establish back-channel communications with the judge. In mid-July he declared a mistrial and the jury verdict was vacated. It was a massive relief, and we all felt vindicated that justice had been done. Nobody will ever know for sure if the judge was persuaded by the ex parte communication or the protests, or a combination of both, or neither. My money would be on the ex parte interaction. Miscavige declared a huge victory for the power of scientologists uniting together. Though the IAS had no part in changing the verdict in Portland, over the years the legend has been created that this was the "first victory of the IAS," which began a long and illustrious history of proclaimed (but untrue or wildly exaggerated) accomplishments and victories.

My next big assignment was to put an end to a new threatened inquiry into scientology in my old hometown of Adelaide, Australia. The President of Church of Scientology International (CSI), Heber Jentzsch, and I flew in with instructions to mobilize the local scientologists and repeat the "successful actions" from Portland. This was my first real involvement with Jentzsch, a much-beloved figure in scientology. He had grown up in a large, polygamous Mormon family in Utah and married Yvonne Gillham, the doyenne of Celebrity Centre (the organization created specifically to attract and cater to celebrities) and scientology royalty. Though he was the President of CSI, this was only to give him an impressive title for the media; he had no internal authority. Heber was the perfect face for scientology to present a reassuring image to the world. Friendly, humorous, and almost grandfatherly in appearance, he was easy to like. So he was used as a figurehead for scientology in meetings with the media, politicians, and leaders of other organizations and religions. Heber and I visited members of Parliament and organized a demonstration down Adelaide's main thoroughfare. The effort to investigate scientology fizzled. Another success in my column.

I had become a warrior on the front lines of the battle to vanquish evil and bring sanity to the planet. I was supremely confident everything we were doing was righteous and vital to the survival of every man, woman, and child on earth. Little did I know that my dedication and certainty in the cause were about to be put to the test by the greatest upheaval in scientology's history.

CHAPTER 8

THE STRUGGLE FOR POWER

In late January 1986, I was heading from the sixth floor of Big Blue's main building to my office on the other side of the complex. As I got into the elevator, Annie Broeker hurried in. I was taken aback—I had not seen her for five years, as she had been hiding with Hubbard, though I had often corresponded with her, especially when I worked directly for her on a special project to find and train a new International Executive Director for scientology. Her orders came in like Hubbard's—transcribed and hand-delivered to my desk, signed "+++" to distinguish them from his "*". It was unlikely that anyone other than me even recognized her. She was not a public figure in the scientology world, and the vast majority of scientologists wouldn't have even known her name, what she looked like, or that she was L. Ron Hubbard's most trusted associate. I wasn't sure if she wanted to engage with anyone, and I was pretty certain she didn't want someone to call her by her name or bring attention to her. She was an old friend, so I said as nonchalantly as I could, as if I had just seen her the day before, "Good morning."

She muttered an almost unintelligible reply and looked down as the elevator doors closed and the car started its descent. She didn't give me a hug as she had always done in the past, or even a warm greeting. Clearly she was preoccupied, and she looked tired. I left it alone.

I arrived at my desk and resumed the flurry of activity that had begun the night before, contacting as many scientologists as possible to attend a hastily arranged event at the Hollywood Palladium the following evening for reasons I didn't know. Annie being in town added to the mystery.

I wondered if the release of Hubbard's long-promised and eagerly awaited OT VIII level was about to be announced. He had teased it back in 1978, claiming it was such an enormous breakthrough that he considered it the "first actual OT level" and changed all the previous levels to "pre-OT levels." He stated he had it all written up but had not released it because it was so powerful that people were not yet ready for it. I speculated the event was either that or some other breakthrough from the Old Man that would guarantee our goal of salvaging the planet. There was always something new to keep the hope going. Whatever it was, clearly something of monumental importance was about to go down.

When I arrived at the Palladium on the evening of January 27, around six p.m., the excitement was palpable. Several hundred scientologists mingled outside and several hundred more packed into the lobby. The foyer buzzed with speculation and anticipation, until it was quieted by a stern voice that boomed over the speaker, saying, "The event starts now," accompanied by weirdly discordant orchestral music laden with heavy percussion, haunting horns, and angelic choruses. It was a direct cue for us to move to our seats, and I took mine near the front with the other OSA executives. Once everyone was settled, the music stopped, and David Miscavige walked out alone and stood at the small wooden podium in the center of the stage, looking even more serious than usual.

"My name is David Miscavige," he began. At this time, most of the scientology world still had no idea who he was—he was very powerful but operated mainly in the shadows—though he had some name recognition with the mission holders. From his tone, I sensed that this was not going to be good news. My stomach began to turn.

Miscavige did not waste time getting to the point, announcing that L. Ron Hubbard "has now moved on to his next level of OT research. This level is beyond anything any one of us ever imagined." My spirits rose: perhaps this was about the new OT VIII and beyond, and it was now a reality.

"This level is in fact done in an exterior state. Meaning that it is done completely exterior from the body. At this level of OT, the body is nothing more than an impediment, an encumbrance to any further gain as an OT."

This is an odd statement, I thought. *The next OT levels are done without a body?*

"Thus, at twenty hundred hours Friday, the twenty-fourth of January, AD 36 [Hubbard's calendar: 'after Dianetics'], L. Ron Hubbard discarded the body he had used in this lifetime for seventy-four years, ten months, and eleven days. The body he had used to facilitate his existence in this MEST universe had ceased to be useful and in fact had become an impediment to the work he now must do outside of its confines."

There was a collective gasp from the audience of 3,500 people. I was as stunned as everyone else. *The Commodore has dropped his body? How can this be? What the fuck?*

What wasn't told to us was that three days earlier, Hubbard had died as a result of an earlier stroke in his Blue Bird motor home on the ranch he had purchased near Creston, California, called Whispering Winds. The only five people with him at the time were Pat and Annie Broeker, handyman and security guard Steve "Sarge" Pfauth, scientologist doctor Gene Denk, and the Senior Case Supervisor International, Ray Mithoff. Mithoff had been called to the ranch a week earlier, after Hubbard suffered the stroke, in order to give him auditing. Notably not present: David Miscavige; Mary Sue (who was living just ninety miles southeast in Los Angeles, after completing her prison sentence in 1984); or any of Hubbard's three children with her—not even Diana, his only child who remained a loyal Sea Org member. (Suzette and Arthur left the Sea Org in the '80s; Quentin committed suicide in 1976.)

Hubbard, or Jack Farnsworth, as he was known to the locals, died in circumstances less than fitting for an almighty leader. It was a bit ironic, as he had taken great care in researching how other great men died. He had specifically noted how Simón Bolívar, the liberator of South America from Spanish dominion, was a tragic figure who, in Hubbard's version of history, made so many mistakes that though he conquered the continent, he died alone and penniless in a ditch. Hubbard was not by any means penniless, but despite his self-proclaimed wisdom and knowledge of all things, to expire from a stroke in a motor home parked in a barn was hardly a noble end.

The concocted story Miscavige presented (perhaps dreamed up with the Broekers; no one really knows), that Hubbard "causatively discarded his body to continue his OT research," was, I realized much later, another stroke of evil genius. Hubbard, far from being the powerful OT at cause over matter, energy, space, time, and thought, was, at the end of his life, a mess. He had suffered several previous strokes as well as pancreatitis, he had been taking strong drugs for the pain, and his mental capacity was seriously impaired—not that I, or any other scientologist, knew that at the time. Without the story of his necessity to "discard his body" to "continue his OT research," Hubbard's death would have thrown a lot of followers into doubt. It may well have been the end of scientology.

Instead, the "acceptable truth" that Hubbard was so far beyond mere mortal status that he had left this physical world on his terms was what we all *wanted* to believe. This was the promise of scientology straight from the mouth of Hubbard: *Follow the path I have laid out and you will transcend the endless cycle of birth and death and realize your full potential as a spiritual being independent of your body and the physical universe.* Even better, it was now possible for the Commodore to finish his job of saving everyone. Yet again, what should have been a crack in the armor of certainty that shielded my mind became instead a reaffirmation and impetus to do even more. Now we had to make sure the goals of the Old Man were achieved no matter what—he had entrusted us with that task while he moved on to bigger and better things.

Hubbard's demise raised an interesting question. As we had all signed up for a billion years of service, we were expected to return lifetime after lifetime to complete our contracts. Hubbard had written that Sea Org members who died would be granted a "21-year leave of absence" before they were expected to report for their next tour of duty, and they would even recall their history in the Sea Org. The motto of the Sea Org, after all, is "We Come Back." But in all my years, I never saw anyone return to duty. The big question was: Would Hubbard come back? Was the Commodore returning to us in twenty-one years, in 2007? Or, because he was LRH, would he require less time off and return sooner? I, like most Sea Org members, I am sure, wondered about this, but never spoke of it to anyone. Questions about LRH and his abilities, intentions, or actions were just not acceptable. Asking would have been interpreted as being critical of Hubbard—questioning him in death was even more unthinkable than doing so when he was alive.

His demise also raised one of the most puzzling inconsistencies: though he'd had the time and foresight to clearly specify he did not want an autopsy done and wished to be cremated immediately, and though his elaborate estate planning had detailed precisely where his money was to go, he had not provided instructions or even a briefing for scientologists on what was to happen to the organization and who was to be his successor.

This was the man who wrote millions of words and delivered thousands of lectures explaining everything from how to wash windows to how to cure yourself of cancer. He routinely sent out "Ron's Journals," in which he updated scientologists on his activities and latest thoughts. Despite his supposed "causative departure" from this earth as he "discarded his body," he neither spoke nor wrote anything that laid out his plans for the future or who would be in charge after he left or how long he was planning on being gone. To not have anything from Ron was an enormous omission that should have been a signal flare to every scientologist. But in the void his death brought to the scientology world, the thought never crossed my mind. It was probably the same for every scientologist. Or if they did think about it, they certainly were not about to voice any concern. It would be doubting Ron to second-guess anything he had done, especially in such an important matter as the future of scientology. It was unthinkable that he would not have had this well planned. I simply assumed in any circumstance like this that there was information I was not privy to that explained any inconsistencies or oddities.

However, a week or so after the event, a document dated January 19, 1986, was distributed to Sea Org members, signed by Hubbard as "Admiral of the Fleet" (he had promoted himself from Commodore), which appointed both Pat and Annie Broeker to the new rank of "Loyal Officer" (a term right from the OT III cosmology denoting those who fought the evil galactic ruler Xenu). They were to be the most senior members of the Sea Organization and thus control all of scientology. It may well have been written by Pat Broeker—it was certainly odd that he was appointed Loyal Officer 1 and Annie, who had been with Hubbard far longer and was far more trusted by him, was Loyal Officer 2. It was also odd that it had not been distributed at the Palladium, as it was dated five days before Hubbard passed, so there had been plenty of time for it to be printed before the event.

Miscavige quickly claimed it was a forgery and had all copies destroyed. What was clear with this sudden retraction was that Miscavige had other ideas about who was going to step into Hubbard's shoes. Miscavige appeared to sense that if he played his cards right, he could seize power. He had eliminated all other potential threats, having taken the original Commodore's Messengers out of the picture, as well as David Mayo. All that stood between Miscavige and complete control of the scientology empire were the Broekers and their allies.

When Hubbard was alive, the Broekers' authority derived from being with him, and nobody could second-guess them. As soon as he was gone, the Broekers had no real organization at their command and only a small number of people they were in communication with, almost all of them via Miscavige. On the other hand, Miscavige had a team of lawyers, his Sea Org minions at Author Services, and most everyone in International Management (which includes CMO International and the International Executive Strata organizations).

Still, had Annie arrived at ASI or the Int Base, assembled the executives, and told us all that Hubbard had made it clear that she was to take over, I believe it would have happened (and in my opinion, scientology would have been far better off, as Annie had more compassion in her pinkie than Miscavige has in his entire body). There may have been a few loyalists who would have taken Miscavige's side, but more would have trusted Annie and that she was carrying out Hubbard's wishes. Miscavige would have been overwhelmed by numbers.

But, for whatever reason, she chose not to assert herself. Instead, she and Pat returned to the ranch in Creston with a dozen or so people from the Int Base to help tend to the property and with whatever other things they were doing. It was a major strategic error. The Broekers were out of sight and out of mind, unknown faces to most of the scientology world.

Miscavige must have seen their return to the ranch as a clear indication that Annie was not going to engage in any overt conflict with him for control of scientology. In that vacuum, he turned his attention to the Broekers' main ally in the visible scientology world: Vicki Aznaran and her Religious Technology Center (RTC) organization. In fact, Vicki had been appointed the first scientology Inspector General by Annie. Miscavige sent his henchmen to her offices in Big Blue and she and her husband, Richard, were frog-marched to Happy Valley, a remote property on the Soboba Indian Reservation in the foothills of the San Jacinto Mountains behind Gilman Hot Springs. Miscavige proceeded to install people loyal to him in RTC. Knowing Annie was not going to save them, the Aznarans left the Sea Org shortly thereafter.

To further secure his takeover, Miscavige began telling his staff at ASI, and some of us who were in his circle, stories of Pat Broeker being a drunk who was in fact never with Hubbard but had been traveling around the country buying exotic animals to populate the Creston ranch. That fit with the fact that Pat began issuing rambling, incoherent "orders" to people, including a plan to "revise" Hubbard's Bridge to Total Freedom. This was blasphemous to any "real" scientologist, and Miscavige made sure everyone soon knew that the Broekers must go, as Pat was Off-Source and Annie was complicit in his betrayal of Hubbard. Miscavige even gave Pat a nickname, "the Bhag," short for Bhagwan Shree Rajneesh, the infamous cult leader from Oregon (and subject of the Net-flix documentary series *Wild Wild Country*). Miscavige claimed Broeker, like Rajneesh, liked to hear himself talk and rambled on endlessly and almost incoherently, spent money like a drunken sailor, and envisioned himself a leader with devoted followers. It was a classic "black PR" cam-paign right out of Hubbard's policy letters on the subject.

Once Miscavige had gotten his own people thoroughly convinced the Broekers did not have the best interests of scientology at heart, he took decisive action. He sent a team to Creston to herd the people Annie had brought there into vans and took them to Happy Valley and the RPF because they were all "slack-offs." Annie and Pat were left at the ranch, but with no allies at all.

While I was not directly involved with these events, nor did I ever visit the Whispering Winds Ranch, I saw the fallout as these people arrived back at the Int Base. Then one night in late 1986, sitting in my office, I got a call from Greg Wilhere, one of Miscavige's most trusted lieutenants at ASI and a friend of mine since the days of the *Apollo*. "You have been selected for a special assignment," he said very seriously. "Tell nobody. Go to your room, get changed into dark clothing, and I will pick you up in the parking lot in thirty minutes." It was clear that I was not to ask any questions.

I soon found out that along with a half dozen other trusted Sea Org members, accompanied by armed private investigators, we were pre-paring to raid a secret remote property I had not even known existed. The Bhag had purchased a small ranch in the California desert near Newberry Springs, quite literally in the middle of nowhere, which had served as a base for Broeker to meet up with Miscavige and then relay things to Creston. It was also intended to serve as a safe house in the event Hubbard was discovered at his Creston hideaway. It was such a secret that even after Hubbard's death, no mention has ever been made of the Newberry ranch in scientology publications, while his Creston ranch has been prominently featured.

We drove from LA to Barstow, where we rendezvoused with the PIs at a local motel. The directive from Greg was simple: "We are going to stage on the road outside the property and await word to enter. We are to locate every file, computer, and piece of paper on the property and load it into the vans. If there are locked doors or padlocks, break them. Do not leave without every shred of documentation that may be there. This is vital to the future of this planet; don't fuck up." I was excited to be part of something extremely important and very secret. This was one of those moments when I knew I had to excel and do everything that was asked of me, as it might be a significant event in the history of scientology, and I was one of the small handful of people directly involved.

Around eleven p.m., we set off from the motel in several rented U-Haul vans, driving the twenty or so miles due east to Newberry. Like a military operation, the PIs were equipped with night-vision goggles, rifles and shotguns, high-intensity flashlights, bolt cutters, and two-way radios. We drove in silence until we took up positions on the side of a road outside the property. We sat there from midnight until six a.m., waiting for word to launch. Though we had walkie-talkies, communication was kept to a minimum. We talked quietly in the van about what it might be like when we went in there and whether we would see where the Bhag had buried the vehicles on the property—one of Miscavige's favorite stories about Broeker was that when he thought someone might have recognized him or believed his vehicle was being followed, he would dig a hole, drive the vehicle into it, and cover it with dirt.

The call never came. We were told to stand down and return home. The adrenaline rush ended abruptly, taking me from alert and on edge to instantly exhausted and hardly able to keep my eyes open. All the anticipation and buildup resulted in nothing. We left and never spoke of it again.

I later found out the reason why: Miscavige convinced Broeker to submit to his will after Miscavige tore the walls out of Hubbard's home at Creston and found bags of unaccounted-for cash stashed behind them. Broeker was smart enough to realize that hundreds of thousands of dollars in brown bags would not look good to the IRS. Unmentioned was just how they had gotten all this cash. The person who had delivered it to Broeker was Miscavige. He was the only point of contact, and certainly Hubbard and the Broekers were not heading to any bank branch to withdraw tens or hundreds of thousands of dollars in cash at a time. That would have sent up red flags. But the need for hard currency was great, since they purchased everything—even properties and vehicles—in cash so there would be no paper trail.

Miscavige had the lawyers he had retained to represent him and scientology on his side. Pat was threatened with being turned over to the IRS for tax fraud and embezzlement. He knew he didn't have a chance, caved, turned over all the files that supposedly contained Hubbard's unreleased research, and hurriedly left scientology and then the country. Miscavige had him surveilled 24/7 by two private investigators just to be sure he didn't make any noise. They followed him from Iowa to the Czech Republic. The PIs were paid millions, and Broeker never uttered another word about scientology.

Meanwhile, in the time-honored tactic of divide and conquer, Annie was separated from Pat. Miscavige pinned the blame on him and convinced Annie she had been a victim of his dishonesty. He then persuaded her to return to the Int Base in Gilman. She was sec-checked and put into a lowly position where she could be monitored. Knowing Annie, I am sure she felt her loyalty to Hubbard and the Sea Org was more important than her personal comfort or status. She sucked it up and returned to Gold as a nobody—and not a single person on the base asked her about her status or what had happened because everyone knew that would be a fast ticket to the RPF.

In mid-1987, Miscavige moved in and officially took over RTC. He had already installed his lieutenants and eradicated the last of those who had been loyal to the Aznarans and Annie. With Hubbard's passing, Author Services had become less and less significant in the world of scientology. There was no longer a need to maintain the pretense of a for-profit secular author's agency as a funnel to run scientology in order to protect Hubbard. When at ASI, Miscavige had called himself chairman of the board; he simply transferred his title to RTC to become Chairman of the Board RTC or COB RTC, often shortened to just COB. In truth, he is not actually on the board of directors of RTC, as that would put him in jeopardy of being roped into lawsuits. His title is unique, setting him apart and above everyone else as the top dog of RTC, the highest-level public-facing organization in scientology. (Hubbard himself had announced its formation to ensure the orthodoxy of scientology in one of his "Ron's Journals" in late 1983, where he had told scientologists to trust only organizations given the seal of approval by RTC. The role of the Church of Spiritual Technology in the hierarchy of scientology was never mentioned.)

When he took over, Miscavige transferred Mike Sutter, the head of the Office of Special Affairs International, to RTC, and I became Sutter's replacement. Miscavige considered nobody else in the regular management echelons competent enough to deal with "external affairs," so I answered only to him, Marty Rathbun, and Mike Sutter in RTC. I had proven myself capable of successfully carrying out special projects for Miscavige, and this was my reward. I was now in charge of all international PR, legal, government relations, and handling enemies—a hefty responsibility. It fell on me to deal with all the scientology messes around the world, whether government investigations, civil lawsuits, or criminal cases.

As a result, I traveled a lot. I was dispatched to Stockholm, Sweden, following the assassination of Swedish prime minister Olof Palme in early 1986. The investigation had homed in on the head of the scientology drug rehab program Narconon. Though the scientologist owned a gun, had been in the vicinity of the murder, and had said some things when first interrogated that heightened suspicion about him, I believed he was innocent. We hired expensive lawyers; I met with the police and provided evidence that supported his alibi. He was eliminated as a suspect and scientology was spared a massive PR nightmare.

I next flew to Paris for an IAS event, then Holland for a meeting with lawyers to gain tax exemption there. Then it was Milan, Italy, for an ongoing criminal case where local scientologists were being charged with fraud. Travel was always on a shoestring budget: cheap hotels if no Sea Org berthing was available in the city; a small daily allowance for meals and taxis.

A great deal of the hopscotching from city to city was to help achieve one of Miscavige's objectives: to deflate criminal cases and crush civil litigation everywhere. They generated too much negative publicity—especially publicity that would attract the attention of the IRS. He was intent on gaining tax exemption, and the time and money devoted to defending against legal cases detracted from that effort.

Once such suit was filed by Vicki and Richard Aznaran in US District Court in Los Angeles, claiming they had been falsely imprisoned and emotionally abused. It was a messy case, as they had engaged Joe Yanny, a brash and effective former RTC attorney who never fully subscribed to the idea that Miscavige deserved unflinching obeisance and as a result had been fired soon after the Aznarans left. The case was being handled by RTC directly, so I was surprised when, out of the blue, I received a call from Richard saying he wanted to meet with me to explore the possibility of settling. He and Vicki only wanted to deal with me. I reported this to Miscavige and he dispatched me to Dallas to meet with them, although Miscavige micromanaged the negotiations. After we had reached an agreement to pay them what they were demanding, Miscavige wanted an additional term added to the settlement that they would "handle" another ex–Sea Org member, Andre Tabayoyon, who was causing trouble because his son was at Gold and had disconnected from him and his wife. Richard insisted on more money for doing so. I agreed, and Miscavige accused me of being a "pussy" for acquiescing. It was a black mark next to my name.

Not all the legal cases were brought by people suing scientology. Many were the result of scientology's proclivity to sue others. One major legal battle had been waged with David Mayo in federal court in Los Angeles (a case in which Joe Yanny had been involved, representing RTC) claiming intellectual property infringement after Mayo opened his Advanced Ability Center in Santa Barbara in early 1983. On top of the litigation, RTC had implemented an intense intelligence and harassment campaign against him and those who supported him. This included physical intimidation, and I had been asked by RTC, specifically Vicki Aznaran, to find people who could be used for this purpose. I had turned to Dennis Clark, an aggressive spokesman for scientology's Citizens Commission on Human Rights (CCHR), who was an imposing physical presence at six foot two and 280 pounds. Joining Clark were local scientologist and Hubbard's former accountant Jim Jackson and a few others, whom Jackson collectively dubbed the Minutemen. They were sent to Mayo's offices and to gatherings of the AAC to disrupt them. These actions gave rise to a countersuit from Mayo and more negative court rulings, including RTC being sanctioned millions of dollars by the court. In the end I settled the litigation with David and Julie Mayo (the same woman I had gone to Buffalo in the blizzard with ten years earlier; they got married after they escaped the Sea Org).

With Miscavige, I also settled the litigation with psychiatrist Frank "Sarge" Gerbode, who had been financing Mayo. Part of that settlement, which Miscavige personally agreed to, included allowing Gerbode to continue using the techniques of dianetics outside the control of the church so long as he didn't use any trademarked terminology. If I or anyone had proposed allowing such blasphemy, he would have derisively rejected it and removed us from our posts. But that was often the way in the world of Miscavige. *Do as I say, not as I do*, much in the same fashion as Hubbard.

Around this time, Mike Sutter and I were sent to Seattle to try to make peace with Vaughn and Stacy Young, a married couple who were acting as expert witnesses against scientology in litigation. Vaughn had formerly been a public relations person at ASI, and Stacy had been one of my subordinates in OSA US before also being promoted to ASI. They both disliked Miscavige intensely. We had installed PIs in the house next to theirs who listened to all their calls on a cordless phone they had been given by a "friend." Strictly speaking, it was not illegal. But it was certainly unethical.

We had nearly reached an agreement with Vaughn and Stacy when one of their tapped phone calls was recorded. A friend told them, "You've got them right where you want them." Miscavige concluded we were being too generous and insisted the terms be changed. Mike Sutter and I followed his orders to change the agreement and the whole thing fell apart. Vaughn and Stacy walked away from the negotiations and continued to be massive problems for years to come.

While I was immersed in saving the public face of scientology, the internal organization itself was also getting an overhaul. In June 1988, with enormous fanfare, Miscavige launched the *Freewinds*, a cruise ship built in the '60s that scientology had purchased and refurbished. It was to become home to the long-awaited OT VIII that Hubbard had promised a decade earlier. With this launch, Miscavige was living up to Hubbard's word, which was important for his positioning with scientologists as the legitimate heir to Hubbard. Until then his accomplishments had primarily been related to "protecting scientology" rather than the more positive spin of advancing people up the Bridge.

Those who had completed OT VII were invited to join the maiden voyage out of the *Freewinds*' home port of Curaçao in the Netherlands Antilles. With about three hundred people in attendance, Miscavige released the first (and last) of Hubbard's unpublished "actual OT levels." Hubbard had stated he had researched many more higher OT levels to be released at some time in the future, but those have never materialized. Miscavige had thought they were in the files Broeker had that we were sent to recover, but that turned out not to be the case.

Even so, the release of OT VIII should have been a huge success, but things didn't go as planned. Soon after the first people "completed" the auditing they were ordered to return to the ship to do "*New* OT VIII." There was never any explanation; it was all "confidential," even to me, as I was only OT V at the time. As was the norm, I didn't think it was odd. *Must be something I don't yet know about as I have not yet attained that level on the Bridge.* What I do know is that others who have done OT VIII told me it was less than overwhelming. Many who had spent decades and hundreds of thousands of dollars to reach the pinnacle of the scientology Bridge were so disgusted when they finally got there that it was the last thing they did in scientology.

Of course, this was never made known internally, though anyone who has not lost their capacity for critical thinking would deduce that the "top of the Bridge" is nothing close to what Hubbard claimed. In typical scientology fashion, Miscavige continues to this day to promise the release of the nonexistent OT IX and X—the "real" OT levels—as another carrot at the end of the pole dangled in front of the donkeys.

Miscavige learned this lesson well from the Hubbard playbook: make promises that give people hope for the future, or even a hope that what they thought they were going to achieve and failed to will soon be possible with another new breakthrough. Hubbard did this from 1950 until 1986, and Miscavige continued the mirage by releasing OT VIII in 1988 and then offering the promise of further OT levels with endless exhortations to the faithful to "get ready for the release of OT IX and X" and an ever-shifting list of requirements for this to happen. Remarkably, scientologists continue to spend large amounts of money on even more scientology services preparing themselves for these nonexistent levels. There is always a new reason and a new solution, and there are always people who keep falling for this ruse. Hope for the future is a powerful motivation.

CHAPTER 9

PR FOR A DEAD MAN

When L. Ron Hubbard was alive, he often asserted how vital his image was for the very survival of scientology, and thus all of mankind. It was *his* image and reputation that kept scientology popular and people flocking to it. Hubbard believed that "all an org has to do is say they 'don't quite hold with my views' for the public to stay away in droves, a thing proven many times. The US government has stated that what is wrong with Scientology is people's high regard of me personally. All this is high PR value, priceless, in fact." To keep that image shiny, Hubbard had a public relations team of half a dozen or so people working on his behalf, giving them the title L. Ron Hubbard Personal Public Relations Officers, commonly abbreviated as PPROs. For many years the PPROs were at Hubbard's side whenever he left the ship. Since the end of his earthly existence in 1986, the job had been almost forgotten.

But in 1990, David Miscavige decided L. Ron Hubbard's image needed burnishing. It was my assumption that this was based on the belief that Hubbard would be coming back, and Miscavige wanted to be ready for him. He had in his mind a list of goals to be achieved and presented when the Commodore returned to Sea Org duty.

For this endeavor, Miscavige turned to me. I had settled into a routine as the commanding officer of OSA International, operating out of an office on the twelfth floor of the Hollywood Guaranty Building (HGB) with a view west down Hollywood Boulevard all the way to the towers of Century City and the coast beyond, when the smog wasn't too bad. The HGB was also where Miscavige had his office, though he listed his address as Ivar Street, which was on the side of the building, and the twenty-four-hour security guards at the front entrance were drilled to say "This is not the address for David Miscavige" and refuse entry to anyone they didn't know—even though the only elevators to Miscavige's eleventh-floor office were ten feet behind their desk.

Miscavige called me to his office and informed me that I should turn over OSA International to my deputy, Kurt Weiland, and take on the role of LRH PPRO Int. Once again, my life shifted to meet the needs of Hubbard, even after his death. While Cathy and the children remained in Los Angeles, I moved into a second-floor office of CMO International at Gilman.

I jumped into the task with the fervor of a true believer. I too was convinced the Commodore would be back at some point, and I wanted to be working directly with and for him when that happened. As the PPRO Int, that would be a given. Head of OSA in Los Angeles, not a chance.

I don't really know if Miscavige fully believed in Hubbard's return; we never talked about it. He acted as though he did and was at least hedging his bets should the Old Man actually reappear. He knew there were plenty of people, like me, who believed Hubbard was coming back. And many of us would be more than happy to explain to Hubbard Miscavige's numerous shortcomings and abuses. There were plenty who despised his dictatorial style and harbored resentment for having been stepped on during his climb to the top. I suspect he wanted a list of good that would outweigh the bad anyone could pin on him. Thus, the Bonnie View mansion at Gold and half a dozen other lavish homes at other remote properties were constructed for Ron to live in upon his expected return. Miscavige was also obsessed with increasing the money in the Sea Org reserves, as this was the ultimate "stat" that

Hubbard relied on to determine whether the church was succeeding and in good hands, and was almost manic in his efforts to sell Hubbard's books by requiring all scientologists to buy new editions. Selling books was the source of Hubbard's royalties and what Hubbard looked at for his "personal statistic." Hubbard wrote dozens of policy letters about how book sales were the best indicator of the health of the organization. There were many other smaller indicators that the fear of Hubbard's return was driving Miscavige, including his fixation with cutting down the reputation of anyone he thought might have Hubbard's ear should he reappear.

One of the first things on my to-do list as PPRO Int was to get Hubbard a Nobel Prize. In the early 1980s, Hubbard had believed he deserved one for his "discoveries" of the Purification Rundown, in which he claimed a regimen of saunas, vitamins, ingesting oil, and huge doses of niacin resulted in drug residues being "sweated out." This program was the cure for the planet's drug problems. Though never proven by actual testing, it is an article of faith among scientologists that the "Purif" is the only workable method of getting someone off drugs. As Hubbard's personal representative at the time, ASI, under Miscavige, was expected to pull off the Nobel Prize. I think Miscavige saw it as a black mark that it had not been done on his watch when Hubbard was alive and he wanted it to happen now. From my perspective, if this "Command Intention" was something Hubbard wanted, and I was now being given the job of getting it, then it was my duty to carry it out or die in the attempt.

I decided the first order of business would be to conduct an image campaign to get Hubbard's name and accomplishments more widely known. This would be a springboard to gaining recognition for his accomplishments, and ultimately the Nobel holy grail. To that end, I initiated PR campaigns about Hubbard—including magazine and billboard advertising. I had to get the ads and billboards approved by Miscavige, and once he deemed them acceptable, funding was no problem. I came up with the tagline "One of the most acclaimed and widely read authors of all time," which became the catchphrase used for everything related to Hubbard. I built a network of "honorary"

PPROs or HPPROs—volunteer scientologists who would help the cause of getting Hubbard's name up in lights. Part of this effort was to try to get Hubbard's books into every library around the world. We had scientologists buy full sets and make "library donations" to be shipped to public libraries. It's a scam that continues to this day—I soon discovered many libraries just throw away such donated books, but nevertheless it helped with the total number of Hubbard books sold, which was the measure of my success. (We never told the donors that most of the books ended up in a dumpster.)

Though I helped sales of his books, I did not get his Nobel Prize. I fairly quickly learned that Nobel Prizes are not awarded posthumously. But that was just a wog rule, according to Miscavige, and I was ordered to figure out how to get the prize committee to change their criteria—a classic example of scientology's "make it go right" attitude. Everything outside the isolated world of scientology was invalid and could be bent to the will of the "most ethical beings in the universe." It was simply a matter of being willing to do anything necessary to make it happen. Luckily for me, eventually the Nobel Prize was forgotten as other matters took precedence, which was another defining characteristic of the Sea Org: Everything was urgent, until the next urgency came along.

Even though I now had a new position, I was still expected to do specific OSA tasks when there was something Miscavige felt was of high importance and he did not trust others to do it. In April 1990, I traveled to Toronto with Miscavige, Marty Rathbun, Mike Sutter, Norman Starkey, and Heber Jentzsch to provide testimony in the criminal case of previous GO members accused of infiltrating the Ontario Provincial Police. Conviction for crimes against the government in Canada would bring the stink of the GO back to the forefront of media and IRS consciousness and hinder our ongoing tax exemption efforts. Miscavige himself led the defense, convinced after Portland that he could turn anything around. We all testified that the GO were "rogue elements" that we had taken care of, but the court handed down convictions despite our testimony. It was another black eye for scientology and yet another problem to add to the difficulties in achieving tax-exempt status, but of course this disaster was never discussed internally, so scientologists outside Toronto didn't know about it.

As part of my job as the head of OSA, I participated in the hiring of Washington, DC, PR firm Hill and Knowlton in 1987. They were well-connected politically, headed by influence peddler Bob Gray. He was what was known as a "fastidious bachelor" who had photos of himself with various US presidents and other very important people adorning his grand office overlooking the Potomac in Georgetown. Miscavige was impressed by the firm's credentials and had a hand in the initial meetings to lay out the terms of engagement. I became the liaison for the day-to-day business of trying to burnish the reputations of Hubbard and scientology—another part of the OSA hat that I took with me to PPRO. Hill and Knowlton was paid handsomely to initially take us on as a client, and then received a large monthly retainer.

It seemed we hired them in perfect anticipation of what was to come: In May 1991, *Time* magazine published a disastrous cover story by Richard Behar titled "The Thriving Cult of Greed and Power." It was the most devastating media hit in the history of scientology to that point. The lengthy article, in what was then the most influential magazine in the world, is summed up by its subtitle: "Ruined lives. Lost fortunes. Federal crimes. Scientology poses as a religion but is really a ruthless global scam and aiming for the mainstream." It was the moment we needed a large firm with influence and contacts most. Instead, Hill and Knowlton's UK parent company demanded Bob Gray terminate his relationship with us. He bowed to the pressure and stopped representing us overnight.

Publicity from the hard-hitting piece and subsequent coverage in other media would, Miscavige believed, make it even more difficult to gain tax-exempt status from the IRS. Hubbard's assets were still in limbo, awaiting CST being recognized as exempt, and he knew the IRS would be unlikely to change their mind about scientology in the face of all this negative publicity.

With Miscavige leading the troops, we went to war. And a righteous war it was. We all believed the *Time* writers and editors were Suppressive Persons who were trying to destroy mankind's only hope and had to be vanquished. We filed a lawsuit against the magazine and sources quoted in the story. We hired private investigators to dig up dirt on reporter Richard Behar.

Regarding Hill and Knowlton dropping us as a client, Miscavige was convinced there was a conspiracy between its UK parent company, WPP, and drug company Eli Lilly. Our CCHR had recently targeted Lilly's antidepressant drug Prozac with negative media appearances, demonstrations, and propaganda pieces that hurt their sales. We filed a lawsuit that alleged Lilly had pressured *Time* to publish the article and Hill and Knowlton to withdraw from representation. As part of the assault on *Time*, we ran an extremely provocative daily full-page advertising campaign in *USA Today* smearing *Time* as unreliable and biased. More importantly, the daily ads reinforced the message of the lawsuit: *No matter who you are, or how big you are, you don't mess with scientology.* While the Lilly case was ultimately settled for a nuisance payment, and we lost the *Time* case after years of litigation, the tenacious war we waged served a valuable purpose of chilling media enthusiasm for covering scientology. We gained a reputation that we were happy to encourage as fierce litigants, and scared plenty of editors away who might otherwise have assigned scientology stories.

In February 1992, Miscavige agreed to be interviewed on Ted Koppel's nightly news show, *Nightline.* He wanted to do the show to present a "positive" face of scientology and respond to the "falsehoods" contained in the *Time* article. *Nightline's* correspondent Forrest Sawyer had traveled to California to shoot footage and conduct interviews for the setup piece a few days before the live interview with Koppel. I chaperoned Sawyer around scientology facilities and arranged his sit-downs with selected scientologists. For his part, Miscavige prepared for the interview intensively. Every day for two weeks, Marty Rathbun, Norman Starkey, and I would fire questions at him as if we were Ted Koppel.

"Mr. Miscavige, how do you respond to the claims in the *Time* magazine article that scientology is merely a money-making operation?" I would ask. Miscavige would rattle off a reply, and then refine it and tell me to ask the question again. The three of us alternated peppering Miscavige with every possible question that Koppel might ask. Miscavige seemed very well prepared and I was convinced he could deal with anything thrown at him.

Two days before the scheduled live interview, we flew to DC and holed up in a room at the Four Seasons in Georgetown doing last-minute intensive cramming. On the evening of the interview, we had arrived in the greenroom just outside the studio when *Nightline's* executive producer Tom Bettag informed Miscavige they planned to extend the show from its normal thirty minutes to an hour and break it into two parts. Bettag explained that each part would be introduced by pieces that Forrest Sawyer had prepared.

"You know what is in your packages and I don't!" Miscavige almost hissed, the seething anger in his voice unmistakable. "You'll ask me things in the first segment to make me look bad when the second piece airs. Show me the pieces right *now* before we go on air." Bettag responded by saying they never showed these intro pieces to the guests. Period. Miscavige hit the roof and threatened to walk out, accusing *Nightline* of ambushing him. Bettag stood his ground and said this was the way things were going to happen. That was, until Miscavige grabbed him by the shirt collar, pushed him against the wall, and screamed in his face, "YOU LIED! You're trying to fuck me over! You handle this or we're all walking out!" This was the only time I witnessed Miscavige physically assault a non-scientologist. It was shocking, but at the time I believed it had been required for the right outcome. And it worked: Bettag was so taken aback, he caved. They agreed to run both packages at the top of the show. Miscavige walked out of the room, still seething mad, and sat down with Koppel, where they watched the intro segments live together before starting the interview.

It was a train wreck. All I could think was *Glad it's not me sitting there trying to deal with Koppel's questions. He is doing a lot better than I would be.* Miscavige was so tightly wound he looked almost crazy at times. He was evasive with many of the questions, while also being accusatory with his vindictive dismissals of anyone who was cited as having a negative experience with scientology. Yet he proclaimed it afterward to be the greatest interview ever on the subject of scientology. Every PR officer or media relations person had to watch a tape of the show to "learn how it is done." When Ted Koppel won an Emmy for this episode, Miscavige claimed, "I won Ted Koppel an Emmy!" and put a replica of the award on display in his office. It was the only live broadcast TV interview Miscavige had ever given; he has not given another since.

The *Time* fiasco became less significant internally once Miscavige had personally stepped into the ring with Ted Koppel and "handled" the situation. Things returned to relatively normal, by Sea Org standards. I continued to look for ways to spread the genius of L. Ron Hubbard. If the media were not going to help, we had to come up with our own vehicles: I figured if presidents have libraries, and great artists have galleries, well, L. Ron Hubbard should have a museum of some sort of his own. With that, we created the L. Ron Hubbard Life Exhibition on the ground floor of the HGB. I spent months putting together a multimedia hagiography of Hubbard, presenting selected achievements in glowing terms while deliberately omitting inconvenient facts. The exhibit contained artifacts collected from his life, photographs, media clippings, and a series of videos expounding on his virtues and accomplishments. It culminated in a grand reveal of hundreds of plaques, recognitions, and proclamations bestowed on Hubbard by towns and cities around the world (most of which were obtained by simply writing and asking for recognition). I organized a festive grand opening where we closed off the street and managed to persuade the president pro tem of the California State Senate, David Roberti, to speak. (Coopting politicians, religious leaders, and other people of stature in the community is something scientology works very hard on. It was part of Hubbard's plan to reel such people in by crowing about the good works scientology does: "You are against drug abuse, right?" and "You want children to have a good education, don't you?" And "If that's the case, then you must support our efforts.")

The exhibition opening was seen as a big success because of the names who attended the event and said nice things. This is deemed an important measure of accomplishment in scientology, as it reflects "acceptance." Once again, it meant accolades for me.

Another way to market Hubbard's genius was to finally get an official biography written, after the Gerry Armstrong debacle had taken that project off course. We already had our own publishing house, so printing a book was easy. More difficult was finding someone to write it. Armstrong had taught us a hard lesson: anyone who got involved in this had to be, above all, a completely dedicated scientologist. I scoured the landscape for anyone who fulfilled that requirement first and also had some writing skills. I settled on Dan Sherman, the spy novelist who was one of the few published authors in the scientology world, and who had also, ironically, befriended Armstrong to set him up to be recorded. He was an OT, as was his wife. His entire life and all his friends centered around scientology. Thus, he was controllable. Dan, with his distinctive gray mullet, small frame, and large vocabulary, was anointed the L. Ron Hubbard biographer.

I brought Dan to the Int Base, set him up in one of the "G Units," a series of stand-alone cabins that had been renovated for visiting celebrities to stay in (including Tom Cruise and Nicole Kidman), and put him to work studying the files that had been gathered on Hubbard's life. Two full-time researchers were assigned to dig up whatever he might need.

At the outset, I was enthusiastic and determined to get the truth out to counteract what I believed were lies about Hubbard perpetrated by those who sought to take him down. Ultimately, however, the task of writing a church-authorized biography on L. Ron Hubbard was a fool's errand. There were too many things that could not be ignored or explained in the man's life. If everything that was a lie, embellishment, or embarrassment was omitted, the biography would be so full of holes that even scientologists wouldn't buy it. Furthermore, if we published a book that was full of lies, we opened ourselves up to being dissected by reviewers and critics.

The inability to put together a real biography was not for lack of trying. An example: Hubbard claimed he was not the father of his daughter Alexis. The researchers spent months pursuing every avenue of inquiry to come up with any shred of evidence that could support Hubbard's claim. They tracked down every possible alternate "father" and even concocted a story based on a lie of Hubbard's that another man was actually her parent. (Hubbard never made the claim publicly, I assume for fear of being sued for libel.) After all the efforts to substantiate Hubbard's claim, we ended up in an even worse position. Now we had diligently followed every lead and knew there was nothing.

There are many similar stories and incidents. We went to enormous lengths to try to come up with evidence that Hubbard's life was as he said it was, since every scientologist knows Hubbard's words are to be taken literally. For example, his claims of wartime experience and injury were particularly important to the myth surrounding his discovery of dianetics and would have to be detailed in any biography. But his naval records didn't align in any way with what he claimed. So, an "expert" was found to provide a plausible explanation. L. Fletcher Prouty had been a naval officer with a bent for conspiracy theories. He concocted a story that Hubbard's military records had been "sheep-dipped" to conceal his actual activities as a naval intelligence officer. In other words, the navy itself created false documents because Hubbard's exploits were so secret that even fifty years later, the government would not disclose the truth. It is a far-fetched if not utterly ridiculous theory, but it suited our purposes, and Prouty became the authority on Hubbard's military career.

One of Hubbard's claims was that he had sunk two Japanese submarines off the coast of Oregon, despite the disagreement of every document released by the US Navy. To prove Hubbard right, a search party was sent to scour the coast with sonar equipment to find the subs. After weeks of expensive searching, nothing was found. This too was explained away—the tides in the intervening years had moved the wrecks out to sea or buried them under the sand.

So instead of publishing a biography that risked opening scientology up to criticism, we followed the example of the LRH Life Exhibition and published issues of *Ron* magazine that covered carefully selected stories about Hubbard's life, such as "Master Mariner" and "The Humanitarian." Each included convenient facts but left huge gaps. For example, there is not a single mention of any of Hubbard's wives or children in the *Ron* issues, and we even digitally erased them from photos that were used. Hubbard noted in one of his policy letters that the hardest thing to see is that which is omitted, and this sums up the official scientology "biography" of Hubbard.

One thing Hubbard wouldn't have wanted omitted was his brushes with celebrities. He was fascinated by them, and he name-dropped constantly, claiming association and interaction especially with Hollywood figures even during his time as a writer of pulp fiction. This fascination continued into scientology, where he began to see them as a means of gaining publicity and acceptance. He even had a list of "target" celebrities to be lured into scientology to help make it popular, and in the early '70s he created the Celebrity Centre—a scientology organization dedicated to the recruiting of celebrities in Hollywood. Miscavige also believed in the value of celebrities, and devoted a lot of time and attention to them. What was important to Miscavige became the priority for his underlings.

Tom Cruise, who became a huge movie star in the 1980s after such blockbuster hits as *Risky Business*, *Top Gun*, *Rain Man*, and *Born on the Fourth of July*, had been introduced to scientology in 1986 by his first wife, Mimi Rogers, an actress and second-generation scientologist. Tom and Mimi married in 1987, but during the filming of *Days of Thunder* in 1990, Cruise became infatuated with his costar Nicole Kidman. Miscavige, who had made a point of getting to know Cruise, had been invited to Daytona to watch the filming. He and his trusted lieutenant Greg Wilhere, now assigned as Cruise's personal auditor, hung out with Cruise at the Speedway, went skydiving with him, and most importantly, helped facilitate Cruise's desire to make Nicole his new wife. Miscavige no doubt saw this as an opportunity to demonstrate his ability to make Tom's wishes come true. Wilhere was assigned to get Mimi to agree to a divorce so Tom could marry Nicole. Like much else that happens with celebrities in scientology, this was highly unusual and would never have happened with a "normal" scientologist.

In fact, scientology claims to have the technology to "handle" marriages. The scientology theory is that marriages fail because one or both partners have undisclosed withholds, and when they confess these to their spouse their desire to end the relationship is dissipated and the marriage is saved. There is even a film written by Hubbard and shown in scientology organizations called *The Married Couple*. No surprise, in the film version the marriage is salvaged, and everyone lives happily ever after. But for celebrities, the rules don't apply. And the bigger your star, the more the rules are bent. Mimi agreed to the divorce after being given the message from on high. In turn, Tom was encouraged to get Nicole into scientology.

Mr. Cruise (as everyone was required to call him as a sign of respect for the work he did disseminating scientology) came to the Int Base in 1990 and brought Nicole with him. I met them both, and because I was Australian I was the preferred choice to drive Nic to the airport if Tom was not around. She was undeniably stunningly beautiful. Yet while Tom was over-the-top enthusiasm from the first handshake or bear hug, she was quieter, more dignified, and could seem almost cold. She never expressed particular eagerness for her scientology courses or auditing; they really didn't come up in our conversations, which were more focused on things like our favorite foods or beaches in Australia. My job was driver and I didn't want to pry. But I also didn't think her lack of gushing fervor was noteworthy. It's very Australian, and I could relate. Talking about yourself, especially in terms of how well you are doing in life, just isn't done. There may have been other reasons too: after all, her father was a psychiatrist, and had she not been Mrs. Tom Cruise, she would not have been eligible to participate in OT levels at all due to her familial connections to psychiatry.

Miscavige was the best man at Tom and Nicole's wedding on December 24, 1990, in Telluride, Colorado, where Cruise had a home. Though I was not there, my old friend Sinar Parman, Hubbard's personal chef, was flown in to cook for the newlyweds. It was the first time I became aware that Sea Org members were used as personal staff for Cruise. It was indicative of how far Miscavige was willing to go to ally Cruise. Other Sea Org members were sent to help set up the house. This became a standard pattern with Cruise. Miscavige would dispatch Sea Org members to do various tasks to "help Tom." Steve Marlowe and John "JB" Brousseau did a great deal of work installing high-end audio/visual equipment for Cruise's houses in Pacific Palisades, Beverly

Hills, and Telluride, as well as in his Santa Monica plane hangar. JB customized cars, limos, and motorcycles for him. He had a custom Blue Bird motor home built under the close supervision of Miscavige's personal driver. Cruise's household and office staff were hand-selected by Shelly Miscavige and reported on his every move.

The world of Tom Cruise became almost as important as the world of scientology to Miscavige. He saw Cruise as the entry point to the most influential people on earth, who could change the perception of scientology. So when Tom and Nicole signed on to director Ron Howard's film *Far and Away*, Ron was brought to the Int Base to be wined and dined by Miscavige and Cruise and introduced to scientology. I have no idea what he thought of his visit, as I never met him, though shortly thereafter I was dispatched by Miscavige to see his partner at Imagine Entertainment, Brian Grazer. As I sat down with Grazer in his office, he told me he liked to meet a new person every week to learn about something he knew nothing about. This week it was to be scientology. I sensed that I had been put on his agenda in order to humor Tom Cruise. Brian was polite and asked a lot of questions and made a good show of being interested—I suspect he believed my perception of the meeting would make its way back to Cruise and he wanted it to be positive. You don't become one of the most successful producers in Hollywood without possessing considerable people skills. I provided an upbeat report of the meeting. Of course, neither Ron Howard nor Brian Grazer ever got involved in scientology, so any apparent interest was more than likely merely an effort to curry favor with Tom. There was a constant effort to utilize Cruise's celebrity to get more important people allied with scientology—especially in Hollywood.

In the early '90s I also began attending international scientology events (referred to within scientology as "Int Events") with Miscavige several times a year, where we and other scientology executives would present the audience with the "good news" from around the world about the "acceptance" of L. Ron Hubbard. Miscavige was the master of ceremonies who gave an overview at the outset and then introduced each speaker. We had to compile and write our own speeches and present them to Miscavige ahead of time for approval. Each speaker covered their own "zone" of activity—for me it entailed gathering information about any recognitions that had been awarded, the number of Hubbard's books that had been sold, newly unearthed information about his accomplishments, new libraries that now had his titles on their shelves, and so on. The speeches would be presented along with visuals (photos, graphs, video clips) shown concurrently on large screens at the side of the stage. Once approved by Miscavige, which was often an arduous process, each speech was loaded into a teleprompter (though in the very early days we had them printed out on paper and had to memorize them so they appeared to be extemporaneous) and we would then present it to the live audience while it was recorded on video and uplinked for airing in scientology organizations around the world the following week. As a result, I became a well-known figure to scientologists. Like the handful of other executives who spoke at these events, I was greeted with a standing ovation when I walked onstage and mobbed offstage by people wanting to shake my hand. Without a doubt David Miscavige was the headliner and the rest of us were the lesser lights, but we were still treated like movie stars by public scientologists (for those who were neither Sea Org members nor staff, these events were the only occasions they interacted with the senior hierarchy).

Though my life as a scientology executive was outwardly glamorous, being featured at scientology events and hobnobbing with celebrities, the pressures and stress of being at the top of the Sea Org hierarchy remained. As always, my personal and family life remained of secondary importance, though I was proud of the fact that my parents had continued their path up the Bridge and had attained OT VIII on the *Freewinds*. This put them at the pinnacle of the world of public scientologists—they were real Operating Thetans who were supposed to be "cause over matter, energy, space, time and thought." They were widely recognized, especially in Australia, as founding scientologists.

I was sitting in my office on the second floor of the Del Sol building at Gold in early March 1991 when Bitty Miscavige walked in and said, "Mike, your brother Andrew is on the phone for you." Bitty at the time was the Commanding Officer of Commodore's Messenger Org International (CO CMO Int) and my boss. Andrew still lived in Australia and was very close to my parents. It was extremely rare for any public scientologist to have a call put through to Gold—even from a family member. I followed Bitty to her office across the hall and picked up the phone. I already knew this was not going to be good news, given how serious Bitty sounded. My brother dispensed with any social pleasantries: "Mike, Barbara"—our mother—he was in the habit of calling her by her first name, even to her face, which is a scientological thing to do—"had a car accident. She fell asleep at the wheel, drove off the road, and hit a tree. Ian [our father] was in the passenger seat and was killed. She is in hospital, very badly shaken, but she will be okay."

I didn't know what to say. I had not seen either of my parents in maybe five years, but I still felt close to them. I barely remember the call after that, but I asked him where he was and if he was with her. He told me he was driving to the hospital and would be there in several hours. Bitty had called in Greg's wife, Sandy Wilhere, who was one of my good friends and had trained as an auditor under Hubbard on the *Apollo*. She took me into session to "run out the loss" just as had been done when Kimberley died. Again, I was numb and consoled myself with the understanding that my father lived on, even though his body was gone.

Several hours later I got another call. Andrew had arrived at the hospital and helped my mother take the phone. She was in shock and understandably distraught. I did my best to calm her. "The police have been here asking me about the accident," she said through sobs. "I think they're going to put me in jail. Michael, I'm scared. Please help me." I reassured her that she was not going to be arrested, and that she needed to focus on recovering. I told her an auditor was being sent to the hospital to help her. I believed that that was the most important thing I could do for her. I did not drop everything and fly to Australia like a normal son would do to help her through her pain, grief, and guilt. I did not even attend my father's funeral. I was too busy with what I had been taught were "more important things": saving the planet.

There are a thousand justifications for this sort of behavior built into the scientology mind-control model. My decision not to go

seemed perfectly right to me. I was convinced that the life and upsets of
a single individual—even one of my parents—could not outweigh the
importance of what I was doing. Of course, the world would not have
come to an end had I flown to be with my mother. Others could have
picked up and taken over what I was doing. Incredibly, I did not see it
that way. It didn't even cross my mind to doubt the tech. My OT VIII
mother had killed my OT VIII father, which meant he must have been
a PTS and connected to a source of suppression, or perhaps he had
decided it was time to move on to a new body. Assuming a new body
was as matter-of-fact to me as moving on to a new job. You decided to
take another position, or you were forced to do so by circumstances
beyond your control—whatever the reason, it was a connected chain
that was simply how the universe worked. Just as my father had left one
body to move on to another, I was about to leave the PPRO Int job,
though not of my own volition.

CHAPTER 10

THE WAR IS OVER

At any time, for any reason—or perhaps no reason at all—anyone in Miscavige's orbit could become *persona non grata*.

Sometime in 1992 I knew I had fallen into disfavor as PPRO Int. Things had not been going well for a few months—then, in October 1992 at the annual IAS celebration event aboard the *Freewinds*, Miscavige had become incensed with me for committing the heinous crime of failing to jump out of my seat to lead a standing ovation when his brother, Ronnie Miscavige, announced the new edition of *What Is Scientology?*, the "encyclopedia of scientology." Incredible as it may seem, this sort of infraction could end one's career. Miscavige believed that a lukewarm reaction (which he defined as anything less than an over-the-top standing ovation with wild applause for minutes) was a bad omen that portended disastrous sales. I had been sitting in the front row, and I remained seated while I applauded the announcement, causing a ripple effect whereby people sitting behind didn't stand either. To Miscavige, the lackluster response was not due to a lackluster presentation but rather to my failure to lead everyone to stand.

Truth be told, I was somewhat peeved that I had not been the one announcing the book. Miscavige had decided a completely new and revamped edition was needed, and because it told the story of Hubbard's life and accomplishments, it fell under my purview as LRH PPRO Int. I had overseen a small team to massively expand and upgrade the version Hubbard had put together, which included replacing the horribly amateur "photo stories" he had shot back in the '70s on the *Apollo*.

For my crime, Miscavige sent me to clean the bilges, a punishment he doled out pretty routinely. It was dirty, dark, noisy, and hot work under the main engines cleaning sludge, oil, and wastewater that accumulated in the very bottom of the ship. Each night I had to bathe in a tub full of fuel oil to break down the grease covering my entire body, and only then could I take a shower and remove the remaining grime with soap. I didn't actually consider the dirty work itself to be degrading; in fact, Hubbard wrote that MEST work (physical rather than mental labor) helped "extrovert" a person who had gotten too "into his head" and thus was not performing well, which is why manual labor was done on the RPF. The work was not really the point. It was the humiliation of being sent to do the lowest grunt duties in front of all the *Freewinds* crew. This was the reason for many of Miscavige's random punishments—to ensure everyone understood their status was very impermanent and he could remove it with the snap of his fingers.

I was escorted home from the *Freewinds* after a few days, before everyone else, and was assigned to live in isolation for a few weeks at Old Gilman House (OGH) on the northeast corner of the Int Base property. It was an aging, ramshackle two-story clapboard house that would have been perfect for Norman Bates's mother in *Psycho*. It was remote from any other building, and it was where troublemakers were sent away from the rest of the crew, guarded and sec-checked. Base crew never ventured there unless they had to. I didn't mind the isolation; it was peaceful, nobody yelling at me, no stress. I didn't mind the manual labor either—clearing rocks and digging trenches—it was a pleasant change spending time outdoors after being a desk jockey and then trapped like a rat in the dark recesses of the ship. I didn't care about the sec-checking every day. By then I had been sec-checked so much it was almost boring. The thing that weighed on my mind was the feeling I had let the team down and was not contributing anything meaningful to the urgent work of clearing the planet.

After several weeks—I don't recall now how many—someone arrived with an order that I needed to get cleaned up and report to the Upper Villas, which was code for COB's office (most of the buildings on the property were still referred to by their names from when it had been a resort). I had no idea what to expect. Had I screwed up something else? Or maybe my punishment was finished, and I was being called back from OGH? I hoped it was the latter.

In an earlier trip to the Upper Villas I had been physically assaulted by Miscavige. It was the first time it happened and came out of the blue. I had arrived outside Miscavige's Officers' Lounge, a large room with a piano, big-screen TV, game tables, and the like, ostensibly for Sea Org officers but reserved for his use exclusively. As was the custom, I was waiting in the dark on the adjoining patio before being summoned inside. Instead, Miscavige burst out of the door and rushed at me like a bull charging a red flag. He pushed me into some bushes and I toppled over backward. He lunged at me again, hitting me in the face and kicking me while screaming, "You cocksucking motherfucker, you've fucked me again, you piece of shit!"

For the life of me I do not recall what my infraction could have been, and I am not even sure I knew at the time. It was never a certainty that you were *not* on the shit list with Miscavige. I do recall being shocked and I also recall that Marty Rathbun was with him, probably to make sure I didn't try to fight back. (Miscavige *always* had some loyal flunkies around to be sure nobody responded in kind.) Miscavige returned to his office, and I sat on the ground, shaken and nursing a bloody lip. His wife and assistant, Shelly, came over to make sure I was okay. She tried to explain, as she often did, "Dave is just very stressed and we have to do everything we can to keep him from being so upset all the time." Then Miscavige reappeared at the door, invited me in, handed me a glass of scotch, and told me to drink it, saying, "It will take the edge off."

There was no apology for his outburst.

He expected me to take my beating "like a man," and then carry on as if nothing had happened. There would be dozens of incidents of Miscavige physically assaulting me to follow, and many, many more with him hitting, kicking, or throwing objects at other senior executives in scientology. The acceptance of this abuse was perhaps the ultimate manifestation of the doctrine of "you pulled it in." It's not what some-one did to you, it's what you did to cause it that all good scientologists look for. No one in the circle who had personal contact with Miscavige would have been there had they not been the most dedicated, hard-core scientologists on earth.

So this time, as I made my way up the hill, I wondered if the same fate awaited me.

I was told to wait outside next to his table with a sunshade umbrella behind the row of offices that were "COB's wing." This was where Miscavige often held court when the weather was suitable. I remained standing (nobody sat down before COB arrived). Miscavige eventually appeared and informed me that he had heard from Jerry Feffer (his personal criminal tax attorney, from the prestigious DC firm of Wil-liams & Connolly) and his wife, Monique Yingling (an exempt orga-nization tax lawyer in DC), that things in OSA were a mess since I had left. They had worked with me previously when I was CO OSA Int and had asked Miscavige for my return. This was highly unusual; these were perhaps the only two people Miscavige was willing to listen to. It was a stroke of luck. "At least someone thinks you're competent," Miscavige said. "I guess they see something I don't see. Get your stuff together and return to OSA Int."

With that, I was back as the big cheese in OSA. Nothing had changed other than the winds of fortune blowing in a different direc-tion, and I was back in favor. You could never predict whether you would be in or out with Miscavige. I think this was deliberate. It was a tactic famously used by Stalin—keep your subordinates divided, fear-ful, confused, and off-balance. No cabal to overthrow the king can form if no one at court is certain of their position. One minute I was digging ditches and the next I was heading up external affairs for all of scientology.

It was clear why Jerry and Monique had interceded on my behalf—they knew I understood what was at stake and would do everything

I could to achieve the ultimate goal: victory over the IRS. That fight was not being won. In fact, it had gotten worse. In 1989, the US Supreme Court ruled "donations" for scientology services were not tax-deductible, as they were quid pro quo transactions, but more damning was a federal court decision affirming the 1988 IRS denial of tax-exempt status to the Church of Spiritual Technology, which stated: "After carefully examining the record and attempting to understand the nominal corporate structure of Scientology it is apparent to the court that it is something of a *deceptis visus*. Real control is exercised less formally, but more tangibly, through an unincorporated association, the Sea Organization."

This ruling had landed like a nuclear bomb. I remember reading the decision with a knot in the pit of my stomach, wondering to myself: *Is it possible to salvage this or has the* Titanic *hit the iceberg?* I could not express these thoughts to anyone; I had to present a tough veneer to the world. "We will appeal this, and we will ultimately prevail like we always do," I told my juniors.

But the reality was that not only was CST not exempt, but the court had also homed in on the big lie that the corporate structure of scientology was mere window dressing because everything was ultimately controlled by the Sea Org. This was a massive blow because it meant Hubbard's estate would remain in probate and could not be distributed to CST, and without Hubbard's money, CST could not preserve Hubbard's "scripture" for eternity per his instructions. This was the single most important thing Hubbard wanted done; even more important than saving the planet today was preserving his technology for all future civilizations. He had predicted that the end of the world would be a fiery nuclear holocaust. He had said often that we didn't have a lot of time. The most important thing Hubbard had decreed must be done, and Miscavige was failing to pull it off. Though we never specifically discussed it with him or among ourselves, I imagine Miscavige felt it was a major blot on his reputation.

Since 1987, Miscavige had been heavily involved with all aspects of the war we waged against the IRS: hundreds of lawsuits, smear campaigns against individual revenue agents, full-page national newspaper advertisements targeting IRS officials and failures, front groups to stir up public outcry, and paid PIs to infiltrate IRS meetings. Every possible avenue was pursued to bring pressure on the IRS, precisely in alignment with Hubbard's goal for OSA: "to bring the government and hostile philosophies or societies into a state of complete compliance with the goals of Scientology. This is done by high-level ability to control and in its absence by low-level ability to overwhelm. Introvert such agencies. Control such agencies." One day in late 1991, Miscavige and Marty Rathbun had been in DC meeting with the lawyers when Miscavige announced he was going to go to the IRS and see the commissioner. The lawyers thought he was joking. Marty recounted to me afterward that he and Miscavige took a cab to IRS headquarters on Constitution Avenue, walked in, and demanded to see Commissioner Fred Goldberg. The meeting didn't happen that day, but the commissioner ultimately agreed to meet a week or two later. It turned out the pressure had worked. Goldberg agreed to review the denial of exemption after Miscavige promised he would turn off the faucet of attacks.

Goldberg appointed John Burke, the assistant commissioner for exempt organizations, to assemble a team to conduct the review. Burke was the perfect choice. A calm, gentle man nearing retirement after a life in service of the IRS, he had nothing to prove and nothing to lose.

I spent a great deal of time in Washington, DC, during the ensuing year. Preparing materials and documents for the IRS became my daily life. I'd fly from Los Angeles to DC every few weeks to meet with Burke's team to present the information. At first, we stayed at the Four Seasons in Georgetown; it had become the home away from home in the days of Hill and Knowlton, whose offices were just a few hundred yards away. But an apartment was eventually rented; we were in DC so often it made economic sense. It didn't much matter, as we spent little time in the hotel or the apartment—we were at the lawyers' offices all day and into the night preparing for our meetings. At the meetings in the IRS offices, Miscavige, Rathbun, Norman Starkey, Heber Jentzsch, Monique Yingling, Tom Spring (another tax lawyer), and I sat on the "church" side of the table, an equal number of IRS people on the other. I attended numerous planning sessions with the lawyers, accountants, and internal staff to decide how to respond to the questions from the IRS and fulfill the demands for documents. There were huge problems we had to overcome—past court rulings, failure to keep proper records, embarrassing chapters in history (the IRS had been a primary target of the GO spying operations), Hubbard policies and writings that were unsavory when viewed in even the kindest light, and a highly unconventional operation that looked and acted nothing like any church anywhere asking to be recognized by the IRS for religious exemption.

In April 1993 we caught a huge break, by way of a horrific tragedy. US government agents had laid siege to the Branch Davidian compound near Waco, Texas. Seventy-six people died in the inferno that ensued, including women and children. It was a terrible black eye for the government that remained a raw, open wound through 1993, and since then, anything that can be interpreted as heavy-handed treatment of even the most fringe religious organizations still makes government officials wary.

Nobody will ever know what impact that had on the ultimate decision, but in the latter half of 1993 the IRS threw up their collective hands, and even in the face of the Supreme Court decision and CST decision acquiesced to granting tax exemption to all scientology churches and related entities, including CST. Though they insisted on a five-year oversight period where the IRS retained the right to review the activities of scientology to ensure compliance with the law as a foil for the criticism they expected when their decision was made public.

Hubbard's insistence on always attacking, never defending, and the relentless unwillingness to ever give in proved to be the winning strategy.

I was not at the final meeting on October 1 when the agreement was signed. For whatever reason I was no longer thought to be needed, but I was one of the few people who knew how close the deal was to being done and expected it to culminate imminently. Right after the meeting, Heber Jentzsch called me in my office on the twelfth floor of the HGB and told me, "It's done." I was elated and relieved. Though not present for the ceremony, I took it as a huge accomplishment. I

could not tell anyone until the news was made official in a joint statement from the IRS.

Many with an understanding of the tax system were not so elated;
in fact, they were aghast when the decision was announced. The *New
York Times* and *Wall Street Journal* weighed in, proclaiming the deal a
travesty in the annals of tax law. Part of the settlement the IRS insisted
on included a hedge against the backlash—only very limited comments
could be made by the IRS or scientology. John Burke retired and never
spoke on the matter.

Tax exemption was the most important accomplishment of Miscavige's reign. It was proof to me and everyone else in scientology that we
were "winning" and that under his leadership, anything was possible.
It was a watershed moment that solidified Miscavige as the undisputed
heir to Hubbard. He accomplished something even Hubbard couldn't
do. He tamed the US government.

The October 1993 IRS exemption was the single most significant
thing to occur in scientology since its formation. The exemption meant
scientology no longer faced extinction by having to pay a billion dollars
or more in tax bills and didn't have to pay taxes on future income. Even
more significantly, it would soon mean no more governmental financial
oversight. No accounting would ever again be needed for the money
scientology took in or spent once the five-year review period was successfully seen out. And with the imprimatur of IRS exemption as a
religious organization, the presumption of protection under the First
Amendment as a legitimate religion was no longer in question.

Miscavige persuaded John Burke that it was a good idea to put out
a statement that could be used to "correct the record" about scientology's true nature as an exempt organization. This was distributed to
government agencies around the world with a basic message: *Scientology is an American religious organization and it now has IRS religious tax
exemption, following the largest review of an exempt organization in IRS
history. There can be no question your government should follow suit and
grant exemption to the local scientology organization in your country.* Miscavige, not one to understand that the entire world does not follow the

lead of the United States, believed this would be the end of all troubles scientology faced anywhere. He thought that because the mighty US government recognized scientology as a tax-exempt religion, so too would the rest of the world.

But first, celebration. This was Miscavige's finest hour, and he made a spectacle of it with a huge presentation given on a massive stage he had specially built at the LA Memorial Sports Arena. On October 8, 1993, the largest crowd of scientologists ever—approximately ten thousand—filled the arena. The event began with a parade of military-style flag bearers accompanied by marching music. Miscavige entered, striding across the enormous stage adorned with flaming sconces and a huge Sea Org symbol, and took his place at the podium. All eyes were on him and remained on him for the next two hours. I had been assigned to chaperone Tom Cruise, who had arrived at the last minute and watched the event from the arena's tunnel closest to the stage. I was not thrilled that I was missing out on the excitement of being front and center in the crowd, but there was nothing I could do.

Miscavige delivered a masterful performance. He dramatically recounted the history of scientology's battle with the forces of the US government as if it were the story of the Romans fending off the barbarians, but when he got to the moment where Rome's defenses were finally breached, he made a thunderous announcement that the IRS had just granted every scientology organization full tax-exempt status. He then screamed, "The . . . War . . . Is . . . Over!" as he punched his finger in the air. The declaration set off a symphony of pyrotechnics that flanked the stage. The audience went berserk, rising as one with thunderous applause, whistling, and screaming that seemed to go on forever. That night, now known to all scientologists as the Turning Point, was a symbol of resilience and triumph. Even today, when any legal or media catastrophe befalls scientology, Miscavige issues the order that all scientologists rewatch the video of this event. It is a moment in time intended to remind everyone that Miscavige remains the undisputed leader of scientology and nobody is going to pry him from his throne. Ever.

*   *   *

DESPITE MISCAVIGE'S WISHES, the exemption did not end the problems all over the world—or even in the United States.

In December 1994, hundreds of secret OT materials found their way onto the internet. This was a huge flap. Protecting the secret upper-level materials was the most important job of the Sea Org, and specifically the designated responsibility of the Religious Technology Center, as it owned the rights to license the OT materials and thus bore responsibility to ensure they were protected. Until then, almost nobody outside scientology had seen the story of Xenu and atomic bombs in volcanoes seventy-five million years ago. At the outset, it was unclear who was responsible, and all hands began a frantic effort to nail down the perpetrators. For twenty years scientology had managed to keep these materials secret—for good reason: Hubbard had claimed that exposure to them could cause people to become ill or even die. It was a matter treated *very* seriously and great precautions had been taken to ensure they never saw the light of day. They were also a massive revenue stream: it cost hundreds of thousands of dollars to be allowed access to the OT levels. We tapped any scientologist who had computer expertise and engaged a group of PIs to collect evidence. This was both high priority and highly confidential. Within the scientology world, at least at the outset, very few people knew of the situation. We did not want scientologists trying to find the material on the internet. Three former scientologists, Arnie Lerma, Dennis Erlich, and Larry Wollersheim (along with two people who had never been associated with scientology, Karin Spaink in the Netherlands and Zenon Panoussis in Sweden), were identified as suspects, and lawsuits were filed against them by RTC for intellectual property infringement in federal court in San Jose, California; Alexandria, Virginia; and Denver, Colorado. In February 1995, federal marshals raided their homes and seized their computers. All had been active in the fledgling internet "protest" newsgroups critical of scientology.

I bounced between the Fairmont San Jose and the Brown Palace Hotel in Denver for months on end, holding meetings with the law-

yers, attending depositions and court hearings, and preparing legal
briefs. (The Virginia case was in a court known as having a "rocket
docket"—hearings were handled quickly with little time to prepare, so
I spent a lot less time there; RTC staff took care of the European matters.) I teamed up with Warren McShane, the president of RTC.

McShane, like a lot of the people working on the PR, legal, and
"enemy handling" aspects of scientology, had formerly been in the
Guardian's Office. In fact, he had been the assistant guardian for
intelligence in New York. He earned a specific reputation with David
Miscavige as "the best liar I know." This explained why a former GO
intelligence man was able to bypass the purge and ended up at the
top of the RTC heap. Warren served a specific purpose for Miscavige. When anyone sued RTC, McShane was designated as the official
corporate representative. So, when asked in depositions, he would say
with a straight face, "Mr. Miscavige is not involved in the day-to-day
activities of the church. Mr. Miscavige was not involved in the decision to file this lawsuit. Mr. Miscavige does not control any finances.
Mr. Miscavige has no knowledge of the activities you are alleging . . ."
This shielded Miscavige from being dragged into legal cases.

The filing of these lawsuits was a strategic blunder. It set the fledgling
internet on fire and activists began appearing from all over, vowing to
destroy scientology and end its assault on "free speech." RTC launched
a new—and virtual—assault that scientology has never recovered from:
legal threats, lawsuits, and attempted criminal prosecutions proved to
be no match for the anonymous worldwide information dissemination
vehicle that was the ever-expanding internet. Scientology was losing the
battle to keep the OT levels secret, and once that toothpaste was out
of the tube, databases proliferated containing all copyrighted works, all
Hubbard lectures, and then internal scientology documents. OSA had
staff assigned to monitor the internet and we soon understood that we
were under siege, though we were accustomed to winning wars of attri-
tion and thought we could outlast this too.

At first the in-house OSA lawyers sent out threats to every person who posted the materials, to the internet service providers, and
even to the phone companies that gave access to the internet. But that

resulted in more sites appearing. It was ultimately a hopeless war, and we spent far too much time, effort, and money pursuing it—because scientologists, and particularly Sea Org members, never give up. Especially not on a righteous cause like protecting L. Ron Hubbard's intellectual properties, the very heart of scientology. Eventually, even we had to admit we had lost. We were playing a never-ending game of Whac-A-Mole—virtually everything ever written by Hubbard or about scientology has now been posted on the internet.

It was during this time period that Miscavige decided to close down the Int Ranch at the Happy Valley property, where children of those based at Gold (including Taryn and Benjamin) lived and went to school. He believed they were a distraction to production, and the law had already been laid down that no Sea Org member was allowed to get pregnant and have children. Miscavige was decidedly not a family man—he once told me that he never planned to have children because "you cannot choose who you get; they could be an SP." In his view, the distraction of children should be nowhere near him. So he decreed they be relocated. Benjamin was twelve at the time and was sent to Clearwater, along with David's niece Jenna Miscavige (Bitty and Ronnie's daughter) and some of the other kids from the Ranch. Others were sent to Los Angeles. There had been reports that kids of some of the Int Base staff who had not been brought to the Ranch but were left in LA basically untended had drifted off into lives of drug addiction. Worried about what might happen to Benjamin with both Cathy and me at the Int Base, I contacted my old friend Tom DeVocht and asked him to become my son's legal guardian and keep an eye on him as best he could within the realities of Sea Org life. I had known Tom since he had come into CMO CW under my care when he was eleven or so. I knew that he was reliable and caring, and that he loved kids. Even when I had been in Clearwater, I'd rarely had time for family visits—maybe thirty minutes twice a year. I am not making excuses for this; it was just the way it was. For example: One time I was visiting Clearwater, in the early 2000s, and I sent a Messenger to have Benjamin come and see me on a Sunday morning. Sundays were the one time of the week when Sea Org members could take a couple of hours to do their errands, so

I wasn't completely surprised that he responded he didn't think meet-ing up with me was as important as getting his laundry done. My son had become a full-fledged Sea Org member, so he didn't have time for family either. That pretty much summed up family life in the Sea Org. At the time, I didn't think anything of it. Actually, I thought, *What fine Sea Org discipline.* I rarely ever saw my son again.

As for my daughter, Taryn, she had become a full-time Sea Org post holder when she was about seventeen. And once a child assumes a Sea Org position, the parent-child relationship, already strained and minimal, becomes nonexistent. The child now answers to someone else and is on the same Sea Org schedule as everyone else—starting at nine a.m. (or earlier), ending at eleven or twelve at night (or later). The rela-tively lax schedule of the Ranch was replaced with full-on Sea Org life. Taryn was just another cog in the wheels of the scientology machine, and that became her full-time role. In the Sea Org, full-time means 24/7, 365 days a year. I would hardly see her again either. Though we were on the same property many times, neither Cathy nor I would even catch a glimpse of her at all for weeks on end, let alone engage in discourse.

MY DAYS WERE endless, crammed with keeping track of scientol-ogy's enemies, conducting programs to neutralize them, putting out fires on the internet, and dealing with the constant celebrity issues.

Perhaps the strangest celebrity encounter I had was with Michael Jackson. I became the go-to person in scientology for Lisa Marie Pres-ley during her marriage to Jacko. Her mother, Priscilla, had become involved in scientology when Lisa Marie was young, and so she had been raised a scientologist. She enlisted me in her efforts to convert Michael to scientology, or at least to convince him to accept it. I gave them both a private tour of the L. Ron Hubbard Life Exhibition. Throughout the tour, Michael was extremely paranoid. He repeatedly dove to the floor, whimpering that he had seen someone taking photographs of him through the windows, though there was no line of sight to any pub-licly accessible location. Lisa Marie laughed it off and explained that he was always worried about the paparazzi. He was so soft-spoken I could hardly hear him, and his comments and questions were disjointed and childish. She had told me she thought Michael understood her because he had grown up in the media spotlight and never really had a childhood, similar to her own experience as the daughter of the King. But it was not to last—they divorced in 1996.

In March 1995 I flew to Wichita, Kansas, to attend the grand opening of a special scientology mission. Miscavige had been pushing hard for celebrities to become more active in promoting scientology, and Kirstie Alley was the first to take the step of putting money into opening a mission in her hometown. After the 1982 mission holder fiasco, few people had stepped up to open new missions, which had diminished the flow of new recruits into scientology. Celebrities doing so would popularize the idea again. Alley was a longtime scientologist who credited scientology with curing her drug addiction. She had become a star on *Cheers* and was close friends with John Travolta, who had been at the top of the scientology celebrity heap before Tom Cruise, though his career was now on a downward trajectory at the time when Cruise's was heading to the stratosphere.

Travolta in fact piloted us all on his Gulfstream from LA to Wichita. I sat across from his wife, Kelly Preston, and played cards with Isaac Hayes and Lisa Marie Presley in the back (they would subsequently be persuaded to open a mission in Memphis). Kelly stunned me when she told me she had lived in Adelaide during her teen years, just a mile from where I lived, and had attended the sister school of the all-boys school where I had spent many years.

Tom Cruise didn't attend, as he was shooting *Mission: Impossible*, but his presence in the scientology orbit loomed larger than ever before. He was the biggest star in the world, and Miscavige was using this to his advantage. Despite the IRS victory, the German government still refused to recognize scientology, believing the organization contradicted the country's values and constitution. The idea of creating a world of supermen (Clears) and replacing wog law and government with scientology principles cut too close to the bone of the earlier master race and its "*Deutschland über alles*" thinking for their liking. Miscavige wanted a campaign conducted against Germany, based on the Hubbard dictate of always attacking: in this case, claiming that the German government was persecuting scientology just like the Nazis had persecuted the Jews. I was instructed by Miscavige to get Hollywood powerhouse lawyer Bert Fields, who was Cruise's attorney, to help out. With Tom's blessing, Bert took the cause of the supposed persecution of our religion in Germany personally. In January 1997, he bought a full-page ad in the *International Herald Tribune* designated "An Open Letter to Helmut Kohl," signed by many of his clients and friends, including Goldie Hawn, Dustin Hoffman, Oliver Stone, and others, decrying the acts of the German government against scientology. The country stood its ground, but the attempt did prove the mettle in Tom Cruise's star power.

With Tom as Miscavige's most important asset, the actor's concerns became scientology's concerns. When Cruise became aware of an unauthorized biography by British author Wensley Clarkson, Miscavige told Cruise, "I will take care of this for you." I was dispatched to London with scientology in-house lawyer Bill Drescher to deal with the publisher and make sure nothing negative appeared in the book. Yes, a church lawyer and the head of the Office of Special Affairs were acting on behalf of Tom Cruise, paid for by the Church of Scientology. With a lot of persistence and veiled threats, we persuaded the publisher to allow us to "review and correct" anything related to scientology in the manuscript. We went to the Blake Publishing offices in West London and collected a copy of the manuscript from the editor. We took it back to our room at the Savoy hotel and spent two days cleansing it of anything negative in return for a promise not to sue. In truth, the book didn't reveal anything new, but it did contain some of what we considered the usual "inaccuracies" about scientology—calling the E-Meter a lie detector and saying that scientologists believe in aliens and that it costs a lot of money. In the overall scheme of things, had we done nothing to the manuscript, it would have made no difference to scientology or Cruise, but it was another "see what I can do for you" feather in Miscavige's cap with Cruise.

In 1997, cracks started to show in the relationship between Cruise and Miscavige during the filming of Stanley Kubrick's *Eyes Wide Shut*. Costars Tom and Nicole were effectively cut off from the world for a year as the notorious perfectionist Kubrick demanded reshoot after reshoot on the highly secretive closed set in London. Losing the day-to-day interaction with Miscavige and spending his time with Nicole had an effect on Tom. He was not checking in with Dave or even returning his calls. Miscavige, fretting that Nicole was pulling Tom out of scientology, sent me to London to meet with Tom's sister Lee Anne at the Dorchester hotel to try to find out what was going on. Lee Anne, a dedicated scientologist following in the footsteps of her brother (he got his three sisters and mother in), claimed everything was fine and they were just busy, but Miscavige didn't buy it.

Not one to give up, Miscavige tasked Marty Rathbun with getting Cruise back in the fold. Rathbun began auditing Cruise under the direct supervision of Miscavige. As Cruise was gradually drawn back into the world of scientology, he rededicated himself to the cause. This created a distance between him and Nicole. Rathbun worked with Bert Fields to hire infamous PI Anthony Pellicano to spy on Nicole and tap her phones. Rathbun also turned their two adopted children, Isabella and Connor, against Nicole by indoctrinating them into the Hubbard teachings of Suppressive Persons. When Tom and Nicole divorced, Miscavige was happy that the "negative influence" of Nicole was no longer dragging Tom away. Cruise thereafter became more fervent in his vocal public support of scientology—and Miscavige.

While Marty was dealing with Cruise, I was tasked with the job of helping John Travolta with some public relations issues. Since the beginning of the '90s, Travolta had been hounded by stories from various alleged male lovers, including one of his former pilots as well as a porn star. I met with John and his attorney, Jay Lavely, to help navigate these land mines. The *National Enquirer* reached out to Travolta and the church for responses. Realizing the potential PR damage a story of gay sex would have on the perfect scientology couple of John and Kelly, we dug up dirt on the sources of the stories and threatened the media with lawsuits. The stories were shut down, and I became a trusted person in John's life. Similar claims have continued to pop up over the years and they have been denied by Travolta or shut down. Gay allegations are land mines for scientology. Scientology publicly claims it is not antigay (despite Hubbard's writings to the contrary), yet the threat of a story describing a scientologist as gay would cause panic internally because for a scientologist, not being "cured" of homosexuality would indicate that the tech doesn't work.

When convenient, our public statements were "We do not get involved in commenting on the personal lives of our parishioners, celebrity or otherwise." In truth, we were very much involved in all aspects of their private lives. This was not reserved exclusively for the two big headliners, Cruise and Travolta. Kirstie Alley and her actor husband, Parker Stevenson, were brought to the Int Base to "resolve their marriage," though Miscavige was not so interested in them personally— Kirstie was past her peak in Hollywood. I was the couple's designated companion while they got their "marriage counseling." I joined them for meals each day for the week or so they were there and engaged them in small talk. They ate in the tiny bar/café in the building that had been converted, theme-park style, to look like an old four-masted clipper ship, next to the large swimming pool reserved for Miscavige and his guests. Despite the circumstances, Kirstie was an entertaining mealtime companion—outrageous, funny, and sometimes inappropriately gross. Parker was an extremely pleasant man whose only apparent flaw was his lack of interest in scientology. We didn't talk about their marriage at all; that was off-limits. But I could tell Kirstie had decided there was no future for her with Parker and so the result was inevitable: divorce. Parker was "not into" scientology. And to the organization, that was all that mattered.

CHAPTER 11

LISA McPHERSON CHANGES EVERYTHING

While the Hollywood marriage counseling was going on, something happened in Clearwater that would become a major inflection point. Its repercussions would forever change the trajectory of scientology.

It was December 5, 1995, and I was working late at night in my Hollywood Guaranty Building 12th floor office when Tom DeVocht called me from Clearwater. This was unusual, as phone calls generally came from those above my command, not below. But Tom was an old friend and Benjamin's guardian, so—anxious that something may have happened to my son—I picked up.

"Hey, Tom, what's up?"

"A woman died in the Fort Harrison hotel," he said without betraying any concern. "We're not sure of her cause of death just yet, but we think she might have had meningitis, so we disinfected and cleaned out the room. Don't worry, I'm taking care of it. Just thought you should know. I'm also calling COB to let him know."

I asked for her name.

"Lisa McPherson."

I'd never heard of her. I asked if there was any media sniffing around.

"No," he replied. "I don't see how the media would even find out about it."

Relieved that nothing had happened to my son, I told him to keep me updated. In a hotel that catered to hundreds of scientologists who flew in to participate in auditing and training, a woman dying was tragic but not unheard of—it had happened before when someone had a heart attack. *Nothing to be concerned about*, I thought, but I added it to the list of things around the world to track as potential problems. The government, media, and general citizenry of Clearwater still made it a fairly hostile environment for scientology, but our operations there were also our primary revenue generator, so anything relating to Flag was given special attention.

We monitored the release of the autopsy, but it was delayed for months due to internal factors within the medical examiner's office. Then, in January 1997, the medical examiner for Pinellas and Pasco Counties, Joan Wood, appeared on *Inside Edition*. We had been alerted she was going to be on the show, so I watched it in my office in Los Angeles with other executives of OSA International. It was sensational and catastrophic and I knew it immediately. She alleged Lisa had suffered from dehydration along with abrasions, bruising, and cockroach bites that covered her body. I didn't believe everything she said, especially not the cockroach bites, as I knew Lisa had not been unattended. I didn't know much else at that point, but I recognized there would likely be serious ramifications. Within hours media across the country erupted in a frenzy of speculation about the beautiful young scientologist who died at our international spiritual headquarters, and seemed to have been denied food and water while being held in some sort of dark dungeon full of vermin.

I was sent to Clearwater, accompanied by in-house lawyer Elliot Abelson, with orders from Miscavige to deal with the fallout. I dutifully downplayed the incident to the press, portraying Lisa as someone "undergoing rest and relaxation" at the hotel who had unfortunately died. I knew when I was speaking to the media that Lisa had been put through something that was far different from "rest and relaxation," but at the time I believed her religious choices were nobody's business outside scientology and did not need to be discussed with anyone.

Plain and simple, Lisa McPherson should never have been at the Fort Harrison. She had been on an emotional roller coaster for some months after moving from Dallas to Clearwater to work for a local scientologist. On November 18, 1995, she was driving down Fort Harrison Avenue when she rear-ended a vehicle towing a boat. Upset, for reasons that remain unclear, she removed her clothes and ran down the street naked. She was picked up by paramedics and taken to Morton Plant Hospital to undergo a psychiatric evaluation. Her boss, scientologist Bennetta Slaughter, was alerted that Lisa was in the psych ward, so she and several people from scientology's Citizens Commission on Human Rights rushed to the hospital to get her out of the hands of the psychiatrists, who were evil incarnate in the eyes of all scientologists. They believed they were saving Lisa from a fate worse than death, yet they may well have done the exact opposite.

Lisa had no immediate family in the area, and so the scientologists managed to get her released into their custody and took her to the Fort Harrison. She was put in room 174, located in the back wing of the hotel, and started to undergo what scientologists call an Introspection Rundown, Hubbard's solution for anyone suffering a psychotic break. Just as he had "researched" on the *Apollo* with Bruce Welch, the first step was to isolate the person in complete silence until they calmed down and could undergo his special auditing procedures. Hubbard asserted it was the *only* technology to deal with this phenomenon. As he put it, "Only the spirit can heal the body." Her thetan needed to be helped. I learned the details of what had happened from interviewing the people involved and reading the contemporaneous reports they wrote. Unfortunately, Lisa was cared for by Sea Org members, mostly hotel maids and housekeepers, who had no clue what they were doing. Lisa was in a full psychotic break, yelling, speaking nonsense, and often physically violent toward them when they tried to give her food. She routinely refused to eat and instead threw the meals around the room. She was never seen by a doctor, unless you count a Sea Org member who had a suspended medical license and who was posted as the Medi-

cal Liaison Officer—her job entailed dishing out vitamins and scheduling appointments for people to see "real doctors" when they needed a
prescription or to fix a broken bone. She was supposed to check in on
Lisa routinely and monitor her physical condition, but like all good
scientologists, she believed Lisa's condition was "spiritual," so her presence was not required; Lisa would be taken care of by the scientology
"technical" people. With little sleep for days on end and her refusal to
eat and drink, Lisa's physical condition deteriorated. Toward the end of
her seventeen days in room 174, she became lethargic and weak. The
"caretakers" were relieved, believing she was finally calming down and
regaining some spiritual peace. It was only when she became totally
unresponsive that they were alarmed.

Instead of rushing her back to Morton Plant Hospital a mile down
the road, or calling 911, they put her in the back of a car and drove her
to an emergency room forty-five minutes away in New Port Richey.
Why? Because a scientologist doctor, David Minkoff, was on call in the
emergency room that evening. They wanted her to be seen by him to
"contain any flap." Lisa never made it. She was dead on arrival at the
hospital.

At the time, though, I believed Lisa McPherson had deliberately
created an inconvenient and unnecessary flap, based on Hubbard's view
of psychosis—that it stems from evil impulses and is born out of an
"obsessive desire to destroy." I fully subscribed to his view that psychiatry was barbaric, and recovery would only come from isolating the person. Once they calmed down, auditing would help them fully recover.
I was quite familiar with Hubbard's tech, having witnessed it firsthand
when he invented it on the *Apollo*. Bruce Welch had eventually come
out of his psychotic state, but he was soon after offloaded from the ship
and I have no idea what happened to him subsequently. Was he cured?
Was he really the proof that the last remaining reason for psychiatry
to exist on earth was gone? It didn't matter; Hubbard's Introspection
Rundown was the proven cure in scientologists' eyes simply because
Ron said it was.

Joan Wood's medical examiner report had determined the cause of
death was a thromboembolism (a blood clot that forms, often in the

legs, then dislodges and blocks a vessel, usually in the lungs) caused by "bed rest and severe dehydration." The manner of death was listed as "undetermined." That final word, "undetermined," was a problem. It meant that further facts would be necessary to make a determination as to whether the manner of Lisa's death was natural (when someone dies of a disease), accidental, suicidal, or homicidal.

Making matters even more complicated, in February 1997, a few weeks after Wood's appearance on *Inside Edition*, Lisa McPherson's estate filed a civil case for wrongful death. With the media now all over the story demanding a full criminal investigation, and the newly filed civil case, David and Shelly Miscavige, along with Marty Rathbun and me, moved to Clearwater to deal with the "McPherson problem" on a full-time basis.

The shit really hit the fan as the Clearwater Police Department, Florida Department of Law Enforcement, and State Attorney's Office (SAO) started intensively investigating the "undetermined" manner of death. We all understood this was very serious when they began demanding to review documents and interview witnesses. We knew this was a situation where we had to prevail, as the consequences of failure were potentially catastrophic. The media, especially the *St. Petersburg Times*, the local paper of record (renamed the *Tampa Bay Times* in 2011), were all over the story. Miscavige, Rathbun, and I remained in Clearwater to oversee our response to the investigation and media attention. We did everything we could to slow the process and make it as difficult as possible for the investigators and civil lawyers to get documents and witness testimony. This was standard practice for scientology litigation: make the cost to the enemy as high as possible in terms of time, resources, and money. It was always to our advantage—we had virtually unlimited funds, as much virtually free labor (Sea Org members in OSA), and the certainty that protecting scientology was the most important thing on earth. It had been a very successful strategy.

But no matter how hard we tried to derail the investigation, eventually, enough facts came out that in November 1998, the state attorney brought charges of criminal neglect and practicing medicine without a license against the church as an entity, offering immunity to all witnesses. I was called by one of our attorneys after she had been contacted by the SAO. I was sitting in the conference room in RTC in the West Coast building (a carryover from when it had been built in 1927 as the West Coast Hotel) on North Fort Harrison Avenue in Clearwater.

"Mike, we just got off the phone with the SAO. They are not bringing charges against any individuals, only two charges against the church."

My heart rate rocketed. This was a catastrophe.

"All the individuals are out of danger," she went on, trying to put a good spin on the news. There were lawyers representing each of the people who had been directly involved with Lisa, as well as attorneys for the corporation. The individuals had faced potential jail time, so from their lawyers' perspective, this was a great relief. The corporation could be found guilty, but that was more of a PR and financial problem. From my perspective as a scientology executive, I had the opposite reaction. A few caretakers being prosecuted was not good, but we could always treat them like the GO—dismiss them as individuals who were not following church policy and move on. The corporation being prosecuted was a much more dangerous prospect.

As cheery as they tried to be, the lawyers didn't call Miscavige directly, which revealed they understood how he'd take it—they spoke to him routinely and would have been put right through. Instead, I became the messenger to bear the bad news. I walked down the hall and into his office to relay what I had just heard, making the mistake of saying the SAO was "only pursuing the church" and not any individuals. Miscavige latched on to that to lash out at me. "You are trying to pretend this is no big deal, you SP, trying to downplay it like this is good news." He always had to have someone to blame. The prosecutors were going after scientology institutionally and I fully understood what an enormous threat that presented. A felony conviction would be grounds for undoing the tax-exempt status of scientology. And now it was headline news everywhere, from CNN to the *New York Times*: "Florida Charges Scientology in Church Member's Death."

Miscavige directed that no stone be left unturned and no bank account left untapped to prove Joan Wood wrong. Her autopsy report was the underpinning of the criminal case and a big factor in the civil case too. We hired the most expensive and prominent experts in the world—including the main defense team of pathologists from the O. J. Simpson case (Cyril Wecht, Michael Baden, and Henry Lee). Miscavige, Rathbun, Ben Shaw (the local head of OSA), and I spent many, many weeks with these pathologists going through detailed medical reports and coming up with theories to undermine Wood's findings. In those weeks and months I learned a lot more about blood clots, blood chemistry, and forensic pathology than I ever wanted to know. I became convinced that Joan Wood had overlooked Lisa's car accident as an underlying likely cause of the blood clot that had resulted in the pulmonary embolism. Wood herself had not examined the body, as the autopsy had been performed by another medical examiner, and bodily fluids were not properly analyzed. No matter my opinion, though, the public perception was unshakable and unfavorable.

To deflect from the deluge of negative media coverage, Miscavige decided to announce a groundbreaking ceremony for the multi-million-dollar, 370,000-square-foot "Super Power building" across the street from the Fort Harrison. He believed this was what scientologists needed in order to be reassured that the McPherson matter was just a blip on the radar, as well as a message to the media that scientology was thriving despite this isolated incident. The building was by no means ready to begin construction, but that was immaterial. This was a typically bold move that I would never have dreamed up—I and everyone else told Miscavige it was genius because to doubt his judgment was a death wish, though I had trepidations about making such a premature public statement that could come back to haunt us. But the immediate problem at hand was always the priority, and we would cross whatever bridge we had blown up when the time came.

This was to be a major affair. Miscavige ordered that all local scientologists and staff attend. Bleachers were constructed, laser lights and pyrotechnics were primed, gold shovels were purchased, and the big event happened. I sat in the audience as the show proceeded with Miscavige smiling as he dug into the dirt and announced, "The sun never sets on scientology." It was classic Hubbard PR tech at work. In fact, it would be fifteen years before the building opened—and then only after a lawsuit was filed claiming the fundraising for the building was fraudulent and the opening was delayed in order to persuade scientologists to hand over more money to complete the building.

The civil case plaintiff (Lisa McPherson's estate) named Miscavige as a defendant in their wrongful death suit. I believed this was simply a litigation tactic to bring pressure to settle the case for a hefty payment. No expense was spared to try to extricate Miscavige from the case. Attorneys were flown in from New York and Washington, DC. But even those high-powered lawyers could not convince the judge that Miscavige should not be included as a defendant. The judge wanted discovery to go forward in the case, including taking Miscavige's deposition, before he could conclude whether Miscavige should not be named as a defendant. It all came to a head in December 1999. The big hearing in the civil case was scheduled for December 15 in Tampa, but Miscavige flew to Los Angeles just a couple of days before. For months, he had been planning another event at the LA Memorial Sports Arena to celebrate the end of the millennium, as his follow-up to the 1993 Turning Point event. Same location, same huge stage, same large audience. He wanted to present a retrospective on the first fifty years of scientology and to tout his accomplishments as he led his followers into a new era of unprecedented growth. He hoped that it would serve to paper over any cracks the McPherson case had created in the confidence of the faithful.

When he departed Clearwater for LA, he told us he was terrified to be leaving the civil case in our hands, as he was sure we would screw it up, but he had no choice but to go. I think he saw the writing on the wall and did not want to be around to share responsibility for the outcome. He could blame us for any bad result and claim it would have been different had he been there. He took Shelly with him. She had been overseeing a huge internal effort to prepare for the turn of the millennium. There had been a general fear across the globe that at the stroke of midnight the world would be thrown into chaos as every computer would shut down because their internal clocks would not be able to cope with changing from the nineteen hundreds to the aughts. We were stockpiling generators, food, fuel, and gold in case banks collapsed. Shelly had taken her role seriously. The most important things to be protected were in Los Angeles with the central computer banks and at the Int Base, so she too could not be in Clearwater until the new year. The stress level was high on all fronts.

The Tampa hearing did not go well. Judge James Moody did not buy the arguments of Miscavige's expensive lawyers. At one point, Marty Rathbun even stood up and tried to argue with the judge that he was wrong in thinking Miscavige had been involved or even had relevant information necessary to the case—all to no avail. Moody ordered that Miscavige was to remain a defendant.

After the December 15 hearing, we drove back from Tampa to Clearwater, preparing to make the fateful call to COB with the bad news. The only reason the call was not made from Tampa was that it was still too early; Miscavige was in California and rarely rose before late morning. I sat alongside Marty in the conference room of the Bank of Clearwater building. "Sir, Moody ruled against us," he reported. Miscavige began screaming in response. His rage was unlike anything we had experienced before, even for someone who typically did not hold his anger in check.

"I knew you motherfuckers would screw this up and ruin my life. I can't trust you to do anything!" The expletive-filled call continued for a few minutes as he accused us and the lawyers of all manner of terrible things, finally reminding us that it was clear he was the only person who could handle anything of importance in scientology. It was a familiar message, but one tinged with more vehemence than we'd ever heard. I feared what was to follow; I was certain we'd reached a tipping point in the world of Miscavige and scientology, and things would not get easier or better.

AT THE END of the millennium, a number of factors converged that I believe brought about the disturbing shift in Miscavige's behavior. Obviously, the stress of the McPherson case was taking a toll, putting him more on edge than ever. But also by then the agreed-upon period of IRS oversight was over. The last annual meeting of the Church Tax

Compliance Committee had been held and Miscavige knew the days
of any government agency having the ability to intrude on the internal
workings and finances of scientology were now finally over. He was free
to rule his kingdom as he saw fit without being answerable to anyone.
And finally, it had now been fourteen years since Hubbard's death, and
the specter of his return loomed. He was the one person who could
snap his fingers and end Miscavige's tenure at the top.

The best evidence of Miscavige's concern about the Commodore
reappearing was the urgent push to finish construction and landscaping
on the opulent multimillion-dollar mansion that he was building for
Hubbard overlooking the Gold Base. Completed in 1999, Bonnie View
was a fully functioning residence with a household staff who laid out
clothes each day in preparation for Hubbard to walk in the door. No
expense had been spared; it was a manor house beyond Saint Hill with
every modern feature, including an indoor pool, two-story library, fully
equipped office, gun room, skeet-shooting range, tennis court, guest-
houses, and a huge garage that held Hubbard's stable of vehicles, all kept
in perfect condition and ready to drive at a moment's notice. I was one
of a very small number of people who have ever been inside the mansion, including the vast majority of staff at the Gold Base. This was not
a museum—it was a home. Ron's home.

The last months of the twentieth century would turn out to be
a watershed period both for me and for scientology generally. Since
that abusive phone call with Miscavige, inklings had begun forming in
the back of my mind. *Is this really scientology?* I wondered. *Am I doing
what is right and what I joined up for?* Doubt was a strange feeling,
as I was conditioned to being certain about everything in scientology.
The absolute conviction that what you are doing is right and just and
saving mankind provides enormous strength to persist and overcome
incredible odds. It's almost a superpower. I felt guilty for having these
thoughts and tried to put them out of my mind. This was not what a
good scientologist, let alone a good Sea Org member, would think.

But it made little sense to me why Miscavige had become so enraged
about a court case—I assumed he could testify that he knew nothing
about Lisa McPherson and he would not be personally liable even if the

case went to trial and damages were awarded. Scientology would pay and nothing would come out of his pocket. His personal reputation would not suffer. He had done nothing wrong. He also knew we were doing everything humanly possible to get him out of the case. It was a thankless task, working day and night to try to protect Miscavige and then being screamed at and abused when things didn't go the way he wanted.

I had joined the Sea Org to advance scientology and Hubbard's objectives, not David Miscavige's. To be sure, he had carefully managed the flow of information to and from Hubbard to position himself as the only person who truly knew what Hubbard wanted, and thus I had been convinced that supporting him was the best way to support scientology. And he had pulled off the impossible by getting tax exemption. I believed in the picture he had painted of his own heroism, to a large degree. But his rage over the civil case smelled different to me, because it appeared to be motivated by what was important to him personally rather than the greater good of scientology.

However palpable these first stirrings of discontent, they were not persuasive enough to overcome my loyalty to Hubbard or my conviction that the very important goal of saving mankind had to be achieved. In times when things seemed crazy, or the physical or emotional pain seemed to be near the breaking point, I would think, *I have suffered worse than this in past lives. My discomfort is nothing compared to the big picture.* These concepts grew out of Hubbard explaining that all Sea Org members had "run planets before" and thus are capable of doing anything against insurmountable odds and personal hardship. The idea that Sea Org members are tough is ingrained from the first days of indoctrination of every new recruit, and it is a source of great pride. I found myself questioning those long-standing beliefs, but they were not easy to crack.

Though Miscavige was beyond furious, he had nobody else he could turn to other than Marty and me to deal with legal cases, lawyers, PIs, pathologists, and the media. So, we carried on, rededicated to trying to prove we were not incompetent idiots who wanted nothing more than the demise of Miscavige, as he repeatedly accused us. To make matters worse for all of us, Robert Minton came to town in late 1999.

Bob was a fifty-three-year-old retired financier from Boston who, in 1997, had heard about scientology's efforts to suppress free speech on the internet. He decided to do something he considered worthwhile with his time, and first took up the cause of Vaughn and Stacy Young, the former Sea Org members who had worked for David Miscavige at Author Services. We had failed to silence them in Seattle, though we tried through our typical Fair Game tactics, including calling Animal Control with an anonymous tip that Stacy, an animal lover, was sheltering dozens of stray and diseased cats and dogs in their rented home. It was of course not true; they had one dog and maybe three cats. Oddly, this was what first got Minton's attention. He put up the money to relocate the Youngs to a new home outside Seattle with a few acres of land for the animals. We had no idea who he was or why he was doing this when his name first showed up—we believed he was some agent of a grander conspiracy; it was not possible that he was simply a person who was willing to spend his own money to help others. Through his contact with Stacy and Vaughn, he learned more about scientology. He became the subject of one of our "noisy investigations" by hired PIs (according to Hubbard's *Manual of Justice*: "When we investigate we do so noisily always. And usually mere investigation damps out the trouble even when we discover no really pertinent facts"). This turned Minton into a crusader to expose scientology abuses—when the McPherson case was opened, he became a full-time advocate.

The resource Minton had was money. He gathered former scientology executives, including Stacy Brooks and Jesse Prince (an executive in RTC under Vicki Aznaran), and moved them into rented homes in Clearwater to form the Lisa McPherson Trust (LMT). I did everything possible—including contacting everyone we knew they could possibly rent office space from to inform them he had made his money through criminal activities (we didn't care if this was true or not). When he could not get anyone to rent office space to him, he decided he would buy a property. We countered by making higher offers on any building in his sights. That eventually backfired, as the building he finally managed to purchase was one we could not persuade the owner to sell to us instead, and was directly adjacent to the old Bank of Clearwater building next door to OSA and across from the West Coast building, where Miscavige had his offices. Minton and his LMT team moved in and began routine protests outside the scientology buildings in Clearwater.

Marty Rathbun and I were berated almost daily by Miscavige about what we were doing to "handle the threat" of Minton and were required to report constantly on his location and activities. To keep tabs, we set up cameras to monitor his building and movements, added security personnel, and hired off-duty Clearwater police officers and stationed them outside our buildings to send a message to Minton that the police were "on our side," while also keeping members of the CWPD happy by providing them with additional income. We mobilized local OT scientologists to engage the LMT personnel and try to distract them. A spy was placed in Minton's group. She went by Laura Terrapin, though this was not her real name. She had previously infiltrated the Cult Awareness Network (CAN), and when she moved down to Clearwater to "help out," she was accepted based on her bona fides from CAN.

The LMT often protested with signs and chants, which started being directed at Miscavige personally, and that added to his anger. SCIENTOLOGY KILLS and WHY DID THE TECH FAIL LISA? were two of the more popular ones, along with DAVID MISCAVIGE HAS BLOOD ON HIS HANDS. He considered Clearwater to be his personal domain and Bob Minton not worthy to lick the soles of his handmade John Lobb shoes.

Marty and I were informed by Miscavige in no uncertain terms that our failure to stop Minton from moving to town had caused irreparable damage to scientology. We felt we had let the team down, and this was confirmed by the sec checking we underwent each day to interrogate us as to what crimes we were engaged in that were preventing us from getting our jobs done. So, we upped the ante by bringing in a number of private investigators and beginning a massive international campaign to silence Minton. Our main PI was Dave Lubow—a protégé of Gene Ingram's who had taken over when Ingram retired to Cabo San Lucas.

Lubow flew to Clearwater, and Marty and I met him in a parking lot downtown a few blocks from the scientology buildings. As we sat in his rental car, I told him, in a tone that left no doubt I was deadly serious: "As of now, you have only one job. Stop Minton. You are to do nothing else. Funding will be provided for whatever you need. Get us your plan on how you are going to accomplish this within the next few days." Lubow said he already had some ideas and would start at once. It was his opportunity to make a name for himself.

Lubow harassed Minton all over the country, visiting Minton's family, relatives, and associates and employing every Fair Game tactic possible. Minton had a financial interest in a car dealership near Boston, so picketers showed up outside with signs saying the owners were religious bigots. He was followed everywhere he went. This was just the noisy part of the campaign. Lubow believed Minton's real vulnerability was his finances, and he pursued a scheme to get Minton's bank accounts frozen in Switzerland. Minton had made money trading in foreign bonds, mostly Nigerian. It was a shady business, but not necessarily illegal. By creating connections through prominent Nigerians in London and the Nigerian Embassy there, Lubow generated enough suspicion about Minton's money that a Swiss prosecutor responded to official requests from the embassy and froze Minton's accounts. I did not know whether Minton had engaged in illegal activities, whether Lubow had bribed people to do his bidding, or if the truth was so murky I could not have unraveled it even if I wanted to. It didn't matter. It was the result that justified the means, and like every other scientology official, I didn't *want* to know what was done in detail. I had plausible deniability if I was ever put in a position of having to respond to questioning by the media or under oath: "I had no idea, and nobody told me, so I am not culpable for whatever you say was done wrong."

We also launched an assault on anyone involved in the Lisa McPherson Trust. When our spy reported that Jesse Prince had marijuana growing on his back porch, we hired ex-DEA private investigators to use their connections to get the police to arrest him. They did so, even though his supposed drug enterprise turned out to be a single plant. Minton had to hire a lawyer to defend Jesse. Jesse was acquitted, but he was now labeled by us as someone who had been arrested for growing drugs.

We planned an operation to get Minton arrested too. Our spy told us that Minton, usually a pretty easygoing guy, was known to snap when pushed too far and got upset when the scientologists "got in his face" while he was picketing. So Rich Howd, one of the local OSA people, confronted Minton on the sidewalk. He very deliberately got right in his face, taunting and goading him. Minton swatted at him with his picket sign to get him out of his way. Howd flopped to the ground like a soccer player trying to get a penalty in the dying moments of a big game, writhing in feigned agony. It was caught on video, as had been planned. The police were called and Howd filed battery charges. Minton was arrested and spent the night in jail. He, like Jesse Prince, was acquitted. But this didn't really matter. The objective had been achieved: we now labeled Minton a "criminal" who had been arrested for "violent assault."

Miscavige instructed Tom DeVocht to tear up the sidewalks in front of the Fort Harrison for "renovations" so the protesters could not walk there. When the sidewalk closures and counterprotesters didn't curtail Minton and his people, a lawsuit was filed to obtain a restraining order. Lawyer Sandy Rosen was brought in from New York to argue the case. Ultimately the judge issued an order that prevented Minton and the LMT from being within ten feet of any scientology building or scientologist.

The protesters stayed ten feet away but were otherwise not dissuaded. It was like an interminable game of cat and mouse. But while stopping Minton was proving difficult, there was more success with respect to the criminal case related to Lisa McPherson's death. In June 2000, State Attorney Bernie McCabe dropped the McPherson case. Miscavige had had personal meetings with the lawyer for medical examiner Joan Wood and with McCabe to present to them the findings of our expensive expert criminal pathologists. They concluded that Lisa McPherson's death had likely resulted from a bruise suffered in the minor car accident that had happened right before she went to Morton Plant Hospital. This, they asserted, was the probable cause of the thromboembolism that was the ultimate cause of death—an accident. They cited detailed scientific evidence based on analysis of her blood, organs, and vitreous fluid in her eyes. Wood could not fight against the conclusions and was persuaded to revise Lisa McPherson's death certificate to reflect the car accident and change the manner of death from "undetermined" to "accidental." The State Attorney's Office had no choice but to drop the criminal prosecution as a result.

We had also managed to get the civil case transferred from Judge Moody in Tampa to Judge Susan Schaeffer in St. Petersburg. Given Moody's rulings, we believed he was bigoted against us and almost any other judge would offer a more level playing field. Miscavige was all in and doing everything he could to prevent the catastrophe of the full story of Lisa McPherson ever being told. He took it upon himself to visit Judge Schaeffer's chambers in an effort to charm her into treating him and scientology favorably. It didn't work, but it never occurred to me how bizarre and misguided it was. Instead, in my distorted view, Miscavige had to take such extreme measures because everyone else around him, including me, had failed to deal with the situation and could not be trusted to do the important work of saving scientology. He was the "only one."

As a direct result of the McPherson matter, measures were taken internally in scientology to prevent any recurrence. It became unalterable policy that nobody in a psychotic state or even with a serious physical condition was allowed to stay in any of the scientology-owned hotels. Working with lawyer Bill Drescher, we drafted and implemented one-sided agreements that everyone who partakes in scientology services is required to sign—forfeiting the right to sue and any rights to access the records of scientology services, and even giving scientology authorization to hold the signee against their will should they have a psychotic episode so they can participate in the Introspection Rundown.

LITTLE OUTSIDE LISA McPherson–related matters intruded into our world in Clearwater, with one exception: dealing with major celebrities. Multi-Grammy-winning musician Chick Corea, a prominent and long-term promoter of scientology, was in financial trouble. Through his musician father, Ron Sr., and their family friend Ron Moss, who was Chick's manager (and the father of actress Elisabeth Moss), Miscavige had a personal connection to Chick. Miscavige brought in Sea Org members to sort out Chick's financial mess. To infuse him with some cash, Miscavige ordered that scientology buy Chick's Mad Hatter recording studio in Los Angeles. Millions were spent on what was destined to be a white elephant. It was no bigger or better than existing underutilized, similar studios at Gold. Ultimately it was made doubly redundant by Miscavige's purchase of the even more expensive white elephant of the old KCET studios on Sunset Boulevard. But this meant that Chick owed Miscavige, just like Tom Cruise, John Travolta, Lisa Marie Presley, Kirstie Alley, and others did after they'd been the recipients of favors.

In mid-2001, while shooting *Minority Report*, Cruise made efforts to bring the movie's director, Steven Spielberg, into the fold. Cruise informed Miscavige that Spielberg was "psych influenced" because his children were seeing a psychiatrist. Shortly thereafter, the scientology front group Citizens Commission on Human Rights picketed Spielberg's kids' psychiatrist's office in the Westwood neighborhood of Los Angeles. When their mother, Kate Capshaw, saw the picketers and realized scientology was behind them, she promptly told her husband, who brought it up to Cruise as unappreciated and inappropriate. Though the action had been very deliberate and coordinated beforehand, when it blew up, Miscavige did what he always did: he found a scapegoat and claimed they had been acting "without authorization." He assured Cruise, and in turn Spielberg, that this had been "taken care of."

Cruise was doing his best to court celebrities other than those with whom he was working on films. Perhaps the most famous were David and Victoria Beckham. Their friendship with Cruise was covered extensively in the media, while behind the scenes a more bizarre scenario was playing out. A professional-grade soccer pitch was constructed on the property at Gold. The ground was leveled, irrigation installed, perfect turf laid, goals raised. A full-time caretaker was appointed from the Gold staff. Of course, nobody working at the property had time to play soccer. It was built for one purpose only: so Tom Cruise could woo his friend David to come to Gold. It never happened. The soccer field remains to this day like a failed field of dreams—they built it, but no one has come.

Apart from celebrity matters, there was one other incident that intruded into our Lisa McPherson bubble. In 2000, David Miscavige's older brother, Ronnie, and Ronnie's wife, my old friend Bitty, announced they were departing the Sea Org. I thought it was a momentary upset that could be smoothed over. Bitty had been targeted by Miscavige for the McPherson matter, as she had been in Clearwater at the time of Lisa's death (though was now back at Int). Bitty had demanded to leave before and I had talked her out of it. Marty Rathbun and I were dispatched by David from Clearwater to Gilman to handle them. Marty was the sec checker, and, because I was their closest friend, David thought I could act as the good guy and persuade them to stay. When they resisted, David offered to give Bitty $100,000 to set herself up outside the Sea Org if Ronnie would divorce her and stay. Ronnie refused. I thought they were making a terrible mistake heading off into the wog world, but nothing I said changed their minds.

Marty and I were ordered by David to get them out of the country so they could not be subpoenaed in the McPherson case. I did not really understand why this was so important, but he was very insistent, and this was not the sort of order to be quibbled with.

We tried many different avenues to find a suitable location and employment for them. Eventually, with the help of former PI Gene Ingram, we set them up in a job selling time-shares in Cabo San Lucas. They at first adamantly resisted leaving the United States and were persuaded to go only when we agreed to Bitty's demand that their daughter, Jenna, who was sixteen at the time, be sent with them. Jenna was in the Sea Org at Flag. Ronnie and Bitty left for Mexico and Jenna was supposed to follow in a few days. We got her on a plane from Florida to LA, but when she arrived at the HGB, it was not quite so simple. Jenna announced to Marty and me: "I am not leaving the Sea Org and you can't make me. I don't want to go with my parents. I think them blowing is a Suppressive Act." She had a point. It was against everything I believed to force someone out of the Sea Org who wanted to be there, and it was also true that abandoning the Sea Org, especially from the

Int Base, carried a Hubbard-mandated SP declare. I had known Jenna since her infancy, and I was well aware she was every bit as stubborn as her mother. This was going to be a big problem. Marty was convinced she could be made to go to Mexico. I knew otherwise. We tried everything we could to persuade her to leave. In the end, our solution to the problem was to make her deal with Bitty and Ronnie. She called them to break the news, with us in the room listening in. Bitty and Ronnie reacted as I thought they would and threatened to come back to the US to collect Jenna. David Miscavige was furious that we had failed to control matters and he had to personally speak to Ronnie to resolve it. Ultimately things calmed down, and Jenna remained in the Sea Org while her parents remained in Mexico.

With Bitty and Ronnie out of the country, I went back to work. My attention went to Buffalo, New York, where the city was trying to evict the local scientology organization, falling back on their eminent domain powers as part of an infrastructure improvement program. Buffalo, like many local scientology chapters, struggled to keep ahead of its creditors, and the organization could not afford to buy another building. So we took up the fight, with Miscavige ordering a lawsuit be filed claiming religious discrimination. In the end, the city decided it would cost less to settle for a nuisance payment that was, however, big enough for us to purchase a much larger new building.

Miscavige deemed this win against the city a huge success and decided to make it an example to the scientology world. Claiming that scientology orgs around the globe were failing because their staff did not know how to sell scientology to the public, he generated a grand plan he later dubbed "Ideal Orgs." The idea was to buy larger, more impressive buildings and renovate them with state-of-the-art media installations to introduce new people to scientology. Buffalo was to be a model for all other local orgs. He outfitted its atrium with dozens of TV screens in high-tech-looking displays. Each showed specific videos that the staff could simply direct members of the public who came in seeking information to watch and learn about all the different (positive) facets of scientology. It was supposed to be the end-all solution to bringing new people onto the Bridge.

Shortly thereafter, Miscavige decided the Tampa org would be next. It was a tiny operation located in a strip mall with no money for a new building, so he ordered CMO CW Messengers Jenny DeVocht and Angie Blankenship to announce that the local scientologists were responsible for raising the funds to purchase a new location. The pressure to donate to the Ideal Org was intense. People emptied their bank accounts and even took out second mortgages to prove they were fully committed. The stigma of having their local org presenting a bad image of scientology to the world was a big motivating factor.

With the rollout of his Ideal Orgs program, Miscavige and his manipulative genius scored again on several counts. First, it was a means of deflecting attention from the lack of new OT levels. Ever since the announcement of Hubbard's death, Miscavige's promise of further OT levels had been on the minds of the most advanced scientologists. Each June, at the annual Maiden Voyage Anniversary summit on the *Freewinds*, Miscavige was routinely asked by OT VIIIs when OT IX and X would be available, and his response was always the same: Hubbard had mandated that they could only be released when every scientology organization on earth was large and prosperous, as Buffalo and Tampa succeeded in becoming. So that meant every OT VIII was responsible for raising the funds to purchase an adequate building of at least forty thousand square feet for their local organization. The onus was on the local scientologists, not the corporate pot. Now when asked about the unreleased OT levels, Miscavige's response was simple: "Is your org ideal yet?" And if it was, then the next question was: "What about the other orgs in your area or country?" The job of a scientologist was never done.

Second, tax-exempt organizations cannot simply amass huge piles of cash. Funds are supposed to be spent for the public good. Hubbard did not believe in charity, so feeding the poor and building schools are just not part of scientology. But the IRS considers purchase of property by churches to be a valid expenditure. The beauty of the buildings is they convert cash into tangible assets that remain on the balance sheet. So Miscavige's main measure of his success—money in the bank plus assets—continued to rise.

Third, the Ideal Orgs focus on purchasing buildings created a significant new—and relatively easy—revenue stream for scientology. Compared to selling scientology training and auditing, which required trained scientologists to deliver the services, collecting money for a building required nothing other than a bank account to deposit it into.

And finally, it provided a PR tool for scientology to claim "massive expansion" by pointing to "new churches" opening. In truth, the buildings are mostly empty.

With the Ideal Org program, Miscavige transformed scientology into a global real estate empire. Headquarters for various scientology entities and front groups have been purchased, from Narconon drug rehab centers, to Applied Scholastics pushing Hubbard "study technology" into the world, to internal publications organizations, TV studios, hotels in Clearwater and Los Angeles, homes and offices where Hubbard once worked, and even a headquarters for the Citizens Commission on Human Rights on Sunset Boulevard in LA, where I was charged with overseeing building a new museum—the Psychiatry: An Industry of Death Museum. The entire presentation was designed to document how psychiatry is "driven by profit" rather than by care for patient well-being. Every video, artifact, and display was an overblown attempt to show how the profession is to blame for the Holocaust, for destroying artists through barbaric "treatments," for hooking children on drugs, and much, much more. There are small kernels of truth contained in the hype—just enough to give it a speck of credibility—while creating the impression that all psychiatrists are conniving monsters out of B movies. I put together a team and approved the design and content of this extraordinary spectacle of over-the-top propaganda. I was convinced psychiatry was the root of all evil on this planet, actively seeking to not only destroy scientology but also enslave all mankind. I did not think it was at all funny, nor even exaggerated. (The fear of psychiatry is one of the hardest ideas to shake when you escape from the mind-prison.)

There is another reason this museum opening was significant. It was the first time I met Leah Remini. I had gotten together with Lisa Marie Presley at the reception afterward, and we walked outside onto the balcony to have a cigarette. Leah was already there, taking her own smoke break.

Lisa greeted her. "Oh, hi, Leah, I see we both had the same idea! Do you know Mike Rinder?" Lisa wasn't one for flowery introductions, or flowery anything. It turned out, neither was Leah. They launched into an expletive-laced discussion—about what, I don't recall, but I remember thinking, *Boy, these two don't hold back.* The fact that Leah felt comfortable enough to include me in what would likely be considered an inappropriate conversation in front of a senior church executive made me instantly enjoy her company. It was a rare break from my highly regimented and usually serious life to encounter a kindred spirit.

CHAPTER 12

RETURN TO CALIFORNIA

Sometime in early 2002, as I sat in my small office in the CMO International building at Gold, the phone on my desk rang. Typically calls were from RTC, summoning me to go up the hill to see COB, or from Miscavige himself. I was surprised; this time it was the receptionist at OSA International in Los Angeles (a few areas in LA could call up to the Int Base on a direct link—it was a single phone system), who told me she had Bob Minton and Stacy Brooks on the line. I told her to put them through.

"Hi, guys, what's up?"

"We want to try to settle matters with scientology and get on with our lives," they declared. "Can we set up a meeting?"

"You know we want the same thing, so I think this would be a great idea," I replied. "I have to coordinate some things first and I will get back to you as soon as possible."

In January 2002, Miscavige had appointed me Commanding Officer of CMO Int and Watchdog Committee (WDC) Chairman—the highest position in the Church of Scientology International. The previous incumbents had all failed; the job was a revolving door. I was just the latest tethered goat about to be sacrificed. I didn't want the position, but my sense of duty required me to do what I could. Fortunately, events from my days in the OSA world were following me and frankly I was relieved as it was a ticket out of a position that I didn't want (and neither did anyone else).

I knew settling with Minton would take priority for Miscavige and I would be off on another special project and someone else would have to try their hand at the impossible task of being CO CMO Int.

Though the McPherson criminal case had been dropped, the civil suit was very much alive, and anything related to it required approval from Miscavige. Minton had been funding the lawyers representing Lisa's estate, and he and Stacy Brooks had been called by us as witnesses in the case in an effort to dig up something discreditable about their activities. I put together a "Completed Staff Work" (a proposal to take action) and sent it to Miscavige. His response was enthusiastic, and he ordered that attorney Sandy Rosen be involved in the settlement. A big, brash New Yorker, Sandy had a sharp mind and an aggressive attitude that won him favor with Miscavige—his only distractions from trying to destroy enemies in the courtroom were contract bridge, the *New York Times* crossword, and Newport cigarettes. He and lawyer Monique Yingling, wife of Miscavige's personal criminal tax lawyer, Jerry Feffer, were two of the few non-scientologists Miscavige trusted, and Monique was also to be present so she could report back to Miscavige on what went down.

I organized everyone's schedules to meet at Sandy's office in midtown Manhattan. Bob and Stacy flew down from Boston with their lawyer. We gathered in a conference room with no windows to the outside world, just a glass wall to an interior hallway. There was a long table with six chairs on each side and one at each end; our team sat along one side of the table, with Bob, Stacy, and their lawyer across from us. Sandy took charge immediately; he informed Minton that he would be happy to negotiate a settlement, but there were a few items he needed to address up front. He proceeded to read off a list of costs, expenses, and damages that Minton had supposedly caused scientology. The total? Seventy-five million dollars. After he announced the figure, he followed up in a menacingly matter-of-fact tone: "And if you don't pay, we will destroy you utterly." Minton, Stacy, and their lawyer looked at each other, stunned. They said they wanted a few minutes to talk among themselves. They left the law office and headed for the elevator. Rosen claimed, "They'll be back," but they did not return. Rosen had pushed it too far and I feared he was not going to be able to close the deal with them.

I traveled back to California. Miscavige was unhappy that the matter had not been resolved in New York. While he had wanted to let Rosen loose and fully agreed with his plan to "tell Minton who was boss," when that strategy didn't work, he claimed that we must have done something wrong. He wanted the McPherson matter behind him. Minton called a few days later and asked to meet with me alone in Clearwater. He did not want Sandy Rosen present and was still upset by the treatment in New York. Miscavige told me to get on the next plane to salvage the situation. I was glad to be the one Minton was still willing to talk to; it was a brownie point for me. Once again, though, Miscavige insisted Monique Yingling be present to report back to him what transpired.

Monique was not a threatening presence like Sandy Rosen. She was a tax lawyer given to wearing Hermès scarves and Cartier watches, but her more genteel manner didn't mean she was a pushover, and she only took her orders from Miscavige himself. Minton and Stacy Brooks agreed to meet at our local lawyer's office in Clearwater after regular business hours.

When Monique and I drove up, Bob and Stacy were waiting in the parking lot. We exchanged pleasantries and then Bob said: "We agreed to meet you here, but we are not going to go into the building."

I was surprised: "You want to have a meeting in the parking lot?"

"Yes," Bob replied. "If this location is the only place you are willing to meet."

I asked them what was inside the building that was so much more threatening than outside.

"You probably have the offices bugged."

I reassured them this was not the case (though they had good reason to be concerned; I had recorded Gerry Armstrong without his knowledge, and the GO had bugged IRS offices).

"You know, guys, I could just as easily record you in the parking lot if I wanted to," I said. Monique chimed in, "It makes more sense to get comfortable. I assure you, we are not recording the conversation." Eventually, they agreed to go inside. We sat down and began to talk about terms of cessation of hostilities. That first night, we spent two hours talking and it turned out they were upset by some of the actions taken by the lawyer representing Lisa's family and that some of the people who had come into the Lisa McPherson Trust had taken advantage of Minton's generosity for their personal benefit.

After several meetings, they agreed to tell what they knew under oath in the McPherson civil case about misrepresentations made to the court concerning the funding of the lawyers. In return, we would call off the dogs in Switzerland and make our "best efforts" to unfreeze Bob's funds. It was a reflection of how shady the whole Swiss operation was that I knew to avoid promising that we would get his funds unfrozen. A guarantee would mean the prosecutor was either corrupt or operating on false information. In this case it was the latter. But I was confident that if I informed Lubow the fight with Minton was over and that he had done his job, somehow Bob's accounts would be freed up by the Swiss.

The glitch was that we could not officially settle with Minton. Had we done so, it would have tainted their testimony. The lawyers for Lisa's family would have claimed the testimony he and Stacy had now agreed to provide had been bought. And they would have been right. It had to be a "gentleman's agreement" that hostilities would end without a formal settlement so they could continue to testify on the stand that they had not "settled with scientology" or received any money. In the end, it was all rather pointless. Judge Schaeffer found Bob and Stacy not to be credible witnesses, unconvinced by their demeanor and suspicious of their about-face. Nobody had predicted this outcome, but when I look back today that was only because we all believed that anything that did not go our way could only be due to suppressive forces at work—not the fact that our constant pleas of righteous indignation and victimhood backfired in gaining sympathy for our positions.

Minton had lost interest in the fight; he did not want to spend any more money on his campaign against scientology. He felt betrayed by those he had been working with (with a few exceptions, such as Stacy). He wanted to return to his pre-scientology days and live his life in peace. He closed down the Lisa McPherson Trust and handed me the keys to the office building he'd purchased. He wanted out so badly he just turned over the $350,000 building as a sign of good faith. All he could do was try to please us and hope we stuck to our end of the deal to get his money unfrozen.

All through these negotiations with Bob and Stacy, I began to see more troubling cracks in scientology that fed my doubts. I now knew, for instance, that Bob was a decent man who had joined the crusade against the abuses of scientology because he thought it was the right thing to do. He had no dog in the fight personally but had suffered enormously because he had stepped forward to say, "This is not right." He had been driven to the verge of suicide for daring to speak up against scientology abuses. Yet we made him out to be a monster. Stacy too is a gentle person with an easy laugh who had been mercilessly attacked because she believed Miscavige was inherently evil and had said so.

My short tenure as CO CMO Int quickly faded into the background. Miscavige appointed someone else to the position, as I had become reimmersed in the world of litigation. I relocated to Clearwater once again to continue dealing with the McPherson civil case.

In November 2002, Mary Sue Hubbard died. Since she had come out of prison, in 1984, she had lived in a house in LA's Los Feliz neighborhood, where she was looked after by a number of Sea Org members who reported to Miscavige. The head agent who had been living with her and informing on her activities for years, Neville Potter, flew to Clearwater. I was sitting in the conference room off the lobby of the Bank of Clearwater building with Miscavige and Marty Rathbun when Neville walked in. He announced to Miscavige with a smug grin, "The witch is dead."

"Finally," Miscavige responded.

The callous disdain for the woman who had been Hubbard's wife since the dawn of scientology shocked me, but I knew not to display any emotion. No matter what anyone thought about Mary Sue Hubbard, she had been loyal to her husband and had always supported him, at great personal cost. She never turned on him, even when he refused to speak to her. It was a remarkable level of devotion. This apparently meant nothing to Miscavige, and it struck a chord in my mind—as with Hubbard, loyalty to him was expected but only reciprocated if he believed you offered him some advantage. But even this realization, added to my other doubts, was still not enough to overcome the chains that bound me to scientology. I remained unwavering in my commitment to Hubbard and the Sea Org, to save the planet or die in the attempt.

With the civil case in a lull and settlement with Minton impossible until the plaintiffs agreed to settle, at the end of 2002 Miscavige sent Marty Rathbun and me back to the Gold Base. As usual, Miscavige was convinced everyone at Gold was either incompetent or working against him. Marty was the Inspector General RTC—the highest position in RTC other than Miscavige himself. Marty was supposed to "get ethics in" on the Int Base (what that meant was never defined, but generally it involved stopping anything or anyone Miscavige found upsetting). I was supposed to assist Marty in accomplishing this, though I had no position in RTC. I was set up with a desk in his office. Soon Miscavige decided Marty was failing as Inspector General and told me to take over. Marty was to now take orders from me. Corporate niceties within scientology were meaningless. And the authority of Miscavige was absolute and unquestioned.

My tenure as the head of RTC was also short-lived. Miscavige decided that Hubbard had been right when he claimed I must have "unhandled evil intentions." A label placed on you by Hubbard is virtually impossible to shed. Only one person seemed to want me to do well: Claire Headley, the head of Internal Affairs RTC. One of the kindest, calmest, and most organized people I've ever met, Claire made what was a miserable, high-stress time at the top of RTC more bearable. Though she was under enormous pressure herself, she would come to my office several times a day to offer kind words and help: "Is there anything you need?" "Here are some vitamins—it will keep your energy up." "Get some sleep, I have everything under control here." Her support was often the only bright spot in my day—empathy is not the currency of the Sea Org, so it meant a lot to me. But no amount of encouragement, vitamins, or sleep would help me avoid the wrath of Miscavige. He soon sent two new people to the base to replace Marty and me: my old friend Tom DeVocht from Clearwater and the head of CST, Russ Bellin.

I was sent back down the hill to CMO Int, just in time for Miscavige to teach the group a lesson. We were all ordered to clean the sewage retention pond in a remote corner of the property. The entire senior echelon of scientology was literally digging shit with shovels—there was not even any value to the work, other than being reminded once again who was boss. If Miscavige ordered you to shovel shit, you saluted and got busy shoveling. We counted ourselves lucky that the punishment lasted only a few days.

I must have failed to appease Miscavige, because his next effort stepped up the game another notch. I was called, along with Marc Yager, who was now the head of the CMO; Guillaume Lesevre, Executive Director International; and Wendell Reynolds, Int Finance Director, to meet COB by the running track far out on the property at ten p.m. We waited for him to arrive; he never waited for anyone, you were expected to wait for him. We all shot each other worried looks, nobody daring to say out loud what we were thinking: *What does he have in store for us this time?*

Miscavige arrived after we had been standing in the dark for about twenty minutes and informed us we were being "offloaded" from the Sea Org on a bus the next morning because we were hopelessly incompetent and "counter-intentioned cocksuckers." To outsiders it may sound like this would be a blessing, an end to the insanity. But to a Sea Org member this was the ultimate humiliation, and it would also mean the end of our relationships with any scientologists, including any family members. He was once again making clear that he completely controlled everyone's fate and that with a snap of his fingers, your life as you knew it could end.

"You have until morning to decide where you want a bus ticket to. You are no longer worthy of Sea Org living accommodations, so I have two tents for you to sleep in tonight. You can pitch the tents in that grove of trees over there and use the bathroom in the sauna that is next to the track."

We spent the night in the flimsy nylon pup tents trying to decide how to respond in the morning. I was the only one who didn't want to beg to stay. I tried to persuade the others that we should go to a country where there was no scientology presence, open an organization, make it a huge success, and restore our reputations. My plan was to respond when asked the next morning that we wanted to be dropped off in Riverside and would make our way from there to India, where nearly a quarter of the world's population had no access to scientology.

It was academic, as the next morning we sat there waiting for his return. He didn't come. Nor the next day. When he showed up a few days later, he interrogated us about one thing or another that had nothing to do with being offloaded. All we knew was that we had not been put on a bus. After we'd spent about two weeks camping out in the pup tents, with the sprinklers turned on each night to wet us down, he drove up on his motorcycle with his ever-present assistant, Lou, at his side. You could hear him coming from a way off, as he rode a customized Yamaha TW trail bike around the property, always faster and louder than everyone else. We stood at attention as he screeched to a stop.

"The incompetent assholes who are supposed to be preparing the annual May ninth event [to celebrate the publication of *Dianetics*] are producing total OPs"—overt products, the scientology term for something bad. "You may be SPs, but you are lesser SPs than these other assholes," he said curtly.

With that, we left our tents, planned the event, wrote the speeches we would deliver, got them approved by COB, and then hopped on a plane to Clearwater, where we put on our tuxedos and addressed the elite of scientology as their trusted leaders. Little did they know a week earlier we had been living in tents after being declared Suppressive Persons by none other than COB himself.

This was all part of the facade. Public scientologists have no clue what goes on behind the scenes in the Sea Org, let alone at the highest echelons of scientology. And they do not dare ask. Not even most Sea Org members know what happens in Miscavige's inner circle.

Cognitive dissonance was reaching a fever pitch for me, but I struggled still. I truly believed that I had a moral obligation to fulfill the billion-year contract I had signed when I joined the Sea Org at eighteen. I was now nearly fifty. In the scientology Code of Honor, Hubbard had written "Your self-determinism and your honor are more important than your immediate life" and "Your integrity to yourself is more important than your body," and I believed that my honor and integrity rested on keeping my word and commitment to clearing the planet. I did not want to see that what I was doing was not only futile—the planet will *never* be cleared—but was in fact hurting people. I also felt an obligation to the marriage vows I had made to Cathy, even though we spent about half our married life in different cities, and responsibility not to abandon my twenty- and twenty-five-year-old children, though in truth, I had effectively already done so.

Meanwhile, the bizarre roller-coaster ride with Miscavige continued, in favor one day, out the next. When I was again on his good side, I was assigned to another special project: to convince the Charity Commission for England and Wales to grant scientology charitable status, and thus exemption from taxation. There is a very different and much smarter system in place in the UK than in the US; one has to prove "public benefit" to the satisfaction of the Charity Commission before becoming eligible to be considered tax-exempt by the revenue service. Tom Cruise, who had been brought into the battle by Miscavige, had arranged for a private meeting with representatives of Prime Minister Tony Blair to plead our case. I flew to London with Miscavige on Cruise's Gulfstream to help with the preparations. The meeting was held in the Dorchester hotel, but I didn't attend—just Cruise and Miscavige went, though I ended up staying in the suite for the night. Quite a change from a pup tent by the track at Gold. The efforts to persuade the UK to grant scientology charity status failed—the government didn't buy into the idea that scientology provided any real value to the world at large.

Bouncing between disgrace and being a vitally needed cog in the machine was difficult to grapple with. I was constantly trying to figure out what I had done right and what I had done wrong. I followed the scientology principle that it was always something I had done or my intentions or thoughts that caused the situation I found myself in. It was an entirely internal mental struggle about my shortcomings— the concept that Miscavige might simply be insane or a sociopath was far outside the thought processes I had been trained into. I repeated a scientology mantra to myself: *What did I do to pull it in?* But even that became increasingly difficult in the face of Miscavige's endless and random whims of who was in favor and who was in disgrace. Nobody lasted at the top of the pile before they were relegated to the bottom. It took me a long time to put the pieces together and realize that every single prominent executive of scientology was removed and disgraced on an almost rotational basis. Each individual instance seemed so justified—these people failed to do their jobs, so their punishment was well deserved. It also made my own failings seem less awful if everyone else was just as bad as me. There are many things about life in scientology that fit the old adage of not seeing the forest for the trees.

While I was by no means the only one, I was certainly among Miscavige's favorite targets. The correlation between how much he perceived anyone as a potential rival and how much they were punished became clear to me over time. I had a few things going for me that put me high on his list: I had worked and trained with Hubbard, I was a well-known figure in the scientology world, and I was one of the few people who had an understanding of the legal, government, and PR scene internationally. Thus he derided me constantly in front of others and routinely slapped, punched, kicked, and throttled me. Just as he did with others. What made me different, though, was that when important matters arose that he did not want to personally involve himself in, he would often call on me. Why I kept answering the call is still hard for me to comprehend. Perhaps I am simply too stubborn to admit that I could be beaten into submission by anyone. It was a strange computation in my mind—as long as I kept going and didn't give up, I was not submitting to his will. Yet the truth is that by carrying on, I was doing exactly what he wanted.

To illustrate the craziness of my shit-to-Shinola day-to-day existence, sometime in late 2003 Miscavige dispatched me to see Tom Cruise's publicist, Pat Kingsley. I had been in the doghouse for some unmemorable reason, and now I was being sent to deal with one of the most powerful women in Hollywood, who represented a stable of superstars. Pat was a very savvy operator and she had been advising Cruise to lay off his scientology proselytizing. She told him the movie studios were investing a huge amount of money, and they wanted him to sell the movies, not scientology. I was supposed to convince her that if this was what Tom wanted to do, she should support him rather than seek to stop him. Miscavige believed she was a suppressive influence on Tom, and he wanted her dealt with. Pat listened politely to my pitch, and was very gracious and professional, but I didn't change her mind about anything. Frankly, she had no reason to change it—scientology was not her client. When I reported back, Miscavige considered me a failure with my soft approach and proceeded with a heavy-handed threat to her delivered by another of his minions. And when she didn't bend, Tom Cruise fired her and replaced her with his sister Lee Anne.

Lee Anne, unlike Pat Kingsley, was a good scientologist first, sister second, and publicist third. She was way out of her depth, and she simply did whatever Miscavige wanted her to. With time, Cruise's public statements steadily became more and more outlandish. He ultimately made a complete fool of himself by jumping on Oprah Winfrey's couch during their infamous May 23, 2005 interview. Shortly after that, he accused Matt Lauer of being "glib" about psychiatric drugs on the *Today* show, and targeted Brooke Shields for taking medication for postpartum depression. He was lauded by Miscavige and those in scientology circles, including me, but laughed at by the rest of the world. He was the perfect example of what a scientology celebrity should be doing—speaking with absolute certainty, unashamed of what we scientologists believed and knew to be true, no matter how batshit crazy.

Miscavige charted his own descent into absurdity. He commissioned very expensive, lifelike custom ventriloquist dolls to be made of me, Heber Jentzsch, and Guillaume Lesevre. They bore a striking resemblance to each of us. He started bringing the dolls to meetings and would ask us questions and have the dolls answer as he imitated our voices. He had little routines for each person: his "Heber" voice sounded like Howdy Doody making childish statements because Miscavige said Heber had the intelligence of a marionette. "Guillaume" had an exaggerated phony French accent because Miscavige hated Guillaume's pronunciation of certain words—and almost every sentence included mention of how much he loved cheese. When he imitated me, he spoke so slowly it was painful, as he routinely chided me for being slow—he once described me to the assembled members of WDC as "the spawn of a retarded sloth's DNA." Miscavige was so amused by these dolls he even had them specially boxed up and brought to England for the annual IAS event.

One day, during one of the endless meetings he lorded over in the Gold Cine Conference Room, he summoned the base electrician, Martin. He sent him off with specific instructions that we were not privy to. Soon thereafter Martin reappeared with two four-foot lengths of one-inch-diameter copper wiring.

"Those are perfect, Martin," said Miscavige. "Now go outside and bury them in the grass in front of the conference room. Put them two feet apart and two feet deep. Right there where I can see them through the window." Once the "grounding rods" were in place, Miscavige ordered me to go outside and hold on to them until he told me I could let go. Everyone, myself included, was mystified. Miscavige then told those who were not OT III or above to leave the room, and he then explained that my body thetans were jumping off me and landing on him, which was causing him great upset, and that by "grounding" me he could stop the flow. I thought Miscavige must have some secret information from Hubbard that explained this bizarre incident—he announced it with such certainty and authority that nobody in the room doubted that my evil "flows" would now be directed harmlessly into the dirt. As I knelt on the grass holding those rods, I once again wondered exactly *what I had done* to cause COB to be so upset.

Many more such bizarre events are indelibly seared in my memory. Miscavige had a technique of posing questions and making accusations that had no correct answer. No matter how you responded, you would be berated. If I said, "Yes, sir," that would result in "That's all you have to say for yourself?" If I disputed anything (heaven forbid), Miscavige would say, "You see, this guy wants to fight me and make me wrong; it's his unhandled evil purposes on display." An "I apologize for . . ." would elicit "Apologize? I don't want your fucking apology, I want you to do it right, you piece of shit." The no-win responses were endless.

I could never outthink him in this game, so I became silent and didn't respond at all, and I wasn't the only one. That set him off even worse—"You motherfucking pie-faced piece of dogshit, don't just stare at me," he barked. Eventually he appeared in CMO International with a pile of white paper plates adorned with Magic Marker. Each one had a smiley face drawn on it, but without the smile—the mouth was a straight line. He called them "pie faces." These paper plate masks were handed out to everyone and we were all required to hold them in front of our faces while he addressed us. "I would rather look at those pie faces than your actual pie faces." We had to keep the pie face masks in place during any interaction with him. As with most of these whims, it lasted a few days and then was replaced by something else to amuse him. I, and pretty much everyone else, became inured to this sort of hazing. We didn't even discuss it among ourselves. Nobody brought up how crazy it was—that would have resulted in a report being written and the complainant being identified as a troublemaker, leading to even worse treatment. There was safety in numbers—if everyone was being abused, it was more tolerable than being individually targeted. This was especially so in the Sea Org, where we had no family to fall back on and no partners we could confide in or talk with about things going on in our lives.

In my case, if I happened to be in the same city as Cathy, we theoretically lived in the same room but often didn't speak to each other even at night, as sleep was at such a premium that unless we got home at exactly the same time (which happened almost never), we fell into bed and went instantly to sleep. If we did have any conversation, neither of us would dare speak our real feelings to the other, as we knew we had to write a report on any such conversation. As for our children, I saw them even less. Benjamin was in Clearwater. Taryn was in Golden Era Productions—though located on the same property, she was in a completely different world on a different schedule in a different building. The only comfort in the Sea Org came from shared experiences with those you worked with—either some success or, in the case of failure or pain, the solace that you were not in it completely alone.

As I mentioned earlier, from the time I was PPRO Int and through the early 2000s I participated in what were known in scientology as the "Int Events." Six times a year there was an international televised briefing to celebrate major events in scientology—Hubbard's birthday, the anniversary of the publication of *Dianetics*, the formation of the International Association of Scientologists, the launch of the *Freewinds*, Auditor's Day (to recognize scientology auditors as "the most valuable beings on the planet"), and New Year's Eve. These elaborate events were seen as opportunities to present the accomplishments and great works of scientology. As always, the information was carefully selected and presented to make it appear we were riding a tidal wave of success, and Miscavige had to approve every word that was uttered and every visual or video that was shown. Heber Jentzsch, Guillaume Lesevre, Marc Yager, and I were involved in almost every one of the events; there were a few others who came and went. Miscavige was the master of ceremonies and took credit as the fearless leader who was making it all happen. Extravagantly staged, captured on six or more video cameras, with fireworks, laser displays, thunderous music, and spectacular backdrops, the events were propaganda tools to deliver the good news to the scientology world exactly as we wanted them to hear it.

Behind the scenes, these events were always "disasters," according to Miscavige. Everyone involved, from the camera operators and sound engineers to the scriptwriters and speakers, was incompetent and could not live up to his standards for a variety of reasons. Especially the speakers: Guillaume's accent. My sloth-like demeanor. Heber sounding like Howdy Doody. Yager looked stupid. Ray Mithoff was "Gumby," and so forth. During rehearsal days we could often be found cleaning the public toilets as punishment for failing to meet Miscavige's expectations, and as a form of humiliation to remind us yet again who was boss. This was just part of life as an "Int speaker" and almost a badge of honor, as we were tough enough to deal with this and then get up in front of thousands of people and deliver a speech.

Usually the storm would subside once Miscavige heard the applause of the crowd and soaked in some "standing Os" on the stage himself. For whatever reason, one year at the annual IAS event held at Saint Hill in England, he was not mollified by the adoration of the crowd. Immediately following the event, he ordered his then right-hand man, Greg Wilhere, to take Heber, Marc, Guillaume, and me and "throw us in the lake" at the bottom of the Saint Hill property. It was a chilly, overcast November afternoon. Wilhere allowed us to take off our shoes and strip down to pants and shirts before we waded into the freezing-cold, almost black water. The bottom was stagnant, slimy mud. Our assignment was to remain in the lake clearing away weeds and debris for a few days, until Miscavige decided he wanted to return to California to prepare for the next event, scheduled for New Year's Eve. As usual, none of us uttered a word of protest or disagreement; that would have made our circumstances even worse. At least we had not been declared SPs and thrown out of scientology. Rather than "We come back," our real motto was "Take it like a man." The lake was one of the places scientologists liked to visit at Saint Hill, but it was declared temporarily out of bounds by RTC without any explanation. Cleaning toilets was one thing; the senior executives of scientology wading around in a slimy lake all day might cause too much consternation with public scientologists.

IN JANUARY 2004, Miscavige started what he called the "A to E room" for Suppressive Persons. In Ron Hubbard's policy letter about dealing with SPs, the steps are laid out as A, B, C, D, and E, hence "A to E." Miscavige declared that the senior officials of scientology (myself included) in CMO International were actively trying to destroy scientology. Of course, it made no sense—if we were truly SPs, we should have been cast out immediately, but like so much else that was illogical if not utterly crazy, we viewed it as merely the latest in what seemed to be an endless series of punishments meted out for our apparent failures and incompetence. None of us could figure out what we needed to do to end the pattern, but each time we hoped the latest thing might be the last.

As designated Suppressive Persons, we had to do the steps A through E. The idea is that you recant your suppressive acts in detail and announce this to the world, pay all debts to the organization, make up the supposed damage you have committed, and redo all scientology courses from the bottom up. I don't recall what I or anyone else had reportedly done at the time to warrant inclusion in Miscavige's latest effort to belittle and humiliate. It could be what he considered an inappropriate facial expression. Or taking too long to answer a question. Or giving the wrong answer. Or no answer. He fostered an environment where nothing was certain, especially any security in your position.

Then Miscavige changed his mind once again and I transformed from incorrigible SP to book editor. I'd be working with L. Ron Hubbard's former son-in-law Jonathan Horwich, whom I had known since the *Apollo* days. He came from a wealthy family and was a renowned audiophile and fastidious about doing things the right way. We had both been in the A to E room but were now tasked with editing all of L. Ron Hubbard's books. We were expected to compare the original manuscript of each book to the existing published edition, correct all typographical, transcription, and punctuation errors, and create indexes and glossaries for each book. That's nineteen books, some with more than five hundred pages. We were told we had to be done in six weeks—an insane target.

Jon and I moved into two small offices in a building called the Ranchos (the name when the Gold property was purchased). We slept barely two hours a night for weeks on end and yet were expected to "edit" Hubbard's rambling and often incoherent writings. It became so ridiculous that people were assigned a single task: to stand over us to ensure we did not fall asleep at our desks. Eventually Miscavige claimed we were sabotaging this project by not working fast enough and declared that like everything else, he would have to do it personally. (It took him three years to complete it.) Jon Horwich soon thereafter escaped the base. I can't say for sure, but this nightmarish experience probably helped him decide there was nothing more for him in the Sea Org.

Despite my "sabotage" of Hubbard's books, I was sent to the *Freewinds* in the Caribbean for the annual Maiden Voyage Anniversary public events in June 2004. But once again, Miscavige decided I was a Suppressive Person, and along with Heber Jentzsch and Guillaume Lesevre, I was assigned to scrape shit from the bilge tanks. At the time, my mother was on board as a public scientologist; she had attended the week of events and then stayed for further study afterward as it was a very long flight from Australia. For weeks I did not see her. But she kept asking about me. She had come halfway across the world and had watched me at the event, but now I was nowhere around. It is another microcosm of the insanity in scientology—my own mother was on the same ship and completely unaware of what I was doing. She knew I would not leave the ship without saying goodbye to her. So, to avoid a flap, I was escorted for a "supervised" visit with her in the main dining room.

Before I saw her, I soaked my whole body in a bathtub filled with diesel oil for an hour to dissolve the grease that had accumulated in every pore, just as I'd done when suffering this particular punishment before. It smelled as bad as it sounds, but it was the only way to remove the ingrained blackness. My entire body from hair to toenails was the color of an auto mechanic's hands. To get rid of the smell of the diesel, I then washed with soap for another hour. I am sure I still smelled terrible despite my best efforts.

I put on a brave face and told my mother everything was wonderful, that I was just really busy saving the world. In fact, I was being held a virtual prisoner, though I still didn't see it that way. She seemed to be doing well, though nobody in that sort of controlled scientology environment will ever say what they really feel if they have any disagreements or upsets. They know it would only result in their being required to pay more money to be taken in session to get to the bottom of their dissatisfaction. It was a dance—I pretended to know that Cathy, Taryn, and Benjamin were all well and happy and that we were the ideal Sea Org family. She pretended she didn't have any questions about what I was doing or why I looked so haggard. This is what is known in scientology as a "good roads, fair weather" interaction. No talk of anything of substance, all is well, nothing to see here.

WHILE I WAS on the *Freewinds*, an agreement was finally reached to settle the McPherson civil case. Suddenly I was needed to meet with Minton and finalize the settlement with him. Miscavige had returned to the US and left us in the bilges until he decided our fate. I was quickly cleaned up and taken to the airport in Aruba. I had a connecting flight to Tampa via Miami, but my first leg from Aruba was delayed and I arrived in Miami too late to make any connection. I heard my name paged to "come to the white courtesy telephone." I picked up and the head of the CMO in Clearwater told me, "Go to Avis, there is a car waiting for you to drive to Clearwater." I had no idea what was going on or why it was so urgent that I get to Clearwater by five a.m. rather than taking the first flight the next morning. Of course, I didn't question it and proceeded to Avis. As an indicator of how out of touch with the world those inside the cocoon of the Sea Org are (especially on the *Freewinds*), I had no idea Hurricane Charley had devastated the west coast of Florida earlier that day. I thought it strange that nobody was manning the toll booths on Alligator Alley and convoys of army Humvees were the only other vehicles on the road. It didn't make any sense until I hit the west coast and saw downed trees, signs, and telephone poles. Natural disasters were not on the Sea Org's radar. So if I was supposed to get to Clearwater "at once," that meant *now*. I arrived at five a.m., and there was nobody around, so I caught a few hours of sleep until everyone was awake.

My orders, relayed from Miscavige by his minions, were to get matters finalized with Minton as fast as possible. He and Stacy Brooks were in Atlanta visiting her mother, so I arranged for Monique Yingling to

fly in from DC and we all rendezvoused at the Four Seasons there—
again from shit to Shinola virtually overnight. There were wrinkles to
iron out and the deal could not yet be signed. We agreed to meet again
at Monique's office in DC once she had finalized the details.

I then flew to Spain for the grand opening of the new scientology
building in Madrid, to be held on September 18, 2004. Tom Cruise
had been dating Spanish actress Penélope Cruz, which was a contributing factor as to why so much money was spent to buy and renovate the
beautiful building there. So it's a bit ironic that by the time it was completed Penélope had broken up with him. Nonetheless, Tom attended
the ribbon cutting to support his best buddy, Dave Miscavige. After
the event, I was with Cruise, waiting for Miscavige and Shelly to arrive
from their office upstairs.

While we stood in the lobby, Cruise turned to me and asked, "Can
you believe Lee Anne can't set me up with a girlfriend?"

Before I had a chance to answer (not that I had an answer), Miscavige walked toward us and asked what we were talking about. Tom
repeated what he had said to me. Miscavige took it to heart. Soon
thereafter a special project, overseen by Greg Wilhere, began in earnest
to hold "auditions" to find Tom Cruise a girlfriend and, ultimately, a
new wife.

From Madrid I flew to New York City for the opening of the new
"ideal" building. (Cruise had an apartment in Manhattan and needed
a place to bring people to teach them about scientology, which is why
that building had such high priority.) Congressman Charlie Rangel had
been persuaded to speak at the ribbon cutting. Miscavige wanted him
to deliver a speech he had written for him lauding scientology. Rangel
refused. Miscavige hit the roof and railed about the incompetence of
those around him for failing to handle the congressman. True to form,
when he was introduced to Rangel, Miscavige was solicitous and polite.
He could always put on a charming public persona, while acting like a
madman behind the scenes.

Sometime later I would take Barbara Walters for a tour of these
premises with Lee Anne—as a condition of her being granted an inter-

view with Tom. I am not entirely sure who came up with this idea; it was probably a combination of Miscavige and Cruise as another step in their plan to make scientology a household word.

In the meantime, I finally traveled to Washington, DC, to complete the settlement with Bob Minton at Monique Yingling's office. Before this, Miscavige had pulled me aside and asked me to figure out how Minton could pay him money personally to compensate him for his "pain and suffering." He told me half a million dollars would be acceptable, but he wanted it to be tax-free. I checked with the lawyers and they all told me it was impossible and could not and must not be done. I told Shelly Miscavige about this and what the lawyers said. She relayed the message to her husband. I believe, though I don't know for sure, that Shelly's failure to "make this go right," rather than just relay to him what the lawyers and I said, was a contributing factor in his deciding she too was trying to suppress him. As with Hubbard, even his wife was not immune to the whims of Miscavige's conviction that enemies were constantly trying to take him down.

While I was in Yingling's office working with her on the Minton settlement, Miscavige constantly called me, screaming at and berating me over the phone. Monique couldn't help but overhear—she asked me, "Why does Dave treat you like that?" I answered that I deserved it. She shook her head. "No, you don't, Mike. You work harder than anyone I have ever met. You are smart and do a great job. I don't think anyone should be treated like that." I didn't want to agree with her—after all, she was not even a scientologist—and to do so would have been tantamount to treason in my mind. But while I didn't show it then, it was finally becoming clearer to me that she was right.

CHAPTER 13

THE HOLE

On November 2, 2005, I sat across from Katie Couric in the NBC *Today* show studio in New York City's Rockefeller Center, with the cameras rolling. She smiled sweetly as she homed in for the gotcha moment no scientology spokesperson wants to be confronted with: "L. Ron Hubbard . . . claimed that seventy-five million years ago, an evil galactic ruler named Xenu killed billions of his people by sending them to Earth in space planes. You can understand why some people might feel this is, at best, pretty unconventional and I guess at worst just plain out there. Right?"

The live interview had suddenly turned into a nightmare and I tried not to let my dread show. I managed to get out a sort of response: "I can understand that, certainly, Katie. That just has no, no basis in reality. This is one of those things that get spread around, one of those old stories . . ."

She persisted: "So he never wrote about that?"

"No. Not in those terms," I deflected. "There is an alteration and twisting of things; and the real point about scientology is that you can find out what scientology is by going into any church, by reading any one of these books, getting them. We try and make them as available as possible so that people can see what scientology is. You won't find anything like that in any of these materials at all."

The *Today* producers had reached out because they were doing a week of shows about religion. With Tom Cruise publicly promoting scientology at every opportunity, it was inevitable that NBC would ask us to participate. Though I was still considered a Suppressive Person by Miscavige as part of the failure of International Management, once again I had been sent to represent scientology because Miscavige had no intention of putting himself in the firing line as he had done with Ted Koppel. He had nobody else he trusted to not make a fool of themselves on national TV—though his treatment of me would not have suggested this, he had confidence I would not make some terrible gaffe, and he complained that Heber, the only other possible spokesperson, presented an "old" image of our "young religion" and that because he didn't understand legal matters he might blunder with some damaging statement that would harm our position. But the trust only went so far—I flew to New York to do the interview escorted by Greg Wilhere. He was along to ensure I didn't try to escape, something Miscavige was always paranoid about, and so he could report back to Miscavige on everything that happened.

The instant the word "Xenu" came out of Katie's mouth, I knew I would have to lie in my response, yet I felt justified due to my belief in what Hubbard had claimed—it was dangerous, even potentially deadly, to expose those not "spiritually prepared" to the story of Xenu. But it stuck in the dark recesses of my mind—was lying for the sake of scientology correct? It seemed easy to rationalize in that instance, but the seed was planted. Somehow live TV with a huge audience magnifies everything.

My performance with Katie Couric was a travesty of dishonesty, but it was exactly what Miscavige expected. I had done well. Back in Los Angeles he informed me that Tom Cruise's powerhouse talent agency, CAA, was not doing its job of successfully killing stories critical of scientology (and therefore Cruise), specifically a piece that Kim Christensen and Claire Hoffman were working on for the *Los Angeles Times* and a forthcoming episode of Comedy Central's *South Park*. He had Cruise's personal assistant, Michael Doven, arrange a meeting with CAA executives Kevin Huvane, Rick Nicita, Paula Wagner, and others from the agency at their office in Beverly Hills.

We gathered in an opulent but windowless conference room. Doven and I sat on one side and the CAA people on the other. After introductions (only Paula, Cruise's agent, and Rick, her husband, had met me before, at one of Cruise's movie premieres) and some pleasantries, Doven, who is not a forceful personality—in fact, I would categorize him as rather meek—began by saying Tom had "some concerns" about how the media was treating him and mentioned the upcoming pieces. I was a little more insistent, telling them that attacks on scientology were attacks on Tom Cruise and that he wanted them to do whatever it took to stop the negative media. Why he was not there making his complaint if it was so important to him didn't cross my mind, though the fact was probably not lost on the CAA people. They said the right things: "Yes, of course," and "We understand and will do everything in our power to prevent this," and "We have a great relationship with the people who run Comedy Central." They were all platitudes, but they were what I needed to hear to report back to Miscavige. This was a strange scenario, attempting to use Cruise's relationship with CAA to pressure the *LA Times* and *South Park* producers to put the kibosh on their pieces. It was uncomfortable and I had the distinct impression that the CAA executives listened out of politeness but walked away from the meeting without having made any specific promises. Indeed, they accomplished nothing. After all, I was not their client. Their job was to promote Cruise's career, not protect scientology. I am not even sure that they didn't secretly agree with what was being said about scientology. Cruise had not persuaded any of them to become scientologists, and he was selling it as hard as he could to anyone he could get to listen.

With the *LA Times* piece that was in the works, Miscavige claimed he was too busy to be interviewed by the reporters, so I was given the job of handling their questions, while still also trying to squash the story. When it became clear the article was going to be published, Miscavige ordered me to deliver a photo of him and Cruise decked out in leathers astride their Ducati motorcycles. He thought that getting this photo would be such a coup for the reporters that it would guarantee a favorable piece.

South Park went ahead with the now famous "Trapped in the Closet" episode on November 16, 2005. As I watched, my stomach churned. From a scientology perspective it was a catastrophe, implying both Tom Cruise and John Travolta were gay, but mostly because it had such a detailed description of the superconfidential OT III materials. The only positive was that it was a cartoon. Although the show displayed a banner reading THIS IS WHAT SCIENTOLOGISTS ACTUALLY BELIEVE during large portions of the episode, we could dismiss it as no more serious than depictions of Wile E. Coyote or Donald Duck. But that was not the case with the *LA Times*. The front-page story was very much not a cartoon. The paper published "Tom Cruise and Scientology" on December 18. Hardly the puff piece Miscavige wanted, it was a rundown of the unusual relationship between Miscavige and Cruise and the special treatment Cruise was afforded as scientology's biggest star. The article included critical quotes from former Sea Org members from the Int Base—whom I dismissed with a standard response as "apostates" and liars (though of course I knew they were telling the truth—they recounted the same things I had experienced and witnessed). There were also some positive words from me describing Tom and Dave as "men who've achieved great success through their force of personality and their drive to excel."

Like most press, neither of these media pieces had much impact within scientology. Everyone inside the bubble is conditioned to ignore the "chaos merchants" in the media and dismiss anything they say as lies. They didn't have a great deal of impact on the world outside either, for different reasons. It was almost an acceptance into the mainstream to be lampooned by *South Park*. No subject or person was off-limits to that show, including every religion, so scientology joined the ranks of Catholics, Jews, Muslims, Mormons, Westboro Baptists, and dozens of others. As for the *LA Times* story, it was about celebrities, and it didn't attract much attention outside LA and New York. At least, that is what we told ourselves and Miscavige to make it seem like it was not so bad.

Downplaying disasters if you have been anywhere near involved with them is a necessary survival skill one learns pretty quickly in scientology. Nobody wants to believe everything is not going incredibly well, so they look for anything that confirms that bias.

Soon thereafter I was dealing with a truly national publication, *Rolling Stone*, and its writer Janet Reitman. As with all major media inquiries, my first effort was to discourage her from doing any story at all, including meeting with her editor, Will Dana, at the magazine's offices in New York. A savvy media guy, who listened to my pitch about how they were missing the real story of scientology, its good works, and its massive expansion, Dana engaged me with a lot of questions. Many other editors in the past had refused to give us the time of day—*I have great faith in our wonderful reporters, talk to them and come back to me after the article comes out.* Dana took a different approach, one that ultimately helped him understand the subject better and helped Janet in writing her story. As time went on and it was clear the story was not going to be a puff piece, Lee Anne contacted Jann Wenner, the publisher of *Rolling Stone*. He responded: "I have great confidence in Will Dana," and was obviously not going to raise a finger to do anything. So we went into charm mode and I prepared a presentation and had Janet take a carefully curated tour of our Narconon drug rehab and other scientology facilities. I had her sit through numerous videos of "accomplishments" produced originally for international scientology events.

In the end her lengthy piece, which ran in March 2006, was a summation of scientology including everything we did not want printed, from Hubbard's history and death to the OT levels and FBI raids. She reported on her visit to the scientology org in New York where they pressured her to buy auditing. And most devastatingly, she told the unvarnished stories of former scientologists—about the destruction of their families, being denied education, and the inside workings of the Sea Org. It was yet another PR disaster for scientology.

THAT YEAR ALSO marked the twentieth anniversary of Hubbard's death. I was certain that Miscavige was truly worried about the possibility that Hubbard would come back to reassume his throne soon. The Old Man was the only person who could unseat Miscavige from what had now become his empire. Personally, I wasn't sure. I hoped he would, because I believed Hubbard would end some of the insanity that had been installed by Miscavige, but I wasn't preoccupied with wondering if he would show up the next day and announce himself.

The challenging media coverage and the fear of Hubbard's potentially imminent reincarnation sent Miscavige further down his desperate, paranoid, and erratic path. He saw enemies around every corner, each trying to sabotage his reputation and all the good work he had done. Those in closest proximity were most often the targets of his impulses to eradicate the perceived threats.

One of those impulses was to reinstate "overboard ceremonies" patterned after Hubbard's on the *Apollo*. Back in the late '60s the Commodore infamously had students' hands tied before having them thrown over the side of the ship to atone for their supposed sins and, he proclaimed, "rise from the deep a better person." The first time Miscavige resurrected the practice, he rounded up everyone in Int Management at one a.m. to march to the large swimming pool reserved for him and his guests near the RTC offices on the north side of the Gilman property. One by one each of us was ordered to walk down the diving board, jump into the pool fully clothed, and "commit our sins to the deep." It was theater of the absurd. Miscavige and his ever-present gaggle of RTC minions looked on as a hundred or so people emerged from the pool like drowned rats, shivering in wet clothes, awaiting his next direction. This became a not-infrequent occurrence; we found ourselves "swimming" with our clothes on every few weeks, though the venue shifted following the first episode to the slimy lake at the back of the property after the swimming pool was deemed too clean for the "traitors and do-nothings."

Things degenerated from there.

Around this time, I got a call: "Report at once to COB's office." I had been summoned to Miscavige's new 45,000-square-foot RTC building, which had been completed in 2004—a large, opulent structure that sat high on the hill overlooking the property, just below Hubbard's mansion.

As I hurried up the hill, five others were doing the same. They all must have gotten the same call. No one wanted to be last to arrive and potentially keep COB waiting. We gathered in the foyer, which was where we typically stood until being led to the marble floors and cherrywood-lined hallways of the second floor and Miscavige's expansive office with its large, custom-built bulletproof desk and thick bulletproof windows. This time, however, we were not taken upstairs but instead ushered by one of his secretaries into a small windowless conference room in the back of the building and told to wait. We all thought we were going to have some sort of meeting with Miscavige there. Instead, we were informed we were to remain in the conference room until we confessed our crimes. A security guard was stationed outside to ensure we did not leave and to escort us to the bathroom when needed. What our crimes were was anyone's guess. As we sat there for hours on end pondering our latest predicament, several more guests joined our little party. Within twenty-four hours there were more than a dozen partygoers, too many to fit in the conference room. We then moved to a larger room on the second floor, and the steady stream of new additions continued. We were handed paper and pens and instructed to write up our O/Ws. We all did as we were told, though at this point I have no idea what I may have written on that paper. This was such a frequent request that I, like everyone else, would struggle to come up with new things and many times just regurgitated the same supposed transgressions over and over with different embellishments to make them sound new. Commonly, these would be in the form of "intentions" or "thoughts," as these could easily be fabricated. "I had counter-intention to COB and did not want to admit to him that I didn't care if the event was well received, so I fell asleep while I was writing my speech."

Sitting in that room, hardly anyone spoke. Nobody wanted to do anything that would bring attention to themselves. We were told to write, so that is what we did. All day. Until we were escorted by security guards to "berthing" on the south side of the property (where we slept under watch) and were then collected again in the morning to start over. Food was brought and set up on temporary tables outside. After a few more days, Miscavige had had enough of the vermin infesting his opulent building and we were relocated again, this time a quarter mile down the hill to the CMO International office building that I was so familiar with.

With that move, "the Hole"—as Miscavige dubbed it—was born. He had a carved wooden sign about four feet by two made and hung on the outside of the building to announce it to anyone who walked by. Three of the four exterior access doors were barred shut, the windows were screwed to only allow them to be opened two inches so nobody could squeeze through to make an escape, and a twenty-four-hour security watch was posted at the only remaining entrance. We were not allowed to leave the building for anything, and were forbidden contact with the outside world.

There were about forty of us at the outset. The building in which I had once had my office was now our prison. Or perhaps the more apt analogy is to a POW camp. When you are sent to prison you know how long your sentence is. A POW camp has no defined end point and is often the venue for brainwashing. We were to remain in the Hole day and night until we had proven to Miscavige that we would no longer try to sabotage him. How this was to be accomplished was to "come clean"—confess our horrible crimes against scientology, Hubbard, and most of all, Miscavige. According to scientology principles, these supposed transgressions were the cause of our alleged failures.

The CMO Int building itself was one of the more ramshackle on the property and was not a traditional structure but two eighty-foot-long double-wide trailers side by side, joined by a conference room and connecting hallway that had been constructed between them. It looked like a large cake box—square with a flat roof, painted white with a "bunting" of fake blue tiles around the top in an attempt to make it blend in with the other buildings on the property. Because it was not built on a foundation, the floors creaked and sagged as we walked. In addition to the smaller conference room that connects the two trailers, there is a larger conference room along one side of the building with cubicles around it, where Watchdog Committee members had their desks, myself included. Since the days of the *Apollo*, little thought had been given to the niceties of office space, unless you were part of RTC.

These offices were never seen by the public, so there was no need for anything to be more than utilitarian. When the HGB had been purchased, there were some PR-friendly offices constructed to be suitable to bring outside people to (the president of CSI had one on the twelfth floor), but most everyone else had modular desks and limited space.

The remainder of the building consisted of smaller offices. There were men's and women's bathrooms, but no showers. There was no dining room or cafeteria either. We slept on the floor or under desks in sleeping bags, with whatever we could find to serve as a pillow. We ate at desks and around the conference room tables. Our "meals" consisted of cold leftovers from the main dining room delivered on large trays—sometimes the menu had been less appealing to those in the dining room, so there were more leftovers; other times there was not enough left to go around for us in the Hole, so we all ate small portions or subsisted on white rice and boiled beans. Every couple of days, security guards escorted the women through a tunnel under highway 79 to a shower room in a large garage, and when they returned, it would be the men's turn. There were five shower stalls and everyone was expected to take no longer than thirty seconds, just like on the *Apollo*. When we first routed to the Hole, we had only whatever clothes we had been wearing, but eventually each person was issued two dark blue T-shirts and two pairs of shorts, which were washed every few days. Personal hygiene was not easy to maintain in these circumstances, and with so many people sleeping, eating, and "working" in a confined space, the odor was palpable, but there was nothing that could be done about it, so we pretended it wasn't a problem.

Miscavige stated that the route out of the Hole was to not only come clean for oneself but to "take responsibility" for others coming clean. What this did was pit everyone against one another. Over about six weeks, we devolved into gathering around a conference table and accusing one another of committing various sins as a means of trying to force confessions. The more you could get others to own up to things, the more you could present yourself as being "with COB."

Part of this employed a Hubbard technique developed in the 1960s dubbed "the Murder Routine." If someone was not coughing up acceptable transgressions, the way to get them talking was to accuse them of committing even more heinous crimes than you could imagine they would be involved in. The theory is that being accused of murder makes it easier for someone to admit to committing a less egregious crime. "No, I did *not* murder my wife, I only cheated on her" is the example Hubbard gave. Confessions extracted by this method were highly dubious.

These daily confession sessions—Miscavige took to calling them "séances"—in the Hole typically began with someone making an accusation that a person had not come clean and was withholding their crimes. If the accused didn't provide a satisfactory answer, they would be told to stand up. More people would join in demanding compliance. If nothing was forthcoming, someone might get in their face and begin screaming at them and threatening to give them a black eye. This stems from a favorite line in a Hubbard policy letter stating that if anyone strayed from the righteous path, then other members could give them a "black eye." And sometimes, more frequently as the days and weeks passed, it devolved into physical altercations, and even torture tactics.

In one memorable example, the former head of Flag, Debbie Cook, was assigned to the Hole by Miscavige, who then tried to get her to say that scientology executives Guillaume Lesevre and Marc Yager had "admitted" they were "sucking each other's cocks."

Miscavige often spoke in the most vulgar and explicitly sexual manner, and he frequently accused people of engaging in various sex acts in graphic detail. I don't know if his proclivity for sexual talk gave him a sort of odd gratification, if it was a way of demeaning people to ensure they understood who was boss, if he wanted to create a "shock and awe" scene, or all of the above. But in keeping with the fundamental teachings of Hubbard, who said that homosexuality could only be cured by auditing or by removing them from society "quietly and without sorrow," many of Miscavige's slurs and insults were homophobic.

Two of his favorite targets were Lesevre and Yager—the highest officials in CSI. Debbie refused to say that they had done what Miscavige was claiming, as there had been no such admission. In typical fashion, he accused her of lying in front of a roomful of people in the

Hole, and when she responded with a denial, he told the crowd, "I don't have time to waste listening to her lies, you had better get the confession out of her." Debbie had not spent her years at the Int Base, though she had been there at times for visits, so she was unfamiliar with the unique ways to survive in this *Alice in Wonderland* world and made the mistake of contradicting those who had reported that Lesevre and Yager had confessed. That was a terrible crime in the eyes of the others in the Hole.

Since she would not agree with Miscavige's claim, Debbie must have had a similar transgression herself—the heinous crime of being a lesbian. This logic stemmed from Hubbard's teachings that if you felt someone's bad actions were "reasonable" or "justified," it was because you must have similar overts of your own. As a result, Debbie, who was happily married to her husband (who had been left in Clearwater when she was brought to the base), was forced to stand for hours in a garbage can with a sign around her neck that read LESBIAN while insults were hurled at her and water was poured over her head.

Similar scenarios played out again and again with all of us in the Hole. When put in the same sort of position Debbie had been in, many simply admitted to whatever the accusation was in order to get it over and done with. Some resisted or tried to explain. In those circumstances, we'd often tell Miscavige when he returned that we had squeezed the confession out, even though this may not have been true. It was what Miscavige wanted to hear.

The numbers in the Hole continued to grow as Miscavige sent more and more people there who didn't do as he demanded. Nobody managed to get themselves released. Eventually almost every person in International Management ended up in the Hole, along with some people imported from Los Angeles, CST, and other locations. There were at least 140 Hole dwellers at its peak—I once made a list. New arrivals were like chickens thrown into an alligator-infested pond, with people fighting to be the one to confront the newcomer. When you had sat for sixteen hours a day for weeks on end trying to write up your transgressions, it was a welcome relief to direct your attention to someone else, and the vigor with which we set upon others was astonishing. It's not like it was safe for those who had been there for a while, though; if they did or said something that attracted the attention of others or Miscavige, they were singled out and castigated as well. As the Hole became more like scenes from *Lord of the Flies* and descended into sadism, what people would admit to under the pressure and threats and physical abuse became increasingly outrageous (and untrue). In any forced confession, the veracity of the information admitted to is inversely proportional to the level of duress under which it was obtained. Every person in the Hole admitted to a litany of supposed transgressions, some of which they may have been guilty of, all of which were embellished, and most of which were simply things they thought would end the pain if they agreed to confess.

To this day, when those who were in the Hole speak about the abuses they experienced and witnessed there, scientology uses the confessions extracted from us to try to discredit the truth of what we say. It's a disgusting element of scientology's Fair Game campaigns to destroy its enemies—of course, when people see handwritten "confessions" but have no idea of the circumstances under which they were written, they tend to give them credence. The written statements from all of us that admit to lying, dishonesty, intentions to destroy scientology, failing at our jobs, and so forth are offered as proof that we are lowlife liars and our claims of abuse are false.

Psychological pain was not the only type inflicted in the Hole. In addition to the chronic lack of sleep and food everyone suffered, which in itself is both physically and mentally debilitating, the threat of physical violence was ever-present. And so was the reality. Slapping, punching, and kicking were the typical punishments for recalcitrance, meted out by the Hole's denizens to one another. And many times it went beyond that. One such punishment was to crawl around the conference table on hands and knees. Sounds innocuous enough, but the floor was covered in rough, high-traffic industrial carpet, not the soft pile of a luxury bedroom. After an hour or so, the rug burns on your knees and palms became extremely painful. And when the exercise was repeated again the next day, before a scab could form, it became excruciating. The scars on my knees from doing this at least half a dozen times are permanent.

Another technique was to sit someone under an open air-conditioning vent while the other vents in the room were closed. Cold air would blast on the person as someone poured water on their head. I saw people shivering uncontrollably with lips turned blue and almost going into hypothermia. After a few months, this method of torture stopped, as Miscavige considered air-conditioning a waste of money and a luxury the Hole denizens didn't deserve.

As always, Miscavige had a particular interest in me. He told the other residents of the Hole that I had not come clean, as my confessions were not salacious enough. About four months into my stint there, he assigned Marty Rathbun to the Hole in part because Marty had failed to make me come clean during the time we had worked together. Marty showed up with an understandably large chip on his shoulder. He brooded for a little while at the indignity of being put in the Hole, but within a couple of hours he began with demands that I come clean, then Murder Routine–style accusations, and soon thereafter he was attempting to strangle a confession out of me in front of the room full of Hole-dwellers. He sat on my chest with his hands around my throat as the mob chanted, "Come clean, Rinder." Cathy, who by this time was also in the Hole (along with virtually everyone else in International Management), got in on the act. She raised her voice above the rest of the mob and shouted, "I know you fucked Vicki Aznaran." She knew no such thing (as it never happened), but she seized on the fact that Miscavige made a big deal about how soft I had been in finalizing the Aznarans' settlement and had paid Vicki more money than she had demanded. Therefore, in scientology-think, I must have had sex with her. It didn't matter how I responded. "That never happened!" was met with jeers from her and others. "Stop lying!" and "Come clean!" "Be honest for once, you piece of shit." This incident was a large nail in the coffin of our marriage. It was the essence of the toxic nature of the environment that in order to try to save her own skin, she had turned on me.

As Marty had me on the ground, throttling me while the crowd bayed, I looked him straight in the eye and said quietly, "Marty, I don't want to play this game anymore."

He looked at me and stopped. In a voice that nobody else could hear, he responded, "Me neither." A few days later he was gone. I thought he had been taken out of the Hole by Miscavige because he was needed for some assignment, but I later learned he had escaped—he had a motorcycle, which he managed to get to, and made a dash through the gate when it opened for someone else.

In that moment with Marty, I decided I was not willing to continue under the existing circumstances. One of two things had to happen: either a drastic change for the better had to take place in the world controlled by Miscavige or I needed to get out of that environment. I had finally come to what Hubbard called "need of change." And yet still I had doubts about what to do—what about my eternity and making it to the top of the Bridge? What about my family? I still loved my children, who were now twenty-eight and twenty-three, even though I never saw them. I loved my mother and siblings, whom I'd also lose if I left. And while the distance between Cathy and me as a result of being so often apart had now widened to a chasm with her wild accusations, I held out hope it could be repaired if given the circumstances and opportunity. Scientology had the technology to resolve all problems. A lot of thoughts swirled through my head each night as I lay on the floor of the Hole trying to catch a few hours' sleep. The easier alternative seemed to be to continue hoping that Miscavige would change, that this was just a phase that would eventually pass. There was absolutely no reason to believe that was the case, but I convinced myself, *Things can't get worse, so they have to get better.* How wrong I was.

My friend Tom DeVocht, who had for a time been Miscavige's golden boy, was also now in the doghouse. He was assigned to the Hole at the same time as the head of CST, Russ Bellin—the two people Miscavige had brought to the base to replace Marty and me. It was pretty much inevitable: if you got too close to the sun, you ended up getting burned.

A few days after Tom arrived at the Hole, he was confronted to come clean by a group of people in the larger WDC conference room. He resisted, and the situation quickly devolved into people punching and kicking him. As he was defending himself, he shouted, "Miscavige is an insane SP! You all better look at yourselves and what you're doing! You are as nuts as him."

It stopped the room cold. Security was alerted and he was quickly hustled out of the Hole and sent to the Old Gilman House. He was too toxic even for the Hole. He had done the unthinkable, calling Miscavige an SP. Tom insisted he wanted to leave the Sea Org. I was assigned to sleep on the floor in front of the door of the room he was put in at OGH so he could not escape in the middle of the night. There was nowhere to run—there were cameras, motion sensors, and high razor-wire-topped fences preventing access to the highway. Sleeping on the floor was the same as in the Hole, but it was nice to have some space and peace for a few hours. I was supposed to persuade Tom to change his mind and stay, because even though he was considered a source of trouble, he could be a bigger threat loose in the outside world. As strange as it seems, Miscavige trusted that I would not "turn." Unfortunately, Tom knew the game only too well and said he would undergo whatever sec checks anyone wanted, but he was not going to change his mind.

I unsuccessfully attempted to talk him out of this plan while we sat in the tiny, poorly lit room with a mattress on the floor where he slept. I tried every angle: "Think what this will do to your mother and sister" (they were both in the Sea Org). "Do you really want to leave Jenny?" (his wife, Jenny Linson DeVocht, daughter of film producer Art Linson). "The wog world sucks, you don't have any education or experience to earn a living, you have been in the Sea Org since you were eleven." And the final catch-all: "What about your eternity? You are throwing away any hope of getting to the top of the Bridge." None of these pitches worked. Because of our long friendship he didn't refuse to talk or become angry with me. He listened and told me over and over that he had made up his mind and it was not going to change.

Despite Miscavige's faith in my resolve, secretly I started to wonder if Tom was doing the right thing and perhaps I should follow him out the gate. He said life at the Int Base was insane and he wanted out no matter the cost, no matter that his mother and sister and wife were in the Sea Org. Jenny had for a long time been one of Miscavige's pets, though she too had been put in the Hole. As soon as Tom said he wanted to leave, she immediately disconnected from him and demanded a divorce. Of course, Tom was right, it was totally insane. But I was torn by having made a loyal commitment to Hubbard and the Sea Org, and I just had not reached the point where I could take the plunge and leave my family. I lay awake outside Tom's door thinking these thoughts through over and over, weighing the upsides against the downsides and imagining what might happen if I left. I was like a man contemplating suicide who put the gun in his mouth many times but just could not pull the trigger.

Each day Tom would announce a countdown to his departure: "I am leaving here in sixteen days." The next day: "I'm leaving here in fifteen days." And so on. And when the appointed date arrived, he said he was walking out the gate and nobody had better try to stop him. He pushed the buzzer on the intercom and told security to open it and let him out. When they refused, he scaled the gate. Security tried to physically restrain him. I was called out of the Hole to deal with the situation. I made everyone back away—though they all knew where I had come from, they also knew that I had been summoned by RTC, so they listened to me. I was concerned physical restraint could lead to false imprisonment or assault charges. I asked Tom if I could take a walk with him.

"You can, but I am not going to change my mind. I am done with this place," he responded.

Together, we walked seven miles into Hemet in 100 plus–degree heat. I engaged in a lot of small talk, reminiscing about times we had spent together and once again trying every avenue I could think of to persuade him to stay.

"Mike, don't waste your time. I have heard every argument and reason a dozen times." He was very calm and simply stated: "I am leaving. I refuse to live life like this anymore."

I knew he was not going to change his mind; I had known him since he was a child. I decided I would do what I could to treat him with some dignity in the hope it might prevent him from becoming an "attacker." He got a motel room and called his brother in Florida to come collect him. His possessions were gathered and inventoried. I delivered them to him when his brother arrived, and as they left, I shook Tom's hand and wished him well. That was a huge faux pas: no Sea Org member in their right mind would ever shake hands with a traitor who was leaving. Someone I had known since my earliest days in the Sea Org, Marion Pouw, had become one of Miscavige's people at ASI and had then moved to RTC. She was assigned to be present at the final handover (Miscavige's trust of me went only so far—at a moment like that, I could have too easily jumped into the truck with Tom). After I eventually left scientology, when everyone was required to write up everything they knew about my nefarious acts, she reported me for shaking Tom's hand. This "handshake incident" became the basis of a subsequent accusation that Tom and I (along with Marty Rathbun) had been engaged in a conspiracy from within to "destroy scientology."

Failing to persuade Tom to stay was not a big blemish on my status with Miscavige at the time. He blamed the sec checkers who had failed to make Tom come clean, and had to claim Tom was a cunning SP, since Miscavige had elevated him to one of his most trusted lieutenants. Under those circumstances, he quickly asserted after Tom was gone (as he had done with others like Mayo and the Aznarans) that it was "good riddance" and things would "go much better now the SP was rooted out." Miscavige continued to seek my help when things flapped. It didn't matter that I was in the Hole; it was the same as when I'd been under guard at OGH or in the bilges on the *Freewinds*. On one hand, he would complain I was a Suppressive Person and tell everyone what a piece of shit I was, and on the other he would send me to deal with important matters as the representative of himself and scientology. I hoped each time that carrying out the assigned task would result in my being permanently reprieved and life returning to some form of normalcy. Hope sprang eternal.

Even after many months of us being in the Hole, Miscavige still could not resist occasionally showing up to remind everyone that he was the big dog.

The infamous musical chairs incident was depicted in HBO's documentary *Going Clear*. It was a twisted version of the children's game with very real consequences, putting Miscavige way ahead of *Squid Game*. He forced everyone to play musical chairs to Queen's "Bohemian Rhapsody" as he looked on, appearing to enjoy himself. He proclaimed that the last person left in the game would be released from the Hole. (Lisa Schroer "won" and was given a short reprieve before being returned some days later.) Anyone not tough enough to fight for a chair when the music stopped would be sent off to some undesirable part of the world the next day. Spouses who were both in the Hole were to be sent to different locations. It was sadistic and he seemed to derive great enjoyment from it. The next morning, outside the Hole was a line of box trucks he had rented to make it appear everyone was being shipped out that day. It was all for show. He had no intention of letting those who had witnessed his sadism out into the world, and he had no problem wasting money on his cruel games.

He also enjoyed coming to the Hole to make announcements about individuals in order to further belittle them and crank up the pressure to come clean. I was his target on more than one occasion, but there was one incident that had a particularly lasting impact. Producers for *Anderson Cooper 360°* had reached out during the media frenzy of 2005, saying they planned to do a show about scientology with several former scientologists, and asking if we'd like to send someone to respond. Miscavige had told me to get back to them and offer them a "better show" by taking them to all the church properties for an "exclusive look" and interviews with celebrities. They bought into it and the process began.

One of Anderson's producers had toured the Flag Land Base and then met with me in New York. Miscavige wanted to slow-roll the show and hope they would eventually lose interest. As part of his plan he ordered me to offer an exclusive interview, with the hook that "nobody had interviewed Mr. Miscavige since Ted Koppel." CNN jumped at the chance, but this gave Miscavige the ability to claim he was "unavailable." He instructed me to offer dates months in advance, and then, as the dates neared, to push them further out. He later changed his mind and decided he would rather be interviewed by Larry King because he asked only "softball" questions. I was caught in the middle. David

Doss, the executive producer for both Anderson Cooper's and Larry King's prime-time shows on CNN, understandably became very pissed off. Months and months passed and eventually David called me and said that he was done with the messing around and they would proceed without Miscavige and would just do the interview with me. By this time I was in the Hole, so I reported the call to Miscavige. (I was the only person in the Hole who ever got outside phone calls, though Angie Blankenship sometimes was called to the phone to speak to Miscavige himself.)

Miscavige then visited the Hole and gave a briefing to the inmates as I stood there: "Rinder screwed up my life again with his incompetence. He offered himself up to CNN to represent scientology. He is so self-important he thinks anyone wants to hear from him. Do any of you want to hear what he thinks?" A chorus of boos in response. "Who does everyone want to hear from?" "You, sir!" in virtual unison. "He told them I was unavailable and he would do the show instead, how do you like that?" People started shoving and screaming at me to try to make themselves look good to Miscavige. "As if I don't have enough to do, now I have to handle this," he sneered as he turned and walked out, followed by his entourage.

I don't know what exactly happened with CNN after that. I think Miscavige had Tommy Davis, son of actress Anne Archer, handle the matter. Tommy wore expensive clothes, drove a BMW M6, and had been assigned as Tom Cruise's handler at the Celebrity Centre. There are few people I have ever met who oozed self-importance as much as him. Tommy became the scientology spokesperson to replace me. Somehow the endless game-playing wore CNN down, and in the end, neither Larry King nor Anderson Cooper interviewed Miscavige.

The Anderson Cooper humiliation increased my doubt about staying in the Sea Org. Being blamed for something Miscavige had orchestrated in minute detail was nothing new; it happened all the time. Whenever anything went wrong, he always found a scapegoat, even if they had done precisely what he ordered. It was the timing and circumstances that made this much more significant than all the earlier incidents. I began actively wondering for the first time since I had arrived on the *Apollo* what would happen if I left the Sea Org. The old mantra "What did I do to pull it in?" had become tedious. Life in scientology was making less and less sense.

IT WAS SUMMER 2005 when I last saw Shelly Miscavige. I had been summoned to LA by Miscavige for something, I don't remember what. As I arrived back at Gold, the security guard at the gate told me I was to report to Shelly's office in RTC immediately. Though the message was urgent, when I arrived, Shelly tried to be nonchalant, inquiring what my business with Miscavige in LA had been. In the middle of the discussion she asked me, "Hey, did you notice if Dave was wearing his platinum or gold wedding ring?" It was completely out of the blue, and she tried to make it sound as offhand as she could. I was floored. Obviously she was not sure whether Miscavige still considered her to be his wife. I tried to remain just as nonchalant in my reaction, saying, "I really don't remember."

I noticed over the next two months that Shelly was no longer around. That may or may not have been unusual; she could have been off at Flag or in Los Angeles with Dave, but I had seen her fear—she obviously knew the writing was on the wall. She had in fact been disappeared, though this was not confirmed to me for some time, when it became apparent she was neither at the Int Base nor with her husband in Los Angeles. At that point, it became very clear to me that if Shelly, the second-most-powerful person in scientology (because she answered only to David, could act with his authority in all matters, and was the only person who could offer any criticism of him), could be thrown to the dogs, nobody was safe. Another piece of the puzzle fell into place in my mind.

I am quite certain Shelly was sent to the CST property in the San Bernardino Mountains. It was the CST headquarters but also a super-secret location that few scientologists even knew existed, where security was paramount. CST had the extremely serious job of preserving Hubbard's writings and lectures for eternity. I was one of a very limited number of people who had ever visited the site, probably no more than a few dozen. It is heavily guarded, inaccessible from any road, and not near any town. It's a self-contained world and the perfect place to hide someone away that you don't want even Sea Org members to know about. Shelly was last seen at the Int Base in 2005 and has not made a public appearance since. Like Mary Sue Hubbard, she became a nonentity, and nobody questioned it.

As the months in the Hole passed, the scales in my mind were tipping to the inevitable conclusion that things were never going to get better and the only solution was to escape. In November 2006, matters started coming to a head. Norman Starkey, the executor of the estate of L. Ron Hubbard and Miscavige's sidekick for years at ASI, was taken out of the Hole by Miscavige to perform as minister for Tom Cruise's wedding to Katie Holmes. As a former captain of the *Apollo* and Hubbard's executor, he had high status and Miscavige had talked him up to Cruise through the years. Though internally labeled a Suppressive Person, Starkey was flown to Italy to participate in the so-called wedding of the century. He got drunk at the reception and tried to hit on Brooke Shields. Brooke's husband, Chris Henchy, complained to Miscavige. Starkey was sent back from Italy in disgrace and everyone in the Hole was punished for what he had done—because it was our fault that we had not handled him. Even for the twisted thinking of the Hole, it was bizarre. How could we be responsible for what Starkey had done in Italy while under the direction of Miscavige? Another piece of the puzzle fell into place. (This wedding was also the beginning of the end for Leah Remini, as it was where she famously asked Tommy Davis, "Where is Shelly?" And he just as famously responded, "You don't have the fucking rank to ask about Shelly.")

Around this time, I and a number of others were taken out of the Hole for another assignment. We were dressed in full Sea Org uniform and driven to Los Angeles to take over the IAS; collect its leader, Janet McLaughlin, and her staff; and bring them back to the Hole. I had earlier been assigned to put a tracking device on Janet's vehicle, as she had become somewhat vocal about her upsets with Miscavige vis-à-vis the fundraising operations of the IAS. The tracking device disclosed visits to the New Zealand consulate and doctors' offices, which suggested that she and her husband were planning an escape back to her home country. She was a huge liability, as she knew all about the finances of the IAS. Janet was the last remaining top executive of any scientology organization supposedly independent of Miscavige's legal control. He had put the heads of CSI in the Hole, followed by the head of CST. Only the IAS remained, and it had come time to exert his complete authority over them as well.

After being briefed in the parking structure of Author Services by Miscavige, with attorney Monique Yingling by his side, we proceeded to the IAS office in Big Blue. We collected Janet and her staff and drove them back to the Hole, but not without drama. Janet resisted for some hours, refusing to move. They were eventually persuaded. Her husband, Colm, was even more adamant he would not cooperate and was physically bundled into a broom closet and held there while Janet and her staff were taken from the building. He was shipped to the *Freewinds* so they would be separated from each other. He was held prisoner there for more than a year. This was all so surreal: like dressing maximum-security prisoners in police uniforms and sending them out to arrest some criminals to join them in incarceration. To top it off, each prisoner then dutifully turned in their police attire and returned to their cell. The level of mind control was astonishing. Both Janet and Colm left a year or more later, but have remained silent to protect their familial connections.

The next and final encounter I had with Miscavige outside the Hole was, in retrospect, the most significant of all in solidifying my decision to leave.

John Sweeney, a reporter for the BBC's investigative show *Panorama*, had reached out in October 2006 wanting to do a story on scientology. He had been directed to Tommy Davis, as I was "unavailable" (in the Hole). Soon thereafter Miscavige called me to the Gold Conference Room. Davis was there, and Miscavige informed me I was to assist in dealing with the BBC and was to be Davis's "slave" and "suck his balls and lick his asshole." Yes, this is what he said. But shortly after we left the meeting, Miscavige called me, telling me privately to report on what Davis was doing. He wanted me to spy on Davis, and also to be a fallback in case he screwed up, adding that I had better not allow that to happen. But to Tommy, I was still the person who was supposed to "suck his balls." This schizophrenic role went on for months with Miscavige calling me almost daily for updates on events while I served as Davis's "assistant."

Davis and I flew to England to meet with Sweeney and his producer, Sarah Mole, in early 2007. We showed them endless videos of scientology's accomplishments in the hope we'd get them to see what we had done for the good of humanity. I returned to the Hole afterward, but my stay was short-lived, as Sweeney showed up unannounced at the annual L. Ron Hubbard birthday event in Clearwater in March trying to obtain an ambush interview with Miscavige. I was quickly put on a plane to Clearwater. Now Sweeney had made a nuisance of himself, so Miscavige told us we needed to know where he was at all times, to be sure Sweeney could never catch him unawares. From then on Sweeney was tracked by PIs everywhere he went, and I personally followed him and his crew across the country to meetings in Berkeley, California, before he finally arrived in Los Angeles.

Sweeney rented a plane and flew over the Gold Base to get aerial footage of the property. No news organization had done this before. Tommy and I rushed to Gold from LA in case he decided to try to get onto the Base. Instead Sweeney and his team returned to Los Angeles, so we rushed back to LA. While we were driving, Miscavige sent Tommy and me disgusting and threatening BlackBerry messages like "I hope you have torn [Sweeney] many new assholes." When he really wanted to make a point, he ended his messages with "YSCOHB," which he demanded we decipher ("You suck cock on Hollywood Boulevard").

We agreed to show Sweeney through the CCHR Industry of Death Museum. This was part of the strategy of media handling dictated by Hubbard policy—direct their attention to the blood, sex, and crimes of psychiatry and talk about what we are doing to end these horrific abuses. Tommy had promised Miscavige he would needle Sweeney into losing his cool. About an hour into the journey through the horrors of psychiatry, Tommy went to work, using techniques practiced in scientology auditor training routines—constantly interrupting, making

repeated digs about Sweeney's professionalism and motives, accompanied by loud throbbing music and sound effects that emanated from
the displays. It was upsetting just listening to it happen to someone
else. Sweeney started to scream at the top of his lungs: "You were not
there at the beginning of that interview . . ." in response to Tommy
accusing him of favoring discredited sources.

But shortly thereafter, Tommy made a major blunder. Sweeney,
upset that this screaming match had occurred, changed the subject and
pressed the issue of wanting an interview with Miscavige. He had been
asking for this since the first day he contacted us. Miscavige had been
pretending to be too busy to have time for anyone as lowly as the BBC.
Tommy answered Sweeney, "I talk to Mr. Miscavige every day and I
would never suggest he grant you an interview."

Sweeney turned to me. "What about you, Mike? Will you ask Mr.
Miscavige to sit down with me?"

"No, I won't, John," I replied.

"Why not?"

"Because you're an asshole."

Producer Sarah and cameraman Bill were behind Sweeney and in
my line of vision. They both instantly cracked up at my response, and
we all laughed, Sweeney included. It broke the tension and was an odd
moment where I felt a connection with the enemies. But this was no
joke to Tommy, who now realized how catastrophic his response had
been. He was full-time devoted to dealing with the BBC and had now
admitted he was speaking to Miscavige daily, obviously about the *Panorama* program. It exposed the lie that the COB was too busy to be
bothered about the BBC. If only Sweeney knew just how much time
Miscavige was spending worrying about him. Tommy realized he had
committed a cardinal sin and that the BBC would now write a letter to
Miscavige and he would have to eat his words. He was savvy enough to
know he would soon be sent to the Hole, so that evening he got in his
BMW and drove to the Wynn hotel in Vegas, where he lay low.

Tommy was supposed to have been heading to London the following day because the premiere of John Travolta's *Wild Hogs* was happening in Leicester Square later in the week. Miscavige was worried

Sweeney would get in front of Travolta as part of the movie press junket and ask him uncomfortable questions, including about Miscavige beating people. With Tommy MIA, I was rushed onto a flight to London and went straight from the airport to brief Travolta in his suite at the Canary Wharf Four Seasons.

John had always been extremely friendly and accommodating to me, as he knew I had helped deal with earlier tricky situations. He had even asked me for my advice when he was sent the script for *Pulp Fiction*—I told him I didn't think playing a heroin-addicted assassin was a good career move or appropriate for a scientologist, which tells you how much I know about movies. As I was talking to him in his suite, his masseur, in a bathrobe, walked into the room. He leaned over and kissed John on the mouth. "I'll be in soon," John said as the masseur headed toward the bedroom. That was pretty shocking, right in front of a senior scientology official. It was just not done. I guess it was indicative of the trust he placed in me. Much has been made of John's sexuality and, whatever the realities of his sexual orientation may be, I firmly believe he would be more open about it if it were not for the stigma he feels due to his strong belief in scientology.

One of the last interactions I had with Sweeney was in the doorway of the Tottenham Court Road scientology building. Sweeney had persisted since day one with inquiries about David Miscavige physically assaulting people. He showed up with a camera crew and I was summoned to come and deal with him. Sweeney asked me point-blank if I had ever been struck by Miscavige. I denied it vehemently and threatened to file a lawsuit if he aired any such allegations. Of course, they were true. And it struck me afterward that now I was lying only to protect David Miscavige's reputation. I was no longer protecting people from the dangers of exposure to secret OT levels, or even protecting the good name of L. Ron Hubbard and scientology. I was lying to protect David Miscavige, and in doing so, allowing him to continue abusing not only the people in the Hole but Sea Org members and scientologists everywhere. Now I was truly on the verge of no longer playing this game, as I had said to Marty that fateful day on the floor of the Hole.

When the BBC show finally aired on May 14, 2007, Miscavige was unable to watch it live, as he was in the US. I had to give him a blow-by-blow over the phone. I was elated: *Panorama* had not aired a single mention of his physical abuse. I believed I had pulled off a miracle and that this might be my ticket out of the Hole and back to a somewhat "normal" life. I am an eternal optimist, even when there is no good reason to be. I got my hopes up once again. But Miscavige didn't see things the way I did. He brushed off the fact that he had dodged the bullet he had been so petrified of and instead began to berate me. "If I had been there handling this, the show would never have aired." Of course, he could have flown to London and visited the BBC and done anything he chose, at any time. He did not.

This was the last straw.

On May 31, 2007, I was still in London preparing a complaint about the *Panorama* program to be lodged with the UK media over-sight body Ofcom. Miscavige sent an order to Bob Keenan, the LRH PPRO UK, informing him that I would not be returning to the United States. Apparently I was not going to be allowed to see my wife or children ever again. I was cc'ed on the dispatch he wrote to Keenan (communications from Miscavige were sent by a type of encrypted email): "How long do you think it will take for you to get MR on a plane to the furthest outreach of Western Australia? I'm not that unkind. I'm willing to give him 10 quid . . . If he can't earn a living on whatever job he gets, he can always sell his body. I could care less."

Miscavige went on to describe what he had learned from the latest "confessions" squeezed from the denizens of the Hole. He was announcing things about the most senior scientology executives to a low-level person in the UK. He referred to the CO CMO Int, Marc Yager, as "the bald-headed guy" and the Executive Director International, Guillaume Lesevre, as "the cheese-eater." This is part of what he wrote:

> Do you know that pimple you saw? Well, I popped it. We're talking two guys buying X-rated movies and masturbating simultaneously in the same room with one being the husband and one being the wife, going through Dean and Deluca [a gourmet grocery store] catalogs as husband and wife and the

bald-headed guy buying the other one cheese as a favor. Right now you are living with a snake. The thing between me and you, buddy, is you don't need to tell me all this other stuff. I know you know. And you know I know. And what he doesn't know is we both know.

This was fairly typical of how Miscavige addressed those in his immediate circle. The depravity of it was a reflection of how much you were trusted—much of what he dictated was sanitized by a unit of transcriptionists. This was an example of pure, unfiltered Miscavige, though even then swear words were deleted or replaced with more acceptable terms.

The false hope I had been relying on for years, that things would eventually improve and that I could figure out what I did to pull this in, dissipated in a blinding moment of clarity. I knew it would *never* get better and no matter what I confessed to, Miscavige would still be a sociopath.

With this last shred of hope dashed, I copied a bunch of documents, made sure I had my passport and all possible cash on me, perhaps two hundred pounds, and waited for the right moment for my escape.

CHAPTER 14

YOU MAKE YOUR OWN TOMORROW

O n June 9, 2007, as I sat in my temporary office in the library on the ground floor of Hubbard's home at Saint Hill, I pulled out my laptop and typed a goodbye note:

> *There is no future for me at this point. I am forever tainted by my past and it doesn't go away. I have thought very hard about this and have not slept for most of the night for the last two days. It has been going on for years and I see no end in sight. I thought that I had come out of it by getting somewhere with the BBC handling, and while it wasn't perfect, I did everything I knew how to do to turn around the disaster. But then things became impossible again, and I don't know how to deal with it anymore. I have introverted and introspected on why I am like I am and what else I have done and my evil purposes until I cannot take it anymore.*
>
> *At this point, I do not think it is a resolvable situation, I have been on a roller coaster since 2003 that I cannot get off and I cannot go on playing this game anymore.*
>
> *I don't want to leave my family, but I think I am hurting them more by being around. Cathy goes through hell and is constantly*

sick and this will just end the cycle for her. Taryn will be devastated, but she will get over it and then not have to worry about me constantly. I don't know about Benjamin, I have not been in touch with him for years.

I really don't have a plan other than to find somewhere to go that I won't be obvious or create problems. I don't know where that will be or even how to get there. At this point, I just want to not be in a state of constant fear and turmoil about what is going to happen to me tomorrow. I am not winning and I am not happy and have no idea where to turn other than to go away.

Mike

I took the note, grabbed my briefcase, and left Saint Hill, headed for the scientology offices at 57 Fitzroy Street in London, figuring it would be easier to escape in the city rather than from the remote estate in the countryside, which was patrolled by security guards and cameras. This trip would not set off any alarms; my routine for the past few months had been to travel to London almost daily to deal with the BBC and return to Saint Hill at night, though on occasion I slept on a mattress on the floor in one of the small offices in the basement at Fitzroy Street.

Close to the Post Office Tower and a few blocks from busy Tottenham Court Road, the London property had been purchased as part of the strategy to invest in real estate. (In this case to "preserve the history and legacy of L. Ron Hubbard," as 57 Fitzroy Street was his old London office that he had rented in the '50s. Other buildings in Washington, DC, and Dublin, along with houses where he lived in Phoenix, Johannesburg, La Quinta, and Bay Head, New Jersey, were all purchased, renovated, and used as part museum, part PR office.)

The forty-five-minute train ride from East Grinstead to Victoria station was calming. Nobody was watching me, issuing me orders, or calling me. The lush countryside passed by accompanied by the comforting sounds of the train and its gentle rocking. I wondered how things were going to play out as I transferred to the Tube at Victoria and headed for Warren Street station.

When Miscavige, who was in Los Angeles, heard I had gone to London, he instructed Bob Keenan, the LRH PPRO UK and his go-to guy of the moment, to get me back to Saint Hill at once. Bob approached me as I was sitting at a desk in the basement room that served as the "office." He looked stern and somewhat tense, as though he was preparing to engage in a fight: "I just got off the phone with the boss," which is how he often referred to Miscavige. "You need to go back to Saint Hill." I knew this was likely my last window to escape. The moment had come to take the leap of faith I had pondered for so long. I made up my mind, but I had to act quickly. "Okay," I responded, "I'll get the next train; I guess at this point there's nothing I can accomplish here anyway." I tried to sound resigned to my fate and as if there were nothing else in the world I would rather do than comply with the wishes of the boss, just as I had done for the last twenty-plus years. I grabbed my briefcase and was out the door before Keenan had a chance to give it much thought and decide he should just drive me to Saint Hill or escort me on the train. I didn't even have a moment to leave my resignation letter.

Once I boarded the Tube, I knew I was safe. Keenan had made a big blunder and now, unless I did something stupid, they would find me only if I wanted them to. But I had no idea what I was going to do.

I got off at Leicester Square Tube station rather than going on to Victoria to catch the train to East Grinstead. I watched the platform to ensure no familiar faces got off behind me. I breathed a huge sigh of relief when I saw nobody I recognized, and my pulse began to return to normal as the train pulled out of the station. I removed the batteries from both of my BlackBerry phones. I walked out into the sunlight and the crowds of London's West End.

I was torn by incredibly mixed emotions. I was still very much a scientologist, and the doubts swirled through my head: *Maybe I have unhandled overts and withholds? Am I really just a Suppressive Person? What have I done to pull this in?* I was also worried about where I was going to sleep that night and where I was going to go. But most of all, I felt the embrace of the realization that suddenly, I was answerable only to myself. I felt the elation of freedom for the first time in decades. Nobody to tell me what to do. Nobody to criticize or punish me. Nobody looking over my shoulder, second-guessing everything I did. I had never been in that position before and it sure felt good.

I walked to Trafalgar Square and sat on the grass in the sunshine outside the National Gallery. It is one of my favorite places. There were a lot of happy, relaxed people around, enjoying a beautiful late-spring day. It was comforting to realize how many individuals in the world were doing just fine without scientology in their lives. I found a nondescript, cheap hotel and paid cash using the money I had scraped together from my personal dollars I had brought with me from the US and the "expense money" I had been issued for transportation and food while in London. I bought myself some toiletries, a duffel bag, and cheap clothes—underwear, socks, shirt, jeans, and sneakers—to replace the business suit and tie I'd been wearing when I left Fitzroy Street. I wandered around the city for a couple of days, staying in a different inexpensive bed and breakfast each night. There are dozens of them around Victoria station that are used to hosting transients with no luggage and don't ask for ID. I had my passport, but didn't want to use my real name to reduce the possibility of being found. I spent some time enjoying London, thinking about life and what I was going to do. Every now and then I would put the batteries back in my BlackBerrys to check for messages; as soon as I had read them, I took the batteries out again and quickly left the area. I knew from past experience that it was possible to track cell phone signals, and I intended to avoid contact until it was on my terms. There were numerous messages from Bob Keenan, starting soon after I was expected at Saint Hill and didn't appear. They began with "Where are you?" and escalated to demands to "report in" and threats of consequences if I didn't, then transitioned to a more conciliatory tone: "The boss wants to talk to you, there will be no consequences if you call in. Everything can be sorted out." From the messages I knew they had no idea where I was, and it gave me a sense of comfort.

I decided to try to reach Ronnie and Bitty Miscavige. I had their phone number in their new location in Williamsburg, Virginia. They had grown weary of living in Cabo San Lucas and one day declared they were moving back to the US. In my role in OSA at the time, I had made contacts through a lawyer and a PI with a person who helped get Ronnie a job as a Realtor. Dave wanted to keep them on his side as much as possible, and didn't want them to be so low on funds that they would be vulnerable to offers from enemies.

My only means of calling them was to go to an internet cafe and pay to make a call to the US on an online phone line. I had no safe cell phone I could use. The connection was poor, but I could not use the BlackBerrys, as OSA could access calls made on them and I did not want them to know who I was reaching out to. I called Ronnie and left a message. I didn't have a way for them to call me back, so I told him I would call again the next day at the same time. Three days in a row with no answer required a new plan. I tried Tom DeVocht. I also had his number to check in with him every now and then to ensure no media or process servers had tried to contact him. Fortunately, Tom answered.

He was surprised and a little suspicious but agreed that I could come to his home in Kissimmee, Florida, near Orlando. I didn't want to book a flight in advance, as I was sure OSA would be monitoring the airline reservations. I knew flights to the US departed in the morning from London. I took the train to Heathrow the next morning. I got there around ten, only to discover that the only direct flights to Orlando left from London's other main airport, Gatwick. I did not have enough time to transfer to Gatwick to make any flight that day. So I bought a ticket from Heathrow to Orlando via Washington, DC, with a family American Express card my parents had given me years before that I had never used. I figured that by the time the charge showed up and my mother noticed it, I would be in the US.

I half expected there to be someone in the transit area at Dulles waiting to intercept me. But the coast was clear. I called Tom from a pay phone in the transit lounge and told him what flight I was arriving on later that night.

Tom was waiting to greet me when I landed. I knew he worried I was an OSA plant being sent to spy on him. I would have had the same concern in his shoes. But our many years of friendship overcame his suspicion and I was soon at his house. He was incredibly understanding and generous. He gave me five hundred dollars to buy clothes. He told me to just relax. To go to Blockbuster and rent all the movies I had not seen in the last twenty years and watch them—I probably consumed twenty movies while at Tom's house, two or three a day, ranging from *Kill Bill* to *Finding Nemo*. We went out to eat and just hung out and talked about our lives and remembered good times as well as less enjoyable experiences. I was in a sort of dream world—it seemed unreal. I was doing what I wanted to do when I wanted to do it. Not since high school, more than thirty-five years earlier, had I enjoyed that sort of freedom. I could take time to do nothing, and though I at first felt ingrained guilt over being "unproductive," I grew more comfortable and at peace as I slept eight or more hours a night for more than a week, something I had not done since I had joined the Sea Org. I also ate well and took vitamins. My physical condition slowly improved, though I continued to smoke, as almost every Sea Org member did.

After about a week I felt settled and tried calling Ronnie and Bitty again, from Tom's house. This time, they answered. I told them I had left the Sea Org and was with Tom in Kissimmee and that I had tried to call them from London. Ronnie explained he had not been able to understand a word of the messages I had left for him, as the connection was so bad it sounded like white noise. He offered to fly me to Williamsburg to stay with them in the self-contained "grandpa unit" they had built in their house for Ron Sr. in anticipation of his eventual escape from the Sea Org. (Ronnie's dad, Ron Sr., was a musician who had joined the Sea Org years earlier and lived and worked at Gold composing and playing music for scientology videos and films. As for everyone else at that base, life was tough for Ron, and Ronnie was convinced he would eventually reach a tipping point and escape.) Ronnie had been so successful as a Realtor that he was now in charge of the same Long & Foster real estate office where I had helped him get a job. He said he could now return the favor and help me get a job. I was gratified by his kindness—we had been through a lot together over the years, and he and Bitty were the best friends I had anywhere. I didn't have to think about the offer; it was what I had wanted in the first place. Ronnie arranged a flight into Newport News two days hence. Tom and I went to Downtown Disney for a final dinner and he dropped me off at the airport the following morning.

I was sad to leave Tom in Florida, though what I most needed was a job, and Ronnie had far more resources to help with this. Our goodbye was one between good friends, so different from the understandable suspicion he had greeted me with when I had arrived.

Ronnie and Bitty were waiting at the airport in Virginia. They were a welcome and familiar sight as I walked into baggage claim in the early afternoon. We drove to the beautiful house they had built in the woods outside Williamsburg, near the York River. It was a calm, quiet place surrounded by old trees with no other homes visible, a wonderful environment to get my bearings. And it was the closest thing I could get to "home." Cathy and I had shared apartments with Ronnie and Bitty for years, and Bitty was one of my oldest friends; I had known her since I was eighteen.

Bitty had also been one of Cathy's closest friends. She insisted I reach out to try to get her and Taryn and Benjamin to come to Williamsburg. I was skeptical but figured I had nothing to lose by asking. I sent off a letter to OSA International (I knew they would open it and get it to Cathy), and within a week received a handwritten response from Cathy dated July 4, 2007. It began:

> *Mike, I got your message about joining you out there and my answer is: Fuck Off. That is the last thing I would want to do and I have no desires to blow or be a wog.*

It went on for a few paragraphs about what a terrible thing I had done and ended with:

> *PS: I'll send the divorce papers and brief the kids.*

It was what I had expected, but it was heartbreaking nevertheless to see it formalized so succinctly and bitterly. I was not trying to escape my marriage; I had been perfectly content to remain married to Cathy for the rest of our lives, despite the fact it had been a Sea Org marriage—as in Sea Org first, marriage a distant second. At this point, my love for her had been replaced by concern for her future and well-being and that of my children. Perhaps if she had come to Virginia right away we might have been able to reconcile, though her response put an end to those ideas. But no matter the circumstances, nothing would change the fact that Taryn and Benjamin were and always will be my children. Her message was too final and too hard for me to accept; I couldn't process the information fully. I knew I was never going to return to the Sea Org. The insanity in that world had become intolerable. In some ways I think I was less upset and less surprised by the letter than Bitty was. She had left before the depravity of the Hole had begun, when it seemed like Cathy and I could handle anything in our marriage. When things were less mad.

Shortly thereafter a shipment of my belongings arrived—all carefully inventoried. Of course, the letter I had sent to Cathy had gone through OSA first, so they knew where I was and whom I was with. Miscavige had decided that it was a better course of action to try to sever connections to me rather than attempt to get me back. He had probably announced to his underlings that he was glad I was finally gone, that I had proven I was an SP just like he'd said all along, though I suspect the fact that I was with his brother and sister-in-law factored into the equation too. The three of us together represented a shitstorm he did not want to stir up. Someone had gone to the trouble of finding and listing every piece of clothing I owned, pens, books, and even half-used tubes of toothpaste and old toothbrushes. But not a single photograph or photo album was sent—and I had many from my childhood and of my family. No shots from my days on the *Apollo*, my wedding, or of Taryn and Benjamin. Nor were there any items that provided evidence of any locations I had been in or of my involvement in scientology. My history had been erased.

Bitty, Ronnie, and I spent a lot of time talking about our lives and experiences. One evening we were sitting on the back porch of their house, talking about their life in Cabo San Lucas and how much they had disliked it. I wondered aloud why Dave had been so insistent that they must be located outside the country: "I know you have his last name, but even if you did get pulled into a lawsuit to testify, why couldn't you just say you didn't know anything and no harm would be done?"

Bitty looked at me, a little surprised. "Don't you know about Lisa McPherson?"

"Yes, of course I do, I spent three years living in Clearwater dealing with that."

"No, I mean what Dave did to Lisa McPherson," she responded.

"What do you mean, what he did?"

I was stunned by what she said next: "Dave was cee-essing [case supervising] her personally; he was the one who ordered she be declared Clear before she had her psychotic episode."

In all the time I had been in Clearwater, and in all the involvement I had with this case, I never knew Miscavige had been personally involved. Suddenly a lot of things made sense. His wild reaction when he was not dismissed from the lawsuit. The disappearance of key individuals who had been working in RTC at the time and obviously knew of his actions. One had been sent to the RPF in Australia, another to be a dishwasher at Gold. And of course, why he was so desperate to keep Bitty and Ronnie out of the reach of any subpoenas when they were no longer under his control in the Sea Org. Knowing this now didn't help me move on with my life, but it did answer some questions and fill in some blanks.

I needed to start making a living. Ronnie had originally told me he could get me a job as a loan officer at Long & Foster, and I interviewed for the position. But it was right at the time of the financial collapse in the real estate world in 2007, and Long & Foster made the decision not to hire any new loan officers—mine was the last interview they did before they shut down their loan department.

Ronnie gave me an introduction to the manager of the car dealership where he had bought his BMW. They didn't have an immediate opening, but their related Toyota dealership in Williamsburg did. I'd always enjoyed cars, and my lack of résumé as a fifty-two-year-old was of no concern—car sales is a ruthless business; you live or die based on how many cars you sell. If you sell nothing, you get nothing. It was a challenge I readily took on—hell, it seemed simple after the things I had done in my former life. I quickly became the top salesman at Casey Toyota. I found a small apartment nearby and furnished it with a bed, a table, a chair, and a TV. Compared to Sea Org living, it was palatial. I opened a bank account, got my own credit card, and bought my first car in a sweetheart deal arranged by the used car manager: a pale gold–colored 2004 Toyota Camry with one hundred thousand miles that was in beautiful condition.

Until now, I had never had an actual income, my own place to live, and the freedom to go wherever I wanted. This was a completely new way of life, and I reveled in it. On my days off I often took long drives. Williamsburg is a beautiful and historic area—I visited nearby Jamestown, Richmond, Virginia Beach, Newport News, and Yorktown. For the first time since high school I was learning about something other than scientology and the worldview of Hubbard. I absorbed a lot about the history of the United States, from the lives of the first English settlers at Jamestown, to the Revolutionary War and defeat of the British at Yorktown, to the Civil War capital of the South in Richmond. US history is not taught in Australian schools, and certainly not in scientology, and I found it all fascinating. Even my job at the dealership was interesting. I met people every day who had lives and experiences and stories that gave me a different perspective from the tunnel vision I had been so accustomed to. I think my genuine interest in hearing from people and talking with them was the key to making me a successful salesman. I still had a long way to go, though.

Since childhood, my life had been strictly centered around the Hubbard view, and that way of thinking cannot be replaced overnight, but the shackles were becoming far less binding and I began seeing things in a different light. While I still considered myself loyal to Hubbard, I certainly felt no allegiance to Miscavige. It was beginning to dawn on me that I bore some responsibility to stop the abuses, even if that somehow harmed the legacy of Hubbard or scientology, but I was unwilling to take any concrete actions yet. Escaping from the oppressive Sea Org environment was only one step toward unraveling the twisted beliefs that had been so heavily inculcated over my entire life.

Perhaps the first big change was realizing that "wogs" are not the uninformed, lower-level humanoids I had been taught they were. The wog world was not crazy—in fact, it was far less crazy than the Sea Org and a virtual nirvana compared to the Hole. Even used-car salespeople were a decent bunch for the most part, and I enjoyed making friends with them, especially an immigrant from Beirut named Said. We spent a lot of time together, and he would cook me authentic Middle Eastern food at his home. A kind, honest man, he really opened my eyes to how wrong my sour view of the wog world had been.

I settled into a pretty standard routine in Williamsburg. I worked five days a week, but because I had no family commitments, I put in longer hours than most, which helped me make more sales. I cooked for myself each night for the first time in my life and spent a lot of my spare time watching TV, catching up on dozens of shows I had never seen—one of my favorites was *Boston Legal* with William Shatner and James Spader. I often visited Bitty and Ronnie on weekends. I saw no evidence of PIs following me, but I was always slightly on edge, expecting something to happen. What I didn't anticipate was contact from someone on the other side of my scientology life. In late 2007, a few months after I began working at Casey Toyota, Sarah Mole, the BBC *Panorama* producer, showed up unannounced, asking for me. I was called to reception and was stunned to see her standing there.

"Hi, Mike, so nice to see you," she said as I approached. I didn't want anyone to overhear, as my scientology past was not known by my coworkers, so I quickly ushered her outside.

"Sarah, what are you doing here?" I tried to sound as nonchalant as I could.

"I heard you left scientology and were selling cars, so I tracked you down and persuaded my bosses to let me fly here to talk to you. I didn't think I could ever get you to come to the phone." She was probably right. Discussing scientology with the media was not on my agenda. I had felt a connection with Sarah, especially in that moment when I called Sweeney an asshole. It seemed she felt similarly, enough that she flew across the Atlantic on the off chance she could get me to talk.

She cut to the chase. "Mike, would you agree to be interviewed now that you have left?"

"I'm sorry, Sarah. As much as I like you and John," I explained, "and feel bad about what I did to make your lives difficult, I am not ready to talk to the media. I am trying to figure out my life and get settled and I don't want to generate attention from scientology."

She understood but persisted: "I flew all this way; are you just going to turn me down like that?"

I smiled. "Yes, I'm afraid I am. But I'll tell you what: if I ever change my mind, I will come to you first." As always, she was gracious, so she didn't push it any further. I think she actually believed me, which was good because I meant what I said.

It was true. I wasn't ready to talk. I was just getting used to my new life, and don't think I had even processed everything fully enough to be able to articulate my thoughts. In the meantime, I now had a small group of ex–Sea Org members in my world. Bitty's son Justin and his significant other lived in Williamsburg, as did one of her sisters, Sarah, and Sarah's husband, Jim. Justin, Sarah, and Jim had all spent years at the Gold Base. Justin was a different generation, but the five of us older people were close and spent weekends and holidays together as a sort of ex–Sea Org family. We were like veterans who had been through a war together. Those sorts of mutual experiences create a strong bond, but they are also isolating, as the only people who really understand what you have been through and how you view the world are others who have also gone through them. The community of ex–Sea Org members, and particularly those who had been at the highest echelons, is an exclusive club. Perhaps even a clique. But for me, and I think everyone else who has left, it is a vital lifeline. Having others who could relate and understand my unique perspective, my insecurities, and even the regular nightmares I had been experiencing since leaving of being back at Gold was the most important element for me of beginning to heal.

Another of Bitty's sisters, Teresa (everyone called her TC), who had also left the Sea Org, came to visit from Denver. We all hung out, now a group of six. Teresa and I connected. She had been raised in a scientology family, we were both ex–Sea Org and both single. It is so much easier to be comfortable with someone who knows your life and who doesn't require endless explanations and definitions of scientology terms. We had an easy, flirtatious rapport, saw each other a number of times, and began a long-distance relationship. I decided to move to Denver—I loved the area from my time there in scientology fighting legal cases. I had no obligations to anyone and wanted to pursue a relationship with TC, so I set out on a new adventure.

TC and I packed up my car and drove across the country in early 2008. It was my first real road trip, and my first time seeing the heartland of the US. Because scientology is so sparsely represented in the Midwest, I had never had cause to visit. Once I arrived in Denver it was an easy transition to working at a much larger Toyota dealership in a big city, with a recommendation from my former manager in Williamsburg. I soon became one of the Denver dealership's top salespeople. I found a nice apartment in a new complex north of the city near TC's house with magnificent views of the Rockies.

Life was relatively happy, but for the recurring nightmares. Every one started the same way: I was back at the Int Base. Every one ended with me waking in a panic because I was unable to escape. Each time, when I inevitably woke up and realized I was in fact in my own bed in Denver and not at Gold, an immense wave of relief would wash over me. Nightmares were not something I had been accustomed to. Now they were an unpleasant routine. I considered them a small price to pay for my freedom.

Outside of the regular nightmares, I often thought about my family, wondering how they were and especially whether my mother was okay. I decided to reach out to them with Christmas cards. The only one who responded was my mother. I had not been in touch with her since I had seen her on the *Freewinds* several years earlier. I didn't bring up anything about scientology other than the fact that I was no longer in the Sea Org and was living in Denver. She continued the conversation, writing to me every few weeks with all the news about my brother and sister and their children and what was happening in Melbourne. She was getting old, and since the terrible car accident that had resulted in my father's death, she had also undergone a heart transplant and suffered a second car accident that put her back in the hospital with various broken bones. She was frail, though always cheerful, and ended her letters with the same message each time: "You are my number one son, and I will always love you. Mom."

I cherished that I had reconnected with my mother, but was sad she was the sole person in my family I was in contact with. I heard nothing from my siblings, nor Cathy or my children, other than divorce papers that scientology's in-house OSA lawyers sent me to sign. The divorce would be simple, I thought—we had no mutual property or bank accounts, and our children were adults. It would just be rubber-stamped and done.

Apart from family, the only thing I missed in my new life was a sense of greater purpose beyond just making money. It is something scientology focuses on: a grand plan to clear the planet, a mission so important that life's hardships and problems are worth enduring. I tried to fill the void by working long hours and going to the mountains to ski and learning to snowboard. I had no desire to return to the Sea Org, but I did yearn for what Hubbard described as "a bigger game."

Some help came from a dead person, or someone I thought was dead. Some months after arriving in Denver, I reconnected with Marty Rathbun. I had heard a rumor that he'd died, likely a story circulated by scientology to keep people from looking for him. He had in fact deliberately vanished from the scientology world, relocating to South Texas, where he had worked as a reporter for a small local paper. If anyone understood my perspective on life, it was Marty. He and I had not just been in the same battle, we had been in the same foxhole and had seen and experienced things that nobody else had.

Marty and two other former Sea Org members from the Int Base— Dan Koon, an old friend who had worked on the *What Is Scientology?* book, and Steve Hall, who had been in the marketing department— spent a long weekend in Denver. It was a memorable few days, recollecting our experiences as we drove to Estes Park in the Rockies, site of the Stanley Hotel, the inspiration behind Stephen King's *The Shining*. There were many jokes and reminiscences about the similarities

between Jack Nicholson's character and David Miscavige. We had all
reached the same conclusion: Miscavige was a madman. The problem
was not with Hubbard or scientology, it was with the COB. At the
time, I felt that Hubbard's philosophy had some bad elements, like
disconnection and some of the ethics tech, but for the most part, his
intent had been to help people. We had been helped. So while it was
easy to point the finger at the sociopath Miscavige, I still saw redeem-
ing factors in Hubbard, and it would take me longer to recognize the
truth about him.

Marty, like me, had come to the realization that he had a responsibility to do something to end the abuses within scientology. He had
been tracked down and contacted by Joe Childs and Tom Tobin, reporters for the *St. Petersburg Times.* We knew them well, as they had written
the vast majority of stories about Lisa McPherson, and Marty and I had
been their primary contacts in scientology when we were in Clearwater.
They had convinced Marty to tell them his story. It was a massive scoop
for them and they were planning to make it into a multipart series. Joe
and Tom traveled with Marty to Denver—it was our first meeting since
leaving the Sea Org—as they wanted me to corroborate his information. Marty did too; in many instances, I was the only one who could
confirm his claims. Details about the Hole and the abuses meted out
by Miscavige had never before seen the light of day in a major publication. Sweeney had not been able to include them in his program due to
legal concerns from the BBC. The libel laws are different in Britain, but
because the BBC is publicly funded, even if they believe they could win
a legal case, if it would cost them millions to fight, they'll often decide
not to air something to avoid being criticized for wasting funds because
they had good reason to believe they would be sued. The *St. Petersburg Times*, unlike the BBC, had years of experience with scientology, including being targeted by Fair Game campaigns. They also knew
Marty and the position he had been in. This was going to be a very big
deal for them. Still, their legal department wanted corroboration, and
of course Joe and Tom wanted me to be on the record. I told them I
would confirm or deny the information they had collected and would
be willing to testify in court to anything I said, but I did not want to be

quoted or identified in their story, due to concern for my mother. She remained a dedicated scientologist and I was afraid if I appeared in the *St. Petersburg Times* speaking out about abuses in scientology, it could shock her sensibilities so badly that, in her frail state, she might expire.

I spent a couple of days with Joe, Tom, and Marty reviewing the details of their reporting and answering questions. I always operated under the assumption that I was being observed by scientology, but I was unaware that I was being surveilled by the very same PIs who had tailed Pat Broeker for twenty years. They had rented an apartment across from mine in Westminster, Colorado, to watch me 24/7 through the window with high-powered cameras and night-vision scopes. They also took my trash and followed me around for $10,000 per week. They were there to keep tabs on my movements and whom I was meeting with, and no doubt trying to dig up any dirt on me. Mine was a pretty boring life: I didn't get drunk, I didn't do drugs, and I wasn't picking up hookers, though I did go to a topless bar with some of the guys from work one night. Ironically, these same PIs ended up suing the church for nonpayment. Joe Childs and Tom Tobin would break that story in 2012 and follow up in 2013 with the fact that the PIs had been surveilling me.

In mid-April 2009, Miscavige, having been alerted by the PIs about Joe and Tom's visit, sent lawyers Monique Yingling and Bill Walsh, along with Tommy Davis and his wife, Jessica, to Denver in an attempt to dissuade me from speaking to the media. Tommy, who had taken off for Vegas during the Sweeney visit to LA in early 2007, had been recovered, sent to Flag to be sec-checked by Jessica Feshbach, and had subsequently married her. He was now apparently back in Miscavige's good books. Tommy and Jessica first went to TC's home and tried to intimidate her, but she slammed the door in their faces and called me, very upset. She had not bargained for scientology banging on her door as a consequence of her association with me, and this played a role in ending our relationship. She had a business and two sons to protect, and I didn't want to visit my problems on her life. Monique then called my cell phone, claiming she "happened" to be in town, and asked to meet for a drink at her hotel. I told her I had just heard from TC and didn't know what she was up to, and I was not going to meet her at the Ritz-Carlton bar. I said I'd call back the following day to let her know if I would meet with her at all.

I then called Marty. He and our friend Jason Beghe (an actor who had very publicly left scientology) flew to Denver that night. I was not about to meet scientology lawyers alone. It would be three on two.

"Let's have some fun with this," Marty said when he arrived. "They're not going to be expecting me and Jason to be with you. We can throw them off balance right from the get-go."

"Yes, maybe we should find a location that will make them uncomfortable," I suggested. "There are some pretty run-down hotels along I-25 near where I live; we could rent a room there."

They agreed, and first thing the next morning, we headed out and looked for a good seedy conference room. In one hotel, a Red Roof Inn I think, Marty opened the doors of a whiteboard mounted on the wall and it fell down and landed on his foot. The hotel manager was worried he might sue, so she offered us half the regular rate. It seemed like the perfect omen and we took the room. I called Monique and told her I would be there at two p.m. If she wanted to talk to me, this was her opportunity.

Monique arrived with Bill Walsh and I met them in the reception area. She knew Marty and Jason were in the room, having been tipped off by the PIs, because when I tried to bring her to the conference room, she refused.

"Shall we meet here in the lobby or the coffee shop? Or I will be happy to get a room."

"It's okay, I have a little room," I said as I headed toward the door to the conference room down the hallway. "I want to record the conversation anyway," I said. I knew that was her concern.

She responded, "I don't want to record the conversation. I am not recording anything, I can assure you, and I would be happy to be searched and I am sure that Bill is too."

I pulled out a tape recorder and turned it on.

She asked me who was waiting in the room. It was an absurd game.

Eventually I called Marty and Jason out into the hallway, and that's where the "meeting" took place.

Monique said she understood I was talking with the *St. Petersburg Times* and asked, "Do you really want to go to war with scientology?"

"I am simply telling the truth and confirming or denying the details of their story."

She probed in different ways whether we could reach a truce: "Let's see if we have a situation where people go their own way and there isn't any more destruction, on either side."

I told her if she wanted to prevent destruction she should turn around, get on a plane back to LA, and stem the destruction coming from within. After about twenty minutes, perhaps realizing she was not getting anywhere with me, she tried a new tack.

"Is there anybody else you would talk to?"

"Absolutely," I responded. "I would like to talk to Guillaume Lesevre."

"Not your family?"

I felt my blood pressure rising. "No, you're the wrong person to talk to me about them." She was not even a scientologist. Now she was trying to dangle my family as some sort of bait.

I continued: "You are out of line trying to manipulate my family as a coin to gain my silence."

The dance went on for a while longer, teetering between veiled threats and peace offerings. It did them no good, as my mind was now made up. I resolved to go on the record with the *St. Petersburg Times*. The lawyers finally left. Shortly thereafter I spoke to Joe and Tom and told them what had happened. I let them know I was ready to be quoted on the record and answer their questions. I was now less concerned about what my mother would think than I was about doing what I could to stop Miscavige from destroying people's lives.

Following the fateful visit from the scientology lawyer brigade, I reached out to Sarah Mole at the BBC to fulfill my promise to her and Sweeney. She then flew to Denver to discuss a follow-up show on *Panorama*. I explained the circumstances surrounding the decision to go on the record and that *Panorama* would be the first video interview I would do.

In June 2009, the series in the *St. Petersburg Times* was published, aptly titled "The Truth Rundown," and I was prominently featured. It was a huge blow to scientology, as it laid bare the truth about Miscavige and life at the Int Base. Scientology wasted no time in responding by targeting the sources and reporters as liars and bigots. I moved to near the top of the scientology enemies list, second only to Marty Rathbun. As a result, I knew I needed to find another job immediately. I had been instrumental in setting up pickets against Bob Minton at a Lexus dealership near Boston, so I knew what would be coming—no single salesman is worth that pain or, more importantly, potential loss of customers to a car dealer.

Marty helped me connect with another former scientologist in the Tampa Bay area who wanted to hire me to help him with his online sales business. As his family were all ex-members, he was not going to be intimidated by scientology. I flew to Florida in August to check out his operations and come to an agreement about what I could do. It seemed a great fit and I decided to move back to Florida.

During this trip, a mutual friend introduced me to another former Sea Org member, Christie Collbran. She had been in the CMO and also had parents and siblings who disconnected from her because she had spoken to Marty. Marty had raved about what a great person she was, and he was right: When we met up, we realized we had a lot in common. She was also beautiful, smart, and artistic. And the more time we spent together talking about our experiences and feelings, the more we grew together. Though I am older than she is, the similarities in our lives, mutual experiences, and shared loneliness through loss of family created a bond between us that remains unbreakable.

Christie had also been raised in a scientology home and had been groomed for the Sea Org. She joined when she was sixteen. When she and her then husband began to understand the extent of the ongoing abuses in scientology as they moved into Miscavige's orbit, she deliberately got pregnant and refused to get an abortion. Her son Shane was born in December 2006, after they were dismissed from the Sea Org.

Once she was out, she attempted to alert her parents to what was really going on behind the scenes in the Sea Org, but they disconnected from her, as did her brother and sister and every friend she'd had since childhood. That any family could abandon a daughter and sister like her for trying to speak the truth from her own experience is impossible to understand except in the context of a belief system that is so rigid and so toxic that it defies any rational analysis. After leaving, she trained herself as a doula to assist pregnant women and new mothers. She now has her own doula agency. She is my best friend and better half. She is also now my wife, but even that unfolded as a story of scientology intrigue.

CHAPTER 15

FAIR GAME

While I was settling into a new life in Florida, Sarah Mole and John Sweeney were putting together their second *Panorama* scientology program, and in December 2009 I flew to London to shoot interviews with them. Marty flew in from Texas. PIs followed us everywhere and we were assaulted by unknown egg throwers in a passing car as we walked down the street near our hotel. The Fair Game campaign against me had begun in earnest.

Sweeney and his team then flew to Clearwater to shoot additional footage for the show. Like clockwork, PIs set up in cars across the street from our house 24/7 and followed us wherever we went. There was no attempt to be subtle; this was a noisy investigation, designed to intimidate. However, I knew every move in the Hubbard Fair Game playbook. It's a mind game. If they didn't succeed in getting into my head, I would win. They tried really hard to make me falter, though, and it was relentless. However, it was not a one-way fight. We were throwing punches too.

Early in 2010, I heard from Christie that Laurie Goodstein, national religion correspondent of the *New York Times*, had reached out to her for a story she was planning on disconnection. I had known

Laurie when I was the spokesman for scientology. Christie was unsure if she should participate and I reassured her that Laurie would do an excellent job. I took Christie to meet her to tell her story. On March 6, 2010, Christie was featured on the front page of the Sunday *New York Times* talking about her experiences with disconnection. As a result, the *Today* show called and Christie was interviewed by Matt Lauer. I accompanied her on the trip to New York. It was strange walking into the same studio I had been in with Katie Couric, now as part of a small group of whistleblowers rather than as a representative of scientology. While we were in New York, Anderson Cooper reached out and Christie also appeared in a segment of *Anderson Cooper 360°*. Now it was not just me: both Christie and I were prime scientology targets.

An old friend from the *Apollo*, Dave Richards, called after seeing me in the media. He introduced me to Robert Almblad, who also lived in the Tampa area. Robert had been with Hubbard on the *Apollo* before I arrived. Like me, he was still a believer in much of the philosophy of scientology but had become disenchanted with the organization, its incessant demands for money, and specifically its practices of making people redo steps of the Bridge. There always seemed to be something new that scientologists were required to do, or redo, and it inevitably cost money. He and many others had become embittered with the repeated bait and switch.

Robert had left the Sea Org decades earlier and had become an inventor of some renown. He developed the first laser key-cutting machine, the kind you find in every Home Depot today. He had also invented equipment used by McDonald's and other fast-food franchises. At that time he was working on a new "safe ice" machine. (Contaminated ice is a little-known but serious problem, especially in hospitals.) Given my experience in PR and dealing with the media, Robert asked me to help him develop and promote his invention. I jumped at the chance to work on something that would give me some sense of larger purpose. I signed on to help him without hesitation. But as TC had found out, associating with me comes at a hefty price. Soon, Robert and his partner were being followed everywhere. Scientology PIs set up a spy office across the street from Robert's workshop and used video surveillance equipment. They even cut down trees in front of his building in the middle of the night so they would have an unobstructed view. They didn't bother getting rid of the evidence: when we arrived the next morning there were three twenty-foot-tall oaks lying in the road. There was no doubt in my mind who had done it, but of course there was no proof.

Scientology also sent in a plant to get close to Robert. Claiming her name was Val Graeve, she befriended Robert's girlfriend's niece, who was staying at their house. She began spending time at Robert's home, gathering information about his activities and plans.

The higher-ups in scientology must have thought this wasn't enough, so they set up another stakeout across the street from my new house. Robert had bought it originally for his son, who had subsequently moved, so he offered it to Christie and me to live in rent-free. It was near his house and office in Tarpon Springs, fifteen miles north of Clearwater. It might seem an odd choice to live near Clearwater, so close to the belly of the scientology beast, but my need of a job and my life with Christie and Shane (his father also lived in the area) dictated it. There was also a big upside in my mind: Benjamin was stationed in Clearwater—I was just twenty minutes away if he ever wanted to leave or needed help.

The PIs installed surveillance cameras and placed GPS tracking devices on my and Christie's cars to follow us. Scientology sent in a spy to get close to us as well: a woman named Heather McAdoo, with a small child the same age as Shane. McAdoo first appeared on the street playing with her son when we were out walking our dog. We saw her almost daily; at first she just said hi, but eventually she struck up conversations with us, trying to get closer.

Soon after Christie, Shane, and I moved to the Tarpon Springs house, my old friend lead scientology PI Dave Lubow showed up to continue the noisy investigation. This time he nonchalantly set up a video camera on a tripod on the sidewalk across the street pointing directly at our front door. He then visited all our neighbors to ask them if they were aware of criminal activity at our address and told them that we were depressing the value of their homes by engaging in mortgage fraud. It's an old tactic, intended to create suspicion and distrust by claiming that there is something untoward going on. Of course, I spoke to each of the neighbors and explained this had happened because I had exposed scientology in the *St. Petersburg Times*. One of those neighbors told Lubow to leave his property and called the police. Lubow disappeared soon thereafter.

In the midst of this onslaught I was contacted by an FBI special agent in Los Angeles working on an investigation into human trafficking violations that focused on the Sea Org members at Gold. The case had grown out of the "Truth Rundown" series, which had included a lot of detail about activities at the base in California. Imprisoning people in the Hole, cutting them off from the outside world, and stripping them of their passports—these were all violations of human trafficking statutes. The FBI agent flew to Florida and I met with her in downtown Clearwater just a block away from Flag. I talked to her for hours and gave her the documents I had taken with me when I escaped in London. I spent many, many hours with the FBI over the next year, on the phone and in face-to-face meetings in Texas and Los Angeles.

The *St. Petersburg Times* continued its reporting after the "Truth Rundown" with follow-up stories from other victims. In response, scientology cranked up its efforts to discredit everyone who had been used as a source in the original series and in subsequent articles, including me. As part of this effort, Monique Yingling called reporter Joe Childs to try to convince him that I was entirely unreliable because I was a terrible, negligent parent. Her proof? She told him that my son Benjamin had aggressive skin cancer, but I had refused to help him and even refused to see my wife when she came to visit me in Denver to inform me about his condition. When Joe told me this, I was flabbergasted. This was the first time I'd heard my son was sick. I told Joe I had no idea Cathy had been in Denver, and Yingling had never mentioned that she was there when we met. Nor did she mention the cancer. If Cathy had in fact been in Denver, she hadn't even tried to call me. Joe reassured me that he knew I was not lying and apologized for being the bearer of bad news.

I was anxious to find out how my son was. Joe said Yingling mentioned he was being treated at the Moffitt Cancer Center in Tampa, so I knew he was still at Flag. I drove to the Fort Harrison to try to see him on April 14, 2010. Marty Rathbun had been visiting us at the time, so we went together and videotaped our trip in case we found out scientology was staging the whole thing. We were stopped by PIs and security guards at the front door who refused us entry; in fact, they refused to even speak to us or relay my request to see Benjamin. Instead, they called the police and issued a trespass warning. I spoke to a Clearwater police officer, who agreed to go inside the building and ask Benjamin if he wanted to talk to me. The officer returned after a few minutes and said he had seen Benjamin, who had told him he did not wish to speak with me. I heard later that he was under watch at the time because he had expressed a desire to leave the Sea Org. It's tragic that he could have walked out the door with the police right then, but the fear of the unknown is enormous and making a decision that will irrevocably change your life with no time to consider your options is almost impossible. It took me many months to finally reach the conclusion that I needed to break out of the bubble.

A bold move like showing up at the Fort Harrison and videotaping the encounter with the guards at the door was an affront to Miscavige. He always feels it necessary to retaliate for any perceived lack of respect for his greatness.

I didn't have to wait long.

Just nine days later I was standing in a secluded parking lot waiting for Christie, who was at a doctor's appointment. While she was inside, I took a call from John Sweeney in London. He needed to do some fact-checking, so he was recording the call. I was stretching my legs, wandering aimlessly next to Christie's car, paying little attention to anything other than the conversation with John and his fact-checker. Suddenly three cars pulled up in the otherwise empty lot. Seven people got out of the two leading vehicles and began walking toward me. Two men in sunglasses whom I didn't recognize, no doubt PIs, got out of the third car and hung back.

The seven people were Cathy, Taryn, and my brother, Andrew,

accompanied by four senior scientology officials: Jenny Linson, Dave Bloomberg, Guillaume Lesevre, and Sue Wilhere. They began screaming at me, right there in the doctor's office parking lot:

"You are a fucking SP!"

"You are going to DIE."

"You are trying to destroy Scientology!"

"You disconnected from your family!"

"You are killing your mother!"

"Stay away from Benjamin."

I couldn't make out who was screaming what, but it was all recorded by the BBC. They sounded stark raving mad. It was as if the insanity of the Hole had been teleported to a shady parking lot in front of a doctor's office in Florida.

I moved toward the car a few yards away, but the mob did everything they could to prevent me from reaching it, jostling me and trying to stop me from getting into my car and then from closing the door. I managed to get into the driver's seat, but my brother got in the passenger side, grabbed the keys, and threw them out into the parking lot. My next move was to try to reach the doctor's office, but now Cathy and the others tried to stop me from getting *out* of the car. All the while, the screaming and cursing continued. Sweeney was listening on the other end and asked me if he should call the police. In short order, the doctor, who had heard the commotion from inside her office, came out to see what was going on. She too asked me if she should call the police and I said, "Yes, right away!" When the doctor appeared—a wog witness—they ceased the physical confrontation, and I was able to get into her office. Cathy and Taryn barged through the door behind me into the reception area. As Christie emerged from her treatment room, they yelled at her: "Whore!" until the doctor demanded they leave her premises.

When they heard the sheriffs had been called, Linson, Lesevre, Bloomberg, and the two PIs hightailed it out of the parking lot. It says a lot that they had flown across the country and were all up in my face accusing me of terrible things but didn't want to be interviewed by a deputy sheriff. They knew their story would not hold up and they might be in trouble for harassment or assault. If they could characterize it as a family dispute, law enforcement was unlikely to take action. So Cathy, Taryn, and Andrew remained (along with Sue Wilhere, the least threatening church official, to ensure the others stuck to the shore story and to report back to Miscavige).

Somewhere in the pushing and shoving Cathy's arm was grazed. I don't know when. I assume it was when she was trying to stop me from closing the car door. The sheriffs arrived and questioned those who remained. They concluded the scientologists had followed me to the parking lot, approached me, and I had attempted to walk away. They noted the graze on Cathy's arm was "incidental contact," though Cathy, Taryn, and Sue tried to claim I had assaulted her. Cathy refused treatment from the paramedics other than to have gauze applied to the graze, refused to go to the hospital, and they noted she said the pain was a 2 on a scale of 1 to 10.

The scientologists told the sheriffs they had just been driving by and happened to see me and that this was a family matter. Those were lies. My brother came from Australia. My daughter, my ex-wife, and the goon squad came from LA. PIs had been following me and there were GPS tracking devices on my car, which is how they knew where I was; the parking lot is not remotely visible from the road. And finally, this was no "family matter." Four senior scientology officials had been flown in from Los Angeles for this specific purpose, and the loudest voice heard on the BBC recording is the screeching shrew Jenny Linson.

I felt drained when it was all over and everyone had left. I called Sweeney back and told him what had happened in the end. I called Marty Rathbun and recounted the incident. Christie and I sat and talked for a long time. I didn't know if Benjamin was in bad health and this was why he had not participated, or if it was a sign he might be wavering. There was a lot I didn't know, but one thing I did: I was not going to give up. No matter what they tried. I would fight until my last breath to expose the abuses of scientology.

A few days after the parking lot incident, Miscavige's former handyman JB Brousseau escaped from the Int Base and made his way to Marty Rathbun's home near Corpus Christi, Texas. Both Marty and I were initially suspicious that JB may have been sent in by Miscavige as a plant. The level of resources scientology was devoting to us was unprecedented, and more elaborate schemes had been developed in the past than sending someone like JB to become a spy. If he was not a plant, his very fresh information about what was going on at the Int Base and with Miscavige could prove invaluable to the FBI investigation. I alerted the FBI that JB had escaped, and they flew me out to Texas with authorization to wear a wire to record my conversations with him.

When I arrived at the Corpus Christi airport, my doubts as to whether JB was for real began to dissipate. A dozen screaming scientologists were waiting at the airport to greet me. I recognized many of them as Sea Org and OSA volunteers from LA. I alerted the TSA that these people were scientologists, and seemingly out of nowhere four FBI agents appeared and herded the troublemakers into a back room.

Earlier that morning, before I had arrived, one of Miscavige's henchwomen, Angie Blankenship, and two others had been sent to the motel where JB had spent the night. They banged on his door, demanding to speak with him. He refused to engage with them. Marty and I had decided that the bellwether on JB (or anyone else for that matter) being a spy was whether they were willing to talk to law enforcement. We knew that a plant would never agree to that. JB readily agreed to speak to the FBI, and the next day, I drove with him to San Antonio to meet at a Holiday Inn near the airport with the FBI agents who had flown in from Los Angeles.

I thought this might be the break the FBI needed. They had expressed concerns that the information they had from me, Marty, Amy Scobee (another long-term former member of CMO Int and WDC who had escaped with her husband), and the others they had spoken to was outside the statute of limitations. Unfortunately, JB's testimony was not enough to tip the scales and, like many other efforts to bring scientology to justice, proved to be another dead end.

Still, the Fair Game campaign only increased with JB now having escaped.

Scientology started a new line of attack: They instructed my family members to send nasty letters to me (the return addresses were the church in Los Angeles) implying I should kill myself. "You should check out of this game and go sit on a rock for a few million years," and other kind thoughts like "You could not actually have a soul." They called me an "overwhelmed, implanted, ev-purp being," and issued the grandest takedown any scientologist can utter: "You are 95% in the American Psychiatric Association camp." It was always 95 percent, not 100, for reasons unknown.

When I didn't respond, they claimed *I* had disconnected from *them*, not the other way round. So I wrote "An Open Letter to My Family," which I published on Marty's daily scientology blog on May 25, 2010 (and subsequently put it on my blog—which I began in 2013 after Marty asked me to take over from him—where anyone can read it today). I still considered myself a scientologist at the time, just not part of the organization. The open letter recounts a lot of facts, including some of the content of the coordinated hate mail my family had sent me. I attempted to be civil and even conciliatory, telling them I understood the position they were in and what they were required to do and that I bore them no ill will.

Publishing the letter made me feel better, but it didn't change my daily circumstances. In fact, things became even more bizarre. A few days later, I was contacted by a reporter in Australia, Bryan Seymour, who asked if I would agree to be interviewed. I checked with the BBC, who still had not finished putting their program together—though I had no legal obligation to give them an exclusive, I felt I owed them the courtesy of checking. John and Sarah were fine with me being interviewed in Australia; they felt I had more than fulfilled my promise to them and wished me luck. In July 2010 Christie and I flew to Australia to do the interview. Scientology sent PIs to follow us there all the way from the US. Bryan is one of the most tenacious people I know. And one of the best. He confronted the PIs on a number of occasions. The interactions were rather humorous, in a very Australian way, as Bryan always called them "mate." A typical first line from Bryan, himself being filmed by his camera crew: "Here's my old friend Chris, how are you doing today, mate?" before asking him why he would work for a nefarious organization.

Despite the usual PI harassment, I tried to make the visit enjoyable for Christie. It was wonderful being "home" again and introducing her to the world in which I had been raised. I took her to the places I went as a kid, the house I'd lived in, and the school I'd attended. We rode on the Manly Ferry across Sydney Harbour, visited the city's famous beaches, and I introduced her to Australian pies and fish and chips. When we were done filming in Sydney, we drove to Melbourne, as I had learned my mother was in an assisted living facility there. I wanted to visit her to tell her I loved her despite everything and simply see her for perhaps the last time before she died. Christie and I went to the nursing home, and the lady in charge said my mother was not there. When I explained that I was her eldest son and had come all the way from the US to visit her, she told me she was very sorry, that Barbara had suddenly gone on an unexpected trip to Adelaide. I knew this must mean that scientologists had spirited her away so I could not see her. I asked if I could leave my mother a note. I wrote it and the woman asked me if I would like to leave it in her room, so I could at least see where she lived. It was a tiny but neat room with little more than a bed, a chair, a chest of drawers, a TV, and a bunch of photos of my father and her children (I was only in group shots with my brother and sister) and grandchildren. It was sad, but I was at least happy she was in a safe location and was being well cared for. Subsequently scientology accused me of "violating her privacy." And they even published a statement from my mother that read:

> Had you knocked on my door I would not have asked you into my space. Your behavior in telling lies to the media about our Church is despicable. I have personally made the effort to find out and judge your actions for myself—and I can't believe you could be so evil. At present there is no future for you as part of our family.

She had no choice but to do what was asked of her. Her entire life was dependent on my brother and sister in Melbourne, and they were also dedicated scientologists.

While I was in Melbourne I also tried to visit my brother's house. Of course, he was not home either, the PIs having tipped him off—he may well have been with my mother. I left a note for him too. Just a few months earlier he had been yelling at me in a parking lot in Clearwater that I didn't understand what effort it had required on his part to get approval to speak to me. Now I had traveled halfway around the world and he was nowhere to be found. So much for the desperate measures he'd had to resort to in order to see me. Obviously, that had been a lie. No public scientologist has authorization to communicate with a family member who is a declared SP like me. Only in a staged and controlled event would such contact be made.

One thing scientologists never admit but always demonstrate: they believe SPs have incredible power to subvert and subdue even the most powerful OTs. My brother and his wife are pillars of the scientology community, massive fundraisers, heads of the OT Committee (consisting of the most dedicated public scientologists in each area who are expected to keep the flock active and engaged in scientology) and the embodiment of all that scientology claims you can achieve. My mother was OT VIII. And yet, I had to be kept away from them at all costs. Why? With a sideways glance or an offhand comment, I might shake the very foundation of their faith?

On September 28, 2010, "The Secrets of Scientology" *Panorama* program finally aired. I flew to London with Christie for the first showing and used it as an opportunity to show her my other favorite city in the world. Of course, we were followed by PIs everywhere. They were so obnoxious that when I took Christie to the Tower of London, the Beefeaters confronted them and ordered them to leave when I complained scientologists were harassing me. I would have imagined it was becoming apparent by then that this tactic was not making me cower and back off from exposing their abuses, but their harassment didn't let up.

In fact, it seemed that they turned it up a notch. The next prong of the Fair Game campaign was to send "reporters" from scientology's

Freedom magazine—particularly a guy named Jim Lynch. He was a washed-up former tabloid writer they hired to hold a microphone in our faces in parking lots, outside our homes, at restaurants, and wherever he could make a nuisance of himself. He was always accompanied by a cameraman and a large bodyguard for intimidation. He would shove a microphone in my face and ask, "Do you still beat your wife?" Lynch used the same sort of ambush tactic on Christie, and with Robert Almblad and his partner.

Finally, they sent "protesters" to harass and picket us at a trade show we attended in Miami with the safe-ice invention. How did they know where we were going? Robert's niece invited Val the spy to come to Miami and hang out with her, as Robert had rented a house near the convention center. Screaming scientologists were waiting in the parking lot with picket signs calling us bigots, haters, and liars as we walked into the trade show. Lynch and his camera crew camped in front of the house we were staying in. They even had the audacity to barge in on a meeting Robert was having in a hotel conference room with one of the companies interested in buying the safe-ice technology.

We were unfazed, though it definitely impacted Robert's funding, as the companies interested in manufacturing and distributing the new technology got cold feet from the harassment.

Both Christie and I still considered ourselves scientologists, though independent from the organization. We had held a July 4th get-together at our house for our like-minded friends to celebrate "Independents Day." We were very close to Marty and his partner, Monique (known to everyone affectionately as Mosey); in fact, they asked if they could be married during the get-together, as many of their friends were present too. I filed the paperwork to perform the wedding on behalf of the "Independent Church of Scientology." Marty and I knew this would drive scientology crazy, and nobody raised an eyebrow in the county records department. There were about sixty people in attendance, a number of whom were former Sea Org members who had been at the Int Base.

The level of brazen harassment kept cranking up. Later in the year, when Marty and I went out to visit the FBI in Los Angeles, we stayed with Jason Beghe at his home in Malibu. When we arrived at LAX, Dave Lubow was waiting for us at baggage claim. "Lubow, what are you doing here?" Marty asked. He curtly responded, "I am going to follow you everywhere." At Jason Beghe's house, Lubow had six PIs in separate vehicles waiting at the bottom of the driveway. On our way to a meeting with the FBI at a restaurant in Santa Monica, the PIs "escorted" us down the Pacific Coast Highway—two cars ahead, one on either side, and two behind. We were completely boxed in. The PIs driving the vehicles wore bandannas to cover their faces. One even donned a hockey mask. We called the FBI en route and told them to come outside the restaurant and watch the procession as we drove by: Marty Rathbun and Mike Rinder with a convoy of six scientology PIs. At another point, Lubow and his team got so aggressive following us that he rammed into the back of our rental car when he was tailing too close.

The FBI were serious about their investigation, but they were fighting an uphill battle. At one point they asked me whether, if I accompanied them onto the Int Base, we could persuade anyone to leave in order to get fresh evidence. I told them I doubted it and that the minute we showed up we would be seen as enemies and the "us versus them" mindset would kick in. They were seriously considering this plan and even showed me aerial reconnaissance shots of the property and asked if I could identify people in the photos. I was stunned at the detail of the images and was easily able to identify some of the people. In some ways I am glad they didn't take the "break down the gates" approach, as I think it would have given scientology a martyr card they could have used for many years. I don't believe it would have accomplished getting anyone out. But I don't know for sure. Just one person breaking ranks might have done the trick, and there is always a chance. In the '70s, nobody had ever thought Michael Meisner would turn himself in.

When JB escaped the Int Base, Warren McShane, the president of RTC, had contacted the Riverside County Sheriff's Department. He complained that JB had "stolen" property (which was untrue), but in the course of doing so also admitted that others on the base could not come and go freely and they did not have possession of their own passports, which were "held by security." This was invaluable evidence for the human trafficking case: a current admission from a church official. It was also evidence that proved the claims made by Marc and Claire Headley in the lawsuit they had filed after their harrowing escapes, documented in Marc's excellent book, *Blown for Good*. One of the FBI agents gave Marc and Claire a copy of the sheriff's report. Their attorney should have filed a request for it with the sheriff's office to obtain it through normal channels. Instead, he just filed it in the case. Scientology claimed the document had been "improperly obtained"—not that anything in it was untrue—and that this proved "collusion" between the FBI and civil litigants.

This was a terrible turn of events. With CSI hiring high-powered former US attorneys to represent them, their reputation for litigiousness and dirty tricks, their unlimited funds to hire lawyers, the difficulty getting evidence, and the barriers presented by the First Amendment, the DOJ bailed. After two years, the FBI investigation was ended without action.

CHAPTER 16

LIFE AS A WHISTLEBLOWER

Even after all the Fair Game tactics and PI harassment, I still separated the philosophical teachings of Hubbard from the actions of Miscavige. I believed Miscavige and his organization were not doing what Ron would do, and their abuses had to be stopped, not just for the benefit of those who were harmed but also to save Hubbard's legacy. This activism had become the higher purpose I had been missing since leaving the Sea Org. While I still had to earn a living, Robert gave me room to do what I felt needed to be done. He had become a target too, simply because he had employed me, and he was now an activist himself who wanted them to be exposed as much as I did.

Lawrence Wright—a meticulous researcher and award-winning writer with an insatiable curiosity and sharp intellect—had been working on a lengthy article for the *New Yorker* since early 2010, detailing scientology's homophobia and how this had driven Oscar-winning writer and director Paul Haggis to question and ultimately leave the fold. At Paul's request, Larry contacted me. I was happy to help him locate sources and information. I had known Paul somewhat when we were both in scientology, but after the "Truth Rundown" series he had reached out due to his disagreements with the organization, especially concerning their lies about disconnection and how they viewed homo-sexuality. From scientology's perspective, Wright's February 2011 piece, "The Apostate," was the worst single article since Richard Behar's in *Time* two decades earlier. The *New Yorker*'s distribution was not nearly as wide as *Time*'s, but its prestigious reputation cemented the article as a serious piece of journalism. It was not only about Haggis and homo-sexuality but a deep dive into the real story of scientology and Hub-bard, containing a lot of ugly history, details of OT III, the Hole, lies about disconnection, attacks on critics, the death of Lisa McPherson, and Fair Game.

Lawrence Wright would be a thorn in scientology's side for the next few years. The article became the genesis of his subsequent bestselling 2013 book, *Going Clear: Scientology, Hollywood, and the Prison of Belief*, and then the 2015 HBO documentary of the same name.

In July 2011, when Larry was working on the book, I arranged for him to come to a second Independents Day gathering, this time on a property owned by the family of a former Sea Org member on a lake outside Houston, so he could conduct some interviews. Christie and I drove to Texas for the get-together, with two PI cars in tow. We were now used to this, so we had a little fun, making them follow us onto random off-ramps and then right back onto the highway, circling shopping mall parking lots, and slowing down until lights turned yel-low, forcing them to drive through red lights to keep up. When we got to the location, we discovered that scientology had placed flyers about Marty and me on car windshields at the nearby Walmart and bought time on the local AM radio station to tell stories about the religious bigots who had come to town. We all laughed at the stupidity of this. But it's not funny that tax dollars of the American public are used to indirectly subsidize this sort of insanity.

I knew there was one person in particular Wright had to speak to: Steve Pfauth. Known to everyone as "Sarge," he was the handyman-slash–security guy who had been with Hubbard during his last days at the Whispering Winds Ranch near Creston, California. It was just Sarge, Annie Broeker, and Hubbard's personal physician, Dr. Gene

Denk. (Pat Broeker was rarely at the ranch and Ray Mithoff was summoned just a few days before Hubbard died.)

Sarge had left the Sea Org within a few years of Hubbard's death, and he'd reached out to his old friend Marty nearly twenty years later to get some things off his chest. Marty had recorded Sarge and shared the recordings with me. The story he had to tell was explosive and it had surprised both of us. We knew it was important. Sarge loved and respected Hubbard more than anyone in the world and had been a loyal and dedicated servant and companion for many years, but he was tortured by what he had witnessed in the final days of Hubbard's life. He recounted his experiences haltingly and sometimes through tears, worried that they would be misconstrued and give a bad impression of his friend. Frankly, there was not a whole lot of room for misinterpretation, but Sarge's reticence made what he said all the more compelling. He was not a man seeking fame or vengeance. He just wanted to unburden himself and for the truth to be known. Both Marty and I knew Larry had to hear what Sarge had told us for himself.

As Sarge explained, toward the end of his life, Hubbard had become increasingly obsessed with disembodied body thetans (BTs) who were bothering him. He said Hubbard, sitting in his Blue Bird motor home, would send him off to gateposts and other odd locations around the property to see if he could see the BT Hubbard was convinced was there. This was shocking news to any scientologist, because any problems with BTs were supposed to be over when someone had attained the level of OT VII. Hubbard, according to the announcement made by Broeker and Miscavige after his death, had advanced *way* beyond OT VII. Even more bizarre, Hubbard had asked Sarge to build a special E-Meter that would blow the BTs away once and for all by passing a massive electrical current through his body. Hubbard said he wanted to end his life by electrocuting himself and the pesky BTs that were haunting him using this E-Meter. Sarge was distraught, unclear how to handle the situation; he was not in the habit of refusing to do what the Old Man ordered, but he also didn't want to be responsible for his death. He hit upon a solution of putting enough current through the meter to give Hubbard a significant shock but not enough to kill him. He didn't know for sure if Hubbard used the device or not, but the meter was returned to him "all burned up" and there wasn't anyone else at the ranch who would have touched it.

Sarge's story discredited everything Hubbard had claimed about his technology and accomplishments. If the OT levels didn't produce the promised result of freeing one from these body thetans, what *did* work in scientology? The final distressing thing Sarge found out from Hubbard: the Old Man had told him he had failed in his mission to save Earth and was going to go off and circle a distant star and was not coming back. (This idea of going in circles around a star is what the Running Program/Cause Resurgence Rundown is based on.)

This was serious stuff, and I had no reason to doubt Sarge's recollections. Though he tried to portray everything in a light most favorable to his friend, his stories were like a jackhammer going to work on my bedrock belief that Hubbard's tech contained all the answers, and I thought about what he said a lot. Even then, I found ways to explain and excuse. *Just because things weren't ideal at the end doesn't mean everything that came before it was invalid or untrue. Hubbard was not perfect; he never said he was.* But it drove me to begin seriously questioning things about Hubbard for the first time in my life.

What finally broke the door down for me was reading Russell Miller's unauthorized biography of Hubbard, *Bare-Faced Messiah*, in 2012. While scientology dismisses his book as bigoted hate propaganda, it is in fact quite even-handed, giving Hubbard credit for his ability to tell a yarn and captivate an audience. Miller meticulously researched Hubbard's life, going back and interviewing his relatives and childhood friends as well as people who knew him at school, in college, during the war, in the early days of dianetics, and forward. He also dug up numerous documents that could not easily be dismissed: ship manifests evidencing Hubbard's travels, contemporaneous newspaper accounts of his activities, FBI files, and personal correspondence. Unless all these people and documents were untrue, or Miller had engaged in a massive fraud himself, his book proved, beyond any doubt, that Hubbard was an inveterate liar. It explained so many of the contradictions that I'd gotten wind of but denied about Hubbard, especially about his wives and children.

The revelations in Miller's book finally broke the spell of Hubbard's infallibility that had been a foundation of my life for nearly fifty years. I saw Hubbard in an entirely new light, no longer a brilliant genius who had solved all the problems of man with insight unsurpassed in history but a brilliant con man who played his role to perfection and who, in the end, had bought his own bullshit.

In time, I realized that attaining "freedom" and happiness—the very carrot of scientology—is more likely when you have the freedom to make your own decisions. I started to understand that I shouldn't rely on what I was "supposed" to think and do according to an ethical code dictated by scientology but on my own understanding of what is right and wrong. It was a scary thought to have no crutch, but ultimately it was extremely liberating. I believe that many who remain in scientology fear letting go of the almost total abdication of questioning that scientology affords them. Under Hubbard's comprehensive dictates and moral rules covering every facet of life, there is little need to think about your choices and decisions.

Christie was going through her own metamorphosis from Hubbard acolyte to critical thinker, and we talked about our feelings and thoughts at great length. It was new territory for us, doubting Hubbard, and it made both of us even more concerned for our family members who were still entangled in the scientology web. It had been somewhat comforting to believe that they might be benefitting in some way from the tech despite all the abuses, so it was devastating to realize as we emerged from our blindness that those left behind were not being helped at all.

THE FIRST DAY of 2012 brought an unexpected surprise that rocked the scientology world. A few minutes after midnight on New Year's Eve, my phone lit up with people texting me about an email that had just been sent out. I read it and immediately understood its significance. It was from Debbie Cook, the long-term head of Flag, who had been forced to wear a sign that read LESBIAN while she was in the Hole.

During her absence the statistics collapsed at Flag and scientology's largest source of revenue went into a nosedive, so Miscavige returned her to her old position to try to salvage matters. But she was just biding her time and eventually escaped with her husband in late 2007, the same year I left. She had been coerced to sign a gag order and remained quiet since then. But in the first minute of New Year's Day she sent out an email to a large number of active scientologists detailing numerous violations of Hubbard policy that had become the norm in the reign of Miscavige. She couched it in terms scientologists would understand, using many quotes from Hubbard's writings, and appealed to them to rise up, do what Ron said, and put an end to the abuses.

Debbie was someone who nearly every important scientologist had met personally; the same cannot be said for Miscavige. She was beloved, and her appeal to scientologists could not be dismissed as the ravings of an SP because she so extensively quoted Hubbard to make her points. Nor was she someone out to make a buck, as she was telling people *not* to hand over their money. Her email spread like wildfire and many people would come to cite it as the first seed of doubt that caused them to begin questioning scientology.

Miscavige was determined to teach her a lesson. After all, he had sent a lawyer to record video of Debbie and her husband, Wayne Baumgarten, signing a gag order in exchange for a $50,000 check and being allowed to leave the Sea Org compound where they had been held before their escape. One of the documents they signed included a stipulation that they not talk to the media. Now they were talking to scientologists—which in some ways was worse.

CSI and RTC hired lawyers in San Antonio, Texas, where Debbie and Wayne lived, to file a lawsuit for breach of contract. Though Debbie had not been in touch with me or Marty Rathbun until that point, when she was sued, she reached out for help. I flew to Texas and through some mutual friends we found a wonderful lawyer to represent her, Ray Jeffrey. Marty Rathbun and I prepared Ray for the case and trained him on the tactics of scientology litigation. Scientology had asked for an expedited hearing as they claimed their rights were being harmed on an ongoing basis. They believed they would steamroll

Debbie, as there was no way a lawyer could be prepared to defend her in a matter of days. They had not met Ray Jeffrey and had not counted on our being able to prepare him.

A lot of media were in attendance as Debbie Cook took the stand in the Bexar County Courthouse on February 9, 2012. Her tearful testimony of abuses and experiences in the Hole was shocking and devastating. She also described two incidents that occurred before she was sent to the Hole—one in which she was forced by Miscavige to watch a friend of hers lick the floor of a bathroom clean, and another in which Miscavige's assistant Laurisse almost broke Debbie's finger. Both Marty and I were also listed as witnesses, so we had to leave the courtroom while she testified. We spent the day strolling along the River Walk speculating about what was happening in the courtroom and how Debbie was holding up on the stand. We should not have worried. Debbie's horror stories just kept rolling out and Miscavige saw the writing on the wall. The scientology lawyers had to urgently stanch the bleeding, so they told the judge they had all the evidence they required, and thus the hearing they had requested did not need to continue. Debbie's testimony blew up all over print media and TV, with stories quoting Ray: "Mrs. Cook was beaten, she was tortured and she was degraded beyond belief. And she was confined in inhumane conditions." Scientology not only didn't follow up in court with all the supposed evidence they had amassed, they dropped their case and settled. Today Debbie and Wayne live comfortable, peaceful lives in the Texas Hill Country.

I returned to Florida after the hearing just in time to find a new place to live, as Robert was selling the Tarpon Springs house. Our family would soon be growing too: Christie was pregnant. She wanted a sibling for Shane, and I wanted a child I could raise in the real world, unlike my children born into the Sea Org. This would be a huge change in our lives, but one we both wanted. We were determined to be settled in a new place before Christie's due date in mid-April. We rented a nice, somewhat smaller house in Palm Harbor, between Tarpon Springs and Clearwater, and moved in. Strangely, our suspicious neighbor Heather

McAdoo suddenly decided she too needed to move, and found an expensive home to rent about five blocks away. This gave her away once and for all as the spy she was. She had been spinning stories about her hard-luck life, and suddenly she was able to rent a four-bedroom house in a nice neighborhood for her and her five-year-old son. She started texting Christie over and over that she wanted to come visit. Christie responded and said we knew she was a scientology plant. She disappeared soon thereafter.

Our son, Jack, was born in our new home on April 15, 2012. I was present, along with a midwife and our faithful white German shepherd, Nikita. Jack was a peaceful, chubby baby with large blue eyes. Shane was five at the time and loved his baby brother from the instant he set eyes on him. From day one, Nikita was Jack's constant companion and playmate; he could pull her ears, ride on her back, or poke her in the eye, and she would remain unfazed, but if anyone or anything approached him that she thought was in any way menacing, her hackles would rise and she became a snarling, intimidating presence.

With Heather McAdoo no longer useful as a spy, and scientology unable to get a house with a sight line to ours, they resorted to a new tactic. They installed a camera in a not-very-discreet-looking birdhouse stand in a neighbor's yard to provide twenty-four-hour surveillance of our street and the front of our home. I noticed it as I was talking to another neighbor, who had just received an anonymous letter telling her to be careful who she associated with. I took a ladder down to the birdhouse and made a short video of me disconnecting the camera, and put it up on YouTube. The neighbors pleaded ignorance, claiming they had been told the birdhouse contained a device to keep birds off their pool enclosure. They didn't seem to have the name of the company that had installed it, though. It was a flimsy lie; they had probably been paid and now didn't want any trouble. A few weeks later I videotaped a garbage truck pulling over a few blocks after it collected our trash to hand over our bags to a ponytailed guy I recognized from the PI headquarters opposite Robert's workshop. I put that on YouTube as well. Toying with scientology PIs had become a form of entertainment for me. They had new tactics; so did I. I began uploading videos of them following me in my car down dead-end streets, or through parking lots where I'd do consecutive U-turns and wave to them going by.

The fun and games with the PIs didn't alter the fact that there was more serious work to be done to end the abuses. And I grabbed those opportunities when they came my way.

Vanity Fair correspondent Maureen Orth asked me to help her with a profile of Tom Cruise. Through her contacts she had heard that higher-ups in scientology had sought to find a girlfriend for Cruise. She had uncovered details about the horrifying ordeal of the grooming of scientologist actress Nazanin Boniadi to be Cruise's mate. I told her I believed that had all begun back in Madrid with Cruise complaining to me that his sister Lee Anne had not found him a partner.

The story was released in September 2012 and it shined new light on the bizarre lengths David Miscavige and scientology would go to for Cruise. My YouTube videos and blog didn't reach a lot of eyeballs, but a major story about Tom Cruise in *Vanity Fair* certainly did. And this one, recounting such an extraordinary tale of his personal life, certainly got a lot of attention.

One of the other people who reached out to me was Leah Remini. She had contacted Debbie Cook after reading Debbie's email in order to get her side of the story. Leah, like all other high-level scientologists, knew Debbie personally. She was also trying to make sense of what had happened to her after she had inquired as to the whereabouts of Shelly Miscavige at Cruise and Katie Holmes's wedding in Italy. She had been sent to Flag and put through hell for that.

Debbie gave her my number. Leah called, and she wanted to know about my experiences, why I had left, and whether what scientology was saying about me was true. As I have sought to do with any scientologist who has reached out to me, I spoke honestly but did not try to convince her what the most appropriate course of action for her would be. It is terribly presumptuous to assume anyone can understand all the dynamics that go into a decision concerning one's future in scientology. Leah had been meeting with executives from scientology, including David Miscavige, and I told her what I knew from experience they were going to do and say. Because they were doing what LRH dictated, my predictions were uncannily accurate. Leah would call me after her meetings and announce, "They said exactly what you said they would." It created a bond between us that has grown even stronger in the succeeding years. Shortly thereafter, she and her entire family left scientology.

Sadly, December 2012 saw another scientology tragedy that was personal to me and illustrative of how toxic the organization and its fundamentalist beliefs are to families. Scientology president Heber Jentzsch had a son, Alexander, who had grown up in the Sea Org with my daughter. Alexander's mother, Karen, left the Sea Org in 1990 and had become a vocal whistleblower twenty years or so later. Though, in 2010, Alexander had also left the Sea Org, he had remained a loyal scientologist and thus had disconnected from his mother. In early December someone alerted me to a mention on Facebook indicating somewhat cryptically that Alexander might have passed away. I reached out to Karen, she in turn contacted the LA County coroner's office, and they confirmed the shocking news: Alexander, only twenty-seven years old, had died. The circumstances of his death were troubling. The scientologist family of his wife had found him unresponsive, and instead of calling 911, they called OSA. Nobody thought to inform his mother. But even more disturbing was scientology blocking Karen from being able to even see his body. Lack of compassion is a hallmark of scientology, but this was a new low.

Earlier in the year we had also learned that Annie Broeker had died. She was my age. Way too young to die. As with the death of Mary Sue Hubbard, there was no public announcement. Marty Rathbun had a vision that Annie had died in January 2012 and contacted Riverside County officials, who confirmed it to be true. In fact, she had died in June 2011. Nobody from scientology told Annie's family members. Marty let them know. Annie's death was another embarrassing failure of the tech—she was as close to Hubbard as anyone had ever been and had been with him while he was supposedly researching the final, advanced, "real" OT levels. For Miscavige, the less anyone ever thought about Annie, the better. There are no doubt scientologists who think she is currently toiling away to save the planet somewhere in International Management.

Many others had reached out to me in the wake of Debbie Cook's email, asking if I could help them, whether it was to get money returned or reconnect with family members. Luis and Rocio Garcia were among them. I tried for months to find lawyers who would take their cases on a contingency fee basis, but everywhere I turned, attorneys told me they were unwilling to assume the risk due to the reputation scientology had worked so hard to establish of using ruthless and expensive litigation tactics. Partly due to my involvement in creating that monster, I felt obligated to find some legal representation for these people. Eventually I located a successful personal injury litigator in West Palm Beach, Ted Babbitt, willing to take scientology on in partnership with two other law firms. He brought a lawsuit in Tampa's federal court in January 2013 on behalf of the Garcias. I spent a great deal of time helping the lawyers understand the policies and practices of scientology as well as the numerous corporations and legal entanglements and relationships. First and foremost, I explained that scientology would spend tens of millions defending a case asking for a few hundred thousand dollars because they feared the floodgates would be opened by the precedent of paying one person. Thousands of people have lost their money to scientology.

Another legal case, one that had been dragging on for years, finally came to a resolution in 2013: my divorce. What had seemed like it would be resolved quickly and simply had turned into a drawn-out process because scientology kept employing delay tactics. The reason? As long as the case was not resolved, the OSA lawyers overseeing it could demand continuously updated financial information from me to see who was supporting me. Eventually, as the five-year deadline of the case filing approached, the judge held their feet to the fire after I asked my old friend Joe Yanny to help out.

With the divorce finalized, Christie and I were finally able to get married, and we tied the knot on June 22, 2013. Our wedding took place on the water just down the road from Flag in Clearwater. About a hundred guests attended, including many old friends from out of town. John Sweeney and his wife even came in from England. Marty gave Christie away and subsequently wrote an open letter to her father scolding him for abandoning his daughter. Sadly, though we were five minutes from where Benjamin was working, he was not there. He might as well have been on another planet.

The venue for the wedding was owned by a local Clearwater couple who had been reading my blog and the "Truth Rundown" series. For having the temerity to offer us the use of the venue as a wedding gift, they became Fair Game targets of scientology.

Soon after the wedding, I was back in Texas to help file another lawsuit. Marty and Mosey had been subjected to very noisy twenty-four-hour-a-day surveillance and harassment by so-called Squirrel Busters (Hubbard called those who disagreed with him "squirrels" because they collected nuts) who knocked on their door, picketed on the street outside their home taunting them, and followed them everywhere in golf carts and cars, being as confrontational, obnoxious, and abusive as they could be. They even rented a pedal-driven paddleboat and paraded back and forth in the canal behind their home, taking photos and shouting at them with bullhorns.

To try to escape the harassment, Marty and Mosey had moved from the coast near Corpus Christi to a place near lawyer Ray Jeffrey in Bulverde, Texas, 150 miles to the north. Ray had become a personal friend through the Debbie Cook case. He was also the former mayor of Bulverde and influential in the local community. He promised them he could provide some measure of protection against the scientology terror tactics. While the picketers and bullhorns vanished, Marty and Mosey discovered spy cameras in the trees pointing at their home. At the time, they were in the process of adopting a child, so they were justifiably worried that scientology might throw a wrench in the adoption. Ray Jeffrey filed suit on behalf of Mosey in August 2013 to keep scientology away from their family.

Mosey had a strong case: she had not been a scientologist but had been victimized by the Fair Game tactics as a means of getting to Marty. Ray was immediately successful, persuading the court to issue a restraining order against David Miscavige, CSI, RTC, and two private investigators who were named in the lawsuit. A dozen high-priced law-yers, including the former chief justice of the Supreme Court of Texas, Wallace B. Jefferson, were representing scientology and Miscavige in the courtroom, but their presence did not impress the judge, nor did their tactics of scorched-earth litigation. Scientology was in another legal battle in Texas with Ray Jeffrey, and they were coming off second best to him once again. But this time Ray was controlling the narra-tive with a plaintiff who threatened to strike a devastating blow against Miscavige's kingdom.

Then, on September 13, 2013, I received an unsigned email from an address I did not know.

> *This e-mail is a courtesy to you in case you have not been informed of events in Melbourne over the past several days.*
>
> *I have met your Mum over the years and always found her to be a delightful lady. I have not seen her for several years.*
>
> *I am sorry to have to tell you that she passed away last Thurs-day. I only found out today. I have just confirmed that she had a farewell service today and her body was cremated at Springvale Crematorium in Melbourne this morning.*
>
> *I know your brother and sister but I am not in comm with them.*
>
> *Mike I offer you my condolences and I am sorry to send you this bad news.*

An anonymous email to inform me my mother had passed away. It was a final cruelty. No contact from my family or any other scientolo-gist who had made up her entire social world for sixty years. They delib-erately made sure I didn't find out she was ill in the hospital—nor even that she had died—until after the service had been performed, as they knew I would have dropped everything and gotten on a plane, unlike when I was in the Sea Org. This incident, like those with Alexander Jentzsch and Annie Broeker, encapsulates the world of scientology. It is always scientology first, family a very distant second. Scientology first, humanity and compassion last. No decency at all.

CHAPTER 17

THE AFTERMATH

HBO's *Going Clear* premiered at the Sundance Film Festival on January 25, 2015. I had devoted considerable time to helping documentarian Alex Gibney and his team throughout 2014 and was excited to see how it turned out, and even more so to see how it would be received.

Some of us who had been featured in the show (Spanky Taylor, Tony Ortega, Sara Goldberg, and Marc Headley) were brought to Sundance by HBO. We all arrived and gathered in the greenroom with Alex, Lawrence Wright, HBO executives, and some of the production crew. Shortly before the lights went down we took our seats near the front of the packed theater. Tobey Maguire was in the row behind us, Alec Baldwin just in front. I was a bit overwhelmed by the magnitude of the occasion; it was an *event*, far beyond what I had imagined. The documentary itself was an emotional roller coaster, and I thought it was a masterpiece: brilliant, wrenching, painful, and an accurate account of the essence of Hubbard and scientology in so little time. Others thought so too. The reaction when the lights came up was overwhelming: spontaneous cheering, a lengthy standing ovation, and an emotional outpouring as Alex, Larry, I, and some of the others who had appeared took the stage to acknowledge the audience. It became the most sought-after ticket at the festival. I knew it was an enormous turning point in the fight to end scientology's abuses. *Going Clear* would bring mainstream attention to what had been mostly treated as a fringe story. Suddenly, the abuses of scientology were the subject of watercooler discussions all over the country.

After the premiere and leading up to the HBO release at the end of March, I did a slew of interviews alongside Alex and Larry, from NPR to a forum at the *New York Times*. A lot of questions centered on the Hole and the harrowing depiction of the musical chairs incident in the film.

Interest in my daily blog posts grew exponentially; many more new people began responding and commenting, and the daily views steadily increased. I now had a much larger and very loyal following; annoyingly to Miscavige, my blog saw a lot more traffic than the official scientology website, despite the fact that the organization poured tens of millions of dollars into it trying to generate interest and traffic.

My life was consumed with whistleblowing. With *Going Clear* I became a far more public figure: reporters, elected officials, and law enforcement increasingly reached out to me for information and insight. Former scientologists also called or emailed, often just to have someone to talk to who understood what they had been through. How strange: I had thought I had been saving the planet with scientology, and now I was dedicated to saving the planet *from* scientology.

Scientology had scared off potential manufacturing partners for safe ice, so Robert returned to developing technology for restaurants, and he didn't require my services any longer. But I still needed to make a living, as whistleblowing did not generate income. In early 2015, I began working with Aaron Smith-Levin, a former Sea Org member who had reached out to me to share his tragic story of disconnection and the cruelties he had experienced. Aaron researched potential investments for financial institutions. It was interesting and challenging work that I readily sank my teeth into. Much of our research entailed determining the likelihood that a new drug would gain FDA approval, the size of its potential market, and the potential profits for pharmaceutical companies. I learned a great deal about what goes into the development and testing of a wide variety of drugs to treat everything from heart conditions to Alzheimer's. My scientology upbringing had ingrained the idea that drugs are generally harmful and that Big Pharma companies vie with their partners, the psychs, for the title of worst people on earth. But the doctors, researchers, and scientists we talked to daily were the exact opposite. And the changes they managed to effect in the lives of millions through new cures or improving quality of life were remarkable. Even "psych drugs," which I and every scientologist were taught to hate, help some people tremendously. This is not to say there aren't terrible abuses in the pharmaceutical industry, but "Big Pharma is destroying mankind" is another scientology fallacy that became crystal clear to me in the course of my work with Aaron. This was fascinating and eye-opening, deepened my new understanding of scientology, and provided me fuel for my whistleblowing endeavors.

I am not sure if it was *Going Clear* that prompted it, but out of the blue, Lisa Marie Presley called me early in 2015. She said she had escaped from scientology in Clearwater in the middle of the night with her family and they were hiding in Nashville. She said she had left because of the mistreatment of Ron Miscavige Sr., David's father, who had escaped the Int Base eighteen months earlier and had been the target of nonstop harassment since, including PI surveillance by a father-and-son team outside his home in Wisconsin that lasted until both PIs were arrested for carrying illegal firearms in the trunk of their car.

Like Leah asking "Where's Shelly?," Lisa had demanded to know why Ron Miscavige was being harassed. David sent his sisters to mollify her by telling stories about what a bad father Ron was. This backfired—Lisa Marie was disgusted, packed up her house in Clearwater, and left. She now wanted Ron's story to become national news. I reached out on her behalf to a lawyer in LA, who in turn contacted, at my suggestion, *LA Times* reporter Kim Christensen, whom I had dealt with so many years earlier. Kim's April 8, 2015, front-page story went into detail about the PIs who had been arrested with a trunk full of weapons including illegal noise suppressors, and how they told the police they had been instructed by David Miscavige himself not to call 911 when they observed what they believed was Ron suffering a heart attack. After speaking with Kim, Ron subsequently appeared in many other media outlets, started a YouTube channel, and wrote a book to try to end the practice of disconnection.

It seemed almost every day a new person would reach out to me who had watched *Going Clear* or read Larry's book. One person I did not expect to hear from was an assistant US attorney in May 2015 who was prosecuting a PI, Eric Saldarriaga, for hacking private email accounts, including mine and Tony Ortega's. Tony also has a very popular daily blog devoted to all things scientology. It was obvious that Saldarriaga's client was scientology: he was convicted and sent to prison. Unfortunately, the FBI could not get enough concrete evidence to also prosecute lead scientology PI David Lubow, who had hired Saldarriaga in the first place. Scientology had nearly been exposed engaging in a felony, which would have caught the attention of the IRS, but had managed to dodge another bullet just like with the earlier FBI investigation. The only silver lining was that Lubow's career as a scientology PI was over. He had become too much of a liability.

Spurred on by the success of *Going Clear*, Louis Theroux, an unconventional British TV documentarian, had been putting together his own unique take on scientology. He recruited Marty Rathbun to consult on the film and appear in it, directing re-creations of events, casting an actor to play David Miscavige and drilling him to be as realistic as possible. Production of the movie was occurring concurrent with scientology's increasingly desperate efforts to derail Marty and Mosey's Texas lawsuit in the appellate courts and ultimately the Texas Supreme Court. During filming, scientology sent two operatives to try to intimidate Marty, asking him whether he was being "paid enough for your foster care" (implying that the adoption of his son was a source of income). The message was unmistakable: *The adoption of your son is now fair game.* Marty was captured by Theroux on camera shortly after the incident, which clearly shook him. "This is really sick," he complains, very upset. "It was a straight adoption."

It is a moment of remarkable insight into both what drives Rathbun and what can only be described as the psycho-terror tactics of scientology.

Louis Theroux wasn't the only person working on a scientology documentary film project. In early 2016 another production company asked me to help them do a program about disconnection. I was willing to help, but as they explained their plan to try to stage "reconnections" of disconnected families, I attempted to dissuade them, as I believed that it was a doomed project. They were determined to move ahead, but while discussions were ongoing, Leah called:

"Hi, honey, do you think you could help me with something?" she asked.

"Sure, what do you need?" I answered.

"I'm working on putting together a scientology TV show, and I want you to assist."

She explained she had been contacted by my old friend from the Int Base, Amy Scobee, who had told her the story of being disconnected from her mother. Leah asked if Amy's mom, Bonny, would be willing to tell her story. When she agreed, Leah sent a camera crew to film her on her deathbed, talking about the pain and horror of disconnection. In an incredibly touching plea, Bonny asked that something be done to stop the cruelty.

"I feel an obligation to do something to try to carry out Bonny's wishes," Leah explained. "I am not sure what form it is going to take yet, but I have a production company who are willing to help me and interest from A&E Network to air it."

"Of course. I'm in. Whatever I can do to help."

I flew to Los Angeles to meet with her, and *Leah Remini: Scientology and the Aftermath* was born.

The show became my full-time occupation for the rest of the year.

While I was working on the show, strange things began happening with Marty and Mosey. Despite the fact that Mosey's lawsuit had been a string of victories, forcing CSI and RTC to appeal all the way to the Texas Supreme Court, Mosey fired her lawyers without warning and dismissed her case in May 2016. To say this was shocking was an understatement. It was just the beginning.

Ron Miscavige's book, *Ruthless*, about the abuses at the Int Base, his escape, and his son David, was also published in May 2016. It generated a lot of media attention—and surprisingly, the wrath of Marty, who despite having earlier praised Ron on his blog for his bravery now launched a broadside attack on Ron's book. It was a complete reversal of course. A few days later, Louis Theroux's *My Scientology Movie* premiered outside the US. Marty, in another twist, wasted no time denouncing it as "dishonest and deceptive" and called Theroux an "ass clown," and the producer a "rimless zero."

From being the loudest and most effective whistleblower against scientology abuses for seven years, Marty had fully turned almost overnight. He began calling me, Tony Ortega, Leah, and others liars, and started defending David Miscavige, who had for years been the object of his endless scorn. He proclaimed that the "abuses" of what he now called "the Anti-Scientology Cult" were worse than the abuses of scientology. It was hurtful in the extreme, not so much to see Marty capitulate but to see him turn on his friends and debase himself. I don't hold it against anyone if they decide fighting scientology carries too big a burden and they walk away. It's a personal choice. But to turn on those he had supported, and who had supported him, and begin lying about them in service of the very people he had so loudly decried, was devastating and unforgivable. Marty and Mosey offered no explanation for their sudden about-face but viciously attacked anyone who even raised a question about what had happened. The only conclusion I can come to is that scientology either threatened what was most important to them—their family and adopted child—or paid them a lot of money, or both.

I had to put the Rathbun drama aside to focus on the production of the ten-episode *Aftermath* TV series. For the first episode, Leah and I flew to Seattle to shoot with Amy and her family. For other episodes, I reached out to those I knew who also had stories of abuse to tell—Mary Kahn, Ron Miscavige, Tom DeVocht, Jeff Hawkins, Marc and Claire

Headley, and Aaron Smith-Levin. I was the main source of stories for the show, and also the in-house scientology expert both behind and in front of the camera. I spent a lot of time in Los Angeles shooting explanations of the strange concepts and language behind scientology for the viewing audience. I also helped edit each episode with Leah and the production team at IPC and our executive at A&E, Devon Graham Hammonds. Leah was passionate about every camera angle and word that appeared on-screen, insisting the show represent these victims properly and in the correct light. Her demand for high-quality production shines through in every episode.

Anyone who knows a bit about scientology understands that producing this show was not routine or normal. Nothing with scientology ever is. There were endless legal threats. Those involved in the production—from showrunners to camera operators, lighting designers to researchers, editors, and production assistants—were followed, harassed, and smeared. A lot of people have to work together to make a TV show happen. They didn't have a dog in the fight, but it became a crusade for them too. Luckily for us, the show was an immediate ratings hit for A&E when it premiered on November 29, 2016. As each episode ran, I heard from more people who wanted to tell of their experiences, so A&E renewed the show for a second season. We had more stories to tell than we could possibly use.

For three seasons, we exposed horrendous pain and suffering inflicted on people as a result of their involvement in scientology. Families torn apart. Children victimized. Women forced to have abortions. People defrauded. A literal trail of death and destruction. And for the first time, the people making the show and interviewing the victims were experts on the subject and brought experience and knowledge to shine light on how scientology worked. Many told us that for the first time, we had personalized the abuses and given them real, believable faces. So many told us they realized, "That could have been me."

I also made some personal amends on the show with people I had been adversarial with in the past, including *Rolling Stone* journalist Janet Reitman, in an episode where Janet told me her assistant had dubbed me "Mr. Scary." I never saw myself that way, but to be fair, a scary presence is a valued trait inside the scientology world, especially for Sea Org members.

Some of the people we spoke to for the show had experiences that shocked even me, a hardened veteran of a lot of Fair Game on both sides of the fence. When we interviewed the victims of actor Danny Masterson, for instance, we were horrified. A well-known scientologist TV star who had been raised in a scientology family, Masterson was accused of raping four women. How they were treated by him as well as by the scientology organization was appalling, and their accounts were too similar to be fabricated. We deferred to the wishes of the Los Angeles County District Attorney's Office, which was considering charges, and decided not to air the episode. (Masterson was ultimately charged in June 2020, and is currently being scheduled for trial.) One other important story that did not make it to air, for multiple reasons, was about my old friend Heber Jentzsch. The President of the Church of Scientology International had been put in the Hole when I was there back in 2006, and had remained there, incommunicado, ever since. When Valerie Haney escaped from Gold in the trunk of a car in 2017 and reached out to me, she told me that Heber was still at Gold, being terribly mistreated. She said he was forced to read scripted videos about how wonderful David Miscavige was while he was being squeezed into a makeshift wooden body brace so he could be upright for the camera because his physical condition had deteriorated so much that he was unable to stand straight. It broke my heart. So when one of his nieces reached out to me and asked if Leah and I would help her do a welfare check on Heber, we readily agreed.

This was the last time I returned to Gold. It brought back floods of memories—few of them pleasant. We remained in the car across the highway outside the main guard booth as Tammy, Heber's niece, approached the gate and pushed the buzzer on the intercom. Nobody responded. I knew there were two or more security guards sitting behind the mirrored glass just a few feet from her, observing and reporting on her every move. They sat mutely watching as this woman, who had never been a scientologist, tried in vain to see her uncle. To them, she was connected to the SPs Leah Remini and Mike Rinder. To those inside the steel gates, she didn't deserve any consideration.

Tammy then went to the Riverside County Sheriff's Department and persuaded officers to visit the property to check on her uncle. The deputies were escorted into a conference room where Heber sat with a minder to ensure he didn't say anything untoward. They were told the minder was his nurse, though I know her well and she had no medical training. The sheriffs didn't ask to speak to Heber alone or see if he was even able to stand without assistance. Scientology higher-ups generally know what they can get away with in situations like this. And law enforcement personnel are ill equipped to deal with scientology, as they do not understand the mindset and lengths adherents will go to in order to present a facade that will avoid a flap.

Tammy returned to Utah, heartbroken. To rub salt in the wound, scientology soon dispatched PIs to her home to threaten her with legal action for having the temerity to try to check on Heber.

While these two stories did not make it to air, thirty-seven others did over the course of the show. Three years of heartbreaking, often tear-jerking, and sometimes scary tales of the nasty reality of scientology. The relentless exposés we unleashed on *The Aftermath* drove Miscavige crazy. In response, he brought in a platoon of lawyers who sent a seemingly never-ending stream of long-winded, outrageous threat letters. Leah ended up reading some of them on air, starting with the very first episode: "[Leah] has shamelessly exploited her former affiliation with the Church as a primary income source" and "Ms. Remini is now joined at the hip with this collection of deadbeats, admitted liars, self-admitted perjurers, wife-beaters and worse . . ." The lengthy letters degenerated further as the episodes went on. None of them ever addressed the facts that had been exposed; they simply attacked with name-calling. Scientology demanded to meet with the producers of the show to present their side of the story. As executive producers, Leah and I asked to attend. They flatly refused, stating there would be no meeting if we were present. They were scared. We repeatedly invited scientology representatives, celebrities, or any scientologist at all to come on the show to present their side. They refused every time.

Along with the legal threats, scientology's Office of Special Affairs also created numerous websites for the sole purpose of smearing Leah, me, and every person who appeared on the show. These fake sites featured videos of victims' family members who were still in scientology. Leah's former "friends" and her estranged and abusive father all made them.

Marty Rathbun also made videos on behalf of scientology denouncing Leah and me and everyone who appeared in *The Aftermath*. He became a mainstay of scientology's weekly response to each episode. It was absurd, but also painful to watch. Yet another example of how toxic involvement with scientology can be to someone's life and dignity.

Unsurprisingly, scientology's responses to *The Aftermath* were especially vicious and voluminous with respect to me. My son Benjamin made a video claiming I was a hater, bigot, and bad father. They created a blog in my daughter's name called Justice4Mom that uses the incident in the doctor's parking lot in Clearwater in 2010 to allege I am a violent wife-beater, complete with lurid made-up details of how Taryn heard "bones crunching," and that Cathy suffered "permanent neurological damage and will be in pain for the rest of her life." They even tried to cash in on the #MeToo movement that grew worldwide in late 2017 as the second season of *The Aftermath* began to air. Cathy and Taryn appeared at #MeToo events and staged pickets and protests holding signs that read #FIREMIKERINDER. Pursuant to Hubbard policy, it is their duty to destroy enemies utterly, if possible, and "cost them their jobs."

Hubbard had said that he could tell the orgs were doing well when the "squirrels" screamed the loudest. I have a different take. The volume and unhinged nature of what scientology says about anything directly correlates to the harm they feel they have suffered. *The Aftermath* had scientology reacting with unprecedented levels of insanity, and that is saying something. They spent more money on lawyers and PIs than for any previous media exposé on scientology. They created more smear websites, hired more fake reporters for *Freedom* magazine, and Miscavige even launched his own TV station with twenty-four-hour-a-day propaganda programming. In many ways, their responses have been the best evidence for what *The Aftermath* set out to show the world: scientology is a toxic cult that for decades has abused and destroyed people. What made it really sting for Miscavige, I am sure, is that *The Aftermath* won two Emmy Awards and numerous other recognitions, making it impossible for him to dismiss it. More importantly from our perspective, *The Aftermath* brought the truth about scientology into the homes of millions of people every week.

I am often asked, "Why do you keep doing this?" I always respond truthfully, "I brought two children into that world and they know no better. I want them to have a chance to think for themselves and make up their own minds."

Until then, I don't plan to stop.

EPILOGUE

By the time of this book's publication, I will have been out of the Sea Org for fifteen years. That's still less than half the span I spent in the mind prison as a professional scientologist, or about a third of my life in total, if I count my scientology childhood.

Happily, I haven't had one of those horrible recurring nightmares about being back at Gold since I began working on this book in earnest. Maybe I am done with them now that I am done writing. It has not been easy, but it has been cathartic. Many times during the process I have woken up in the middle of the night—not because of a trapped-at-Gold nightmare, but rather because my thoughts were churning, remembering things and places and people and details. I would worry about whether I had them right yet, or question whether it was important to include them. I took to keeping a pad and pen next to my bed to jot down notes—it was the only way I could go back to sleep. If I didn't make a note, I just couldn't get the thoughts out of my mind.

There are a lot of stories about what I experienced as a scientologist that I could not fit in the space of this book. They might have been important at the time and may have been *very* important to the people they impacted, but they didn't move this story forward. Some events, like Lisa McPherson's saga, probably warrant an entire book. Either way, I would like to apologize to anyone I may have hurt or been unkind to whom I have not had a chance to contact personally. There are many, and I hope if you have read this far you may have a better understanding of what compelled me to act in the way I did.

As I said, I don't plan to stop this work. I am proud of the changes I and the other whistleblowers exposing the abuses of scientology have brought about. We have heard from those who have left in recent years that as a result of all the negative publicity, the Hole has been dismantled. Some relatives of dying family members have even been allowed to visit, even though they are declared SPs. We have also heard that Sea Org women are no longer coerced into having abortions. The outside pressure has made a difference. But there is much, much more that needs to be done.

Two years ago, Christie and I formed a nonprofit organization with Luis Garcia, Aaron Smith-Levin, Marc and Claire Headley, and lawyer Ray Jeffrey. The Aftermath Foundation helps people escape from scientology and gives them somewhere to turn for resources to assist them in this difficult transition. We have helped dozens of people, and the work continues.

Leah and I have become ambassadors for Child USA, an organization focused on protecting the rights of children, especially against abuses by religious organizations. I now sit on the board. We are changing the laws in numerous states across the US with legislation enacted to make it possible for victims to pursue their day in court.

PEOPLE OFTEN ASK me, "What are your religious beliefs today?" I find it a difficult question to answer.

I am still no fan of any organized religion, and I have not joined a religious congregation. But I do enjoy the sense of community that religious organizations bring, and have become friends with outspoken scientology critic Pastor Willy Rice and his wife, Cheryl, at the Calvary Church in Clearwater. I have attended Christmas services and events at the church, and the people I have met there are uniformly wonderful. Kind, honest, and moral. I enjoy their company. To me, they represent all that is good about religion.

Christie and I sent Jack to preschool at our local Methodist church. We attended school functions at the church, the annual Nativity play, and various church fundraisers. Again, a wonderful group of kind, self-less people.

Christie reads lots of books on the subjects of mindfulness and spirituality, like Michael Singer's *The Untethered Soul*, and has persuaded me to read a couple too. They contain a lot of useful tips for happiness and general well-being. I tend toward more pragmatic titles, like Martha Stout's *The Sociopath Next Door*—which taught me a lot about the mindset and tactics of L. Ron Hubbard—and Viktor Frankl's *Man's Search for Meaning*. When I embarked on the task of drafting this book, I turned to Anne Lamott's *Bird by Bird* for excellent advice on how to write.

None of these things have convinced me to put my fate in the hands of God, Jesus, a self-help guru, or Buddha. Perhaps I am gun-shy, having been so badly burned by my utter faith in L. Ron Hubbard.

Yet still I consider myself a spiritual being, not merely a corporeal entity.

If I had to state it simply, I believe religion is the search for peace and happiness. This is what those who are devoutly religious hope to find in their particular teachings. And I am very happy for them if they do. I firmly believe everyone has the absolute right to believe anything they wish, so long as their actions do not harm others. I have found a path that works for me: I believe the biggest freedom I gained in leaving scientology was the ability to make my own choices, no longer bound to thinking and doing what L. Ron Hubbard or scientology instructed. My personal road to peace and happiness has been to do what *I* know is right. This is not easy to define, but I feel it. Others may disagree with what I decide is right, but I cannot control that. It works for me and brings me joy, a sense of fulfillment, and good karma.

I could never start a cult and make a lot of money based on this principle, as it is the antithesis of cult think. Maybe that's why it works for me.

FINALLY, THE MOST important thing in the world to me is my family, closely followed by my friends. Christie is my better half and I adore her with all my heart. I could not love Jack and Shane more. Neither Christie nor I have any parents or siblings who are in contact with us, so we have built our own family of choice. These are the people— many former Sea Org members, all former scientologists—with whom we spend our holidays and vacations. And we are incredibly thankful for them.

My two elder children and even my ex-wife are welcome to join us at any time. So too are Christie's family members. We will always welcome the phone call or ring of our doorbell—just like when Tom DeVocht welcomed mine from London.

If they ever do, unconditional love and a whole new world await them.

AFTERWORD

With the publication of *A Billion Years* on September 22, 2022, my world became a tornado of activity.

Of course, scientology's reaction was entirely predictable. To begin, they had various lawyers send letters to the publisher threatening dire consequences should the book see the light of day. Also typically, they waited so long that even if they had made any sort of valid claims or demands, the book had already been printed and shipped to Amazon and bookstores around the country. One especially strident one, threatening terrible consequences, arrived the day *after* publication. Fortunately the legal team at Simon & Shuster and all the executives and my editor at Gallery Books knew exactly what to expect and remained unperturbed.

The wonderful Jennifer Robinson, my publicist at Gallery, set up a series of media appearances to launch the book, with an exclusive first interview scheduled to air on CBS *Mornings* the day of release. I flew to New York City the week before to be interviewed by Jim Axelrod, and also sat down for an interview with the CBS sister show *Inside Edition*. The timing was to allow them to edit together their pieces for airing. The interview with Jim lasted about two hours; he asked a lot of probing questions. I was impressed with his preparation and knowledge of the subject.

Hindsight being 20/20, I should have realized that other networks may have been a better choice. The parent company of CBS is Paramount. It also happened to be the parent company of Simon & Schuster so, at first glance, this seemed to be a good plan. Unfortunately, and more importantly, Paramount movie studios is the home of Tom Cruise, fervent scientologist and generator of massive revenue for the corporation. A lot more revenue than my book would ever bring in. We had ventured onto a far-from-level playing field, as would soon become clear.

Scientology sent David Miscavige's personal lawyer, Monique Yingling, to CBS headquarters in New York to try to stop the segment from airing. How ironic that one of the last things I had done in London before my escape was accompany Monique to BBC headquarters to demand a meeting with the director-general of the BBC to prevent John Sweeney's *Panorama* exposé of scientology from airing. We had been unsuccessful. The BBC refused to even meet us, content to rely on the integrity of their reporter and the *Panorama* producers. Unsurprisingly, given the corporate structure, Monique had better luck with CBS. From my years of experience, I had a good idea how she would conduct the meeting: She would bring a binder containing "Dead Agent" material on me—a term Hubbard coined for someone who has been discredited as a source of information, akin to a spy who has been exposed and is thus executed for treason. Such binders contain anything discreditable that scientology can dig up from their files, with great emphasis placed on any admissions of lying. She would likely say something to the effect of "scientologists [particularly including Tom Cruise] should not be victims of smear campaigns without having their voices heard." She would then, as always, make dire threats to the network of what would happen when scientology filed their inevitable massive lawsuits. These days, most media outlets understand scientology's legal threats are toothless—despite similar letters, they didn't sue the *St. Petersburg Times* for their devastating Truth Rundown series, nor *The New Yorker*, Random House or HBO for *Going Clear* (the book and documentary film respectively), *Vanity Fair,* CNN, or even A&E for *The Aftermath.*

About forty-eight hours before the scheduled airtime, Simon & Schuster was informed by CBS that there would be a "delay" in airing the segment. The book release date was set in stone, whether the CBS *Mornings* show aired or not. Notwithstanding strong protests from Simon & Schuster that CBS had reneged on their agreement to air the segment with me on the publication date, in return for exclusivity, CBS held firm. In fact, it took more than two weeks until the segment did finally see the light of day, at which time it included not only the interview with me but parts of an interview with Monique Yingling, even though she had not read the book. I found it amusing that scientology couldn't come up with a single scientologist they trusted to do the interview to represent their side of the story—rather they used a non-scientologist lawyer. I credit Jim Axelrod for putting Yingling on the spot, particularly when she was forced to admit scientology had amassed billions of dollars in assets—something that had never previously been publicly acknowledged. She did, however, accomplish one objective. By delaying the airing of the segment, she disrupted the planned media rollout of my book.

Simon & Schuster and I forged ahead regardless, and I did numerous interviews with other media: TV, print, radio, and podcasts. There was a great deal of interest and overwhelmingly positive responses to the book.

The first major review was published by *Kirkus Reviews*, an extremely influential but notoriously hard to please book review site. It was better than I could have hoped for.

Many other positive reviews followed. *A Billion Years* hit the *USA Today* national bestseller list and has remained the number one bestselling book in the scientology category on Amazon since the day of release. The publisher and I were very pleased. And while every media outlet or podcast I appeared on received the standard scientology efforts to intimidate them into silence, it is gratifying to know how little impact these threats had. Some of my all-time favorite interviews occurred in the wake of the book release, sometimes two or three or more a day, and this continued for months. CBS was the only media outlet that blinked, as far as I know, and the only sour note of the entire publicity process was the impact of the delay by CBS on the book making it onto the *New York Times* bestseller list, which needs to happen the first week of release and is often stimulated by an interview segment airing on a national show.

Throughout the process of my promotion of the book, scientology continued to do everything they could to otherwise muddy the waters. I was at the top of their enemies list at this point, and they spent enormous amounts of money from their tax-free "war chest" that is used to destroy their enemies on Google ads to appear at the top of the results page when anyone searched for my book title or my name. The ads claimed to provide the "real story" of the book and of me, though they simply linked to the scientology smear sites calling me a wife beater and a liar. Eventually, scientology even published a series of "books" on Amazon, purporting to be synopses of *A Billion Years* with deceptive covers and titles making them seem like Cliff Notes summaries. Some people were deceived into buying them, not realizing until the fake books arrived that these contained only rehashes of the smear sites. As usual, scientology did not dispute specifics in the book. Rather they simply claimed I am a liar, an "apostate" who cannot be trusted, and that I was trying to make money by riding on the "good name and popularity" of scientology. They didn't disprove the incidents and experiences I recounted or even claim any specifics were untrue.

There is one particularly amusing anecdote I can now recount. John Sweeney's publisher, Humfrey Hunter, had agreed to release *A Billion Years* in the United Kingdom and Australia. Because of the nature of libel laws in the UK, Humfrey's legal counsel (Jonathan Coad) recommended putting Miscavige on notice before publication. Jonathan offered to send me a draft. I was expecting the typical legal letter, and was wholly unprepared for the brief, pithy missive he proposed be forwarded, informing Miscavige's counsel that the book was coming and made certain claims about him, asking him to respond to the following:

The allegations against your client are serious and include the following:

    1. That he frequently physically assaulted members of the Church;

    2. That he has effectively incarcerated his wife;

    3. That he is an inveterate liar;

    4. That he is insane.

I would be most grateful if I could hear from you ASAP.

Very Best Wishes,

Jonathan Coad

Miscavige's lawyer never responded. I still laugh every time I read this.

No doubt because *A Billion Years* was written primarily for my children, scientology felt the need to have a response from Taryn and Benjamin. An "Open Letter" from them, I am sure actually written by someone in the Office of Special Affairs, was sent out to the media. It's a strangely cobbled-together collection of talking points that begins by accusing me of not being a good father—a rather odd approach given this is in large part what the book is about.

The letter ends with this: "a real father does not make the rejection and denunciation of their religion a condition for reuniting with his children," an assertion typical of the topsy-turvy world of scientology. I have never placed any such condition on my relationship with them. In fact, I told them they could believe anything they want in an open letter I published on my blog almost a decade ago. It is they who are required by scientology policy not to communicate with me because I am an SP.

While my immediate family were performing as die-hard scientologist are wont to do, I had a very pleasant surprise from a totally unexpected vector.

For most people, family reunions are a normal if sometimes tiresome or unwanted part of life. Not for me. Since my parents were, and my siblings, elder children, and nieces and nephews are scientologists, a family get-together with me and them is never going to happen. That's why it was wonderful when my cousin Craig reached out, after seeing I had scheduled a book event at the University of Pennsylvania. He asked if he could come up from Washington, DC, to attend the event and if we could have a meal together. Craig is the eldest son of my father's sister, and really the only non-scientology family member I had any connection with while growing up. A year older than me, Craig had spent Christmases and other holidays with my family during our formative years. Fifty years ago I had visited him and his long-term girlfriend, Vicki (now his wife), to tell them I was leaving Adelaide to join the Sea Org. They had tried to talk me out of it, saying I should use my scholarship to Adelaide University to embark on a real career.

Obviously, I didn't listen. I knew he had since moved to the US and was a successful lawyer. When I was still in the Sea Org he had reached out to me, but I was not interested in a "wog" contact so never followed up even though I had visited DC dozens of times.

As it turns out I really enjoy a family reunion. Even if it's a very small one. After the book event we shared a late dinner and talked and talked and talked, filling in the details of what had happened in our lives over five decades. He and Vicki have three daughters and a son, and six beautiful grandchildren so far. Craig told me their family was what they lived for and they regularly get together even though they are scattered across the country. He explained that he had reached out in part because when he read that my son Jack had no relatives in his life (he has never met any of his grandparents, aunts and uncles, cousins, or even his half-brother and -sister) he wanted me to relay a message to him that he has an entire family that he is part of, and asked that we come to visit so we can all meet. He gave me photos of all of them so Jack could see many loving people he has in *his family*. Same for Christie and me. We are part of their clan and the love is unconditional. This was incredibly touching, and when I got home and told Jack, he was thrilled. Due to intervening circumstances, we have not yet made it to visit our "new" family, but intend to do so as soon as we can.

In the wake of the book gaining a wider audience, we continued our work at the Aftermath Foundation, the nonprofit organization established by Christie and me and four other "exes" to help scientologists, especially Sea Org members, escape and begin their lives anew. The book spiked interest and as a result we experienced our most productive year by far. Though the identity of those we help is always kept confidential, some want their stories told, and we recently produced our first video about one of those people, Serge Obelinsky. His is a heart-wrenching tale of the cruelty of scientology policies, but thanks to the Foundation and some other amazing people, it has a movingly happy ending. We have more stories we plan to tell publicly, and all the while we are making it possible for people to escape the abuses of scientology on a daily basis.

I also continued work with the nonprofit organization Child USA. Founded by University of Pennsylvania professor Marci Hamilton, who is featured in an episode of *The Aftermath*, Child USA has helped secure huge advances in the rights of victims of child sexual abuse across the United States. My involvement with Child USA continues to be something of which I am very proud.

While all of this was happening in the public arena, various important developments related to scientology came to the forefront, following a lot of behind-the-scenes preparatory work. Valeska Guider Paris, a former SO member whom I knew well and who had lived in my and Christie's house for a while with her husband, Chris, asked if I would help her and two other former childhood Sea Org members, Gawain and Laura Baxter, with a lawsuit they were planning. She wanted me to brief their lawyers on scientology policy and tactics in litigation.

Valeska and the Baxters went on to sue David Miscavige and various scientology entities for engaging in human trafficking and other abuses. As with most scientology legal cases, it dragged out due to delay tactics on the part of scientology, who sought to have the matter decided by "religious arbitration"—a made-up scientology "justice procedure" that is wholly controlled by scientology, conducted by scientologists in good standing, and only final once approved by scientology officials. In other words, it is a one-sided kangaroo court that prevents any accountability or justice. They managed to persuade a judge that such arbitration was a good idea, so the victims were ordered to appear before those they claim abused them to determine whether they had in fact been abused as children. Scientology Clearwater spokesman Ben Shaw claimed this decision meant they had "won the case," a perhaps inadvertent but clear admission that their arbitration is nothing more than a sham. This is so bizarre it is almost unbelievable. The order to participate in scientology arbitration is under appeal at the time of writing.

Conversely, the same court ruled in favor of the plaintiffs on another important matter: the personal involvement of David Miscavige. Miscavige, like Hubbard before him, goes to enormous lengths to avoid being served in any legal case. Miscavige has constructed an elaborate wall of barriers to prevent such personal service. He has been successful in this for many years. Yet a plaintiff diligent enough in making and documenting every effort to comply with the law can eventually succeed. The lawyers for Valeska and the Baxters accomplished this feat after more than a year of painstakingly documented attempts. For the first time, the court determined Miscavige was deliberately avoiding service and ruled that he was now officially a defendant in the case. This may prove very significant in future cases.

Behind-the-scenes legal work in which I was involved also came to fruition in another matter. When Leah Remini and I found out about the alleged rapes of Danny Masterson, at the time we were first shooting *The Aftermath*, we reached out to the victims and interviewed them. Their experiences shocked and incensed us both, and we helped them report to law enforcement and prosecutors. We didn't air the planned episode so as not to jeopardize any possible prosecution. Frustratingly, the decision on whether to proceed with a case against Masterson dragged on and on, but eventually the Los Angeles district attorney charged Masterson with three counts of rape. He was tried in Los Angeles in November 2022. Disappointingly, the outcome after many weeks was a hung jury. The prosecutors requested a new trial, which was held in April and May 2023. This time, on May 31, Masterson was convicted of two of the three counts of forcible rape and sent directly to jail. On

September 7 he was sentenced to life in prison. Finally, his victims saw a measure of justice for the horrific crimes he committed against them.

The Masterson verdict is hugely significant. A celebrated scientologist from a prominent scientology family, who was raised on scientology principles, was now convicted of violent rapes. It generated a huge amount of media coverage, none reflecting well on scientology, and further driving home the idea in the minds of the public that scientology is something to be concerned about.

There is a lot more to come in the Masterson saga. The criminal judge was careful to keep the case limited to the actions of Masterson. Consequently, a lot of evidence about scientology's involvement in the aftermath of the rapes did not come out in the course of the criminal trial because it was not relevant. However, Masterson's victims filed a civil case, where this will be more relevant, naming not only him but also a number of other scientology individuals and entities. This is common; the family of Nicole Brown Simpson sued OJ Simpson civilly and won even though he had been criminally acquitted of the murder of their daughter.

The Masterson civil case was put on hold pending the completion of the criminal proceedings. Before that pause, scientology's effort in this case to send these victims to scientology "arbitration" was overturned on appeal. Following the sentencing, the stay in the case was lifted and the victims (now plaintiffs) will have their day in court to determine the involvement and culpability of scientology and the potential of damages to be paid by scientology and Masterson. This case casts a far wider net than the criminal prosecution and is shaping up to be a potential Waterloo for scientology.

Finally, on the legal front, Leah Remini filed a lawsuit of her own naming David Miscavige, Religious Technology Center, and Church of Scientology International. Her complaint lays out the policies, pattern, and practice of scientology seeking to destroy its enemies, and then many specific instances detailing how these policies have guided the targeted actions of scientology to harass her and ruin her career and life. She seeks court orders that would prevent scientology from conducting such campaigns against her or anyone else in the future. Should she prevail it will put an end once and for all to scientology's Fair Game practices.

Concurrent with these significant legal actions unfolding, a whole new avenue of exposure of scientology abuses has sprung to life. One of the people featured on *The Aftermath*, Aaron Smith-Levin, began doing YouTube videos detailing the inner workings and stories of abuses in scientology. It proved very successful, and I soon began a YouTube channel of my own, as did Marc Headley. When we began collaborating and livestreaming our exposés together, "SPTV" was born. Soon, others added their voices, and there are now dozens of YouTube channels telling the truth about scientology, loosely affiliated under the "SPTV" banner. This is no doubt driving Miscavige crazy. He has spent tens of millions of dollars on the ill-fated Scientology Network (a streaming TV service)—which continues to flounder with no audience to speak of. SPTV racks up more views every day than the costly, slick propaganda that appears on the Scientology Network. The thought of a constantly infuriated Miscavige makes me smile.

On another front entirely, six months after the hardcover publication of *A Billion Years*, I contracted a nagging cough. I visited the doctor, was diagnosed with bronchitis, and was given cough medicine and antibiotics. I took what was prescribed but the cough didn't recede. I went back two more times, and was eventually referred to a pulmonologist. She sent me for a CT scan of my lungs. When the results came back she informed me that I had fluid accumulating on my right lung and that I needed to have it drained. The procedure is called a thoracentesis. Unfortunately, the first appointment I could get was two weeks out. My cough continued to worsen and my breathing became very labored. I called the doctor and was directed to visit the local hospital emergency room. I was soon admitted and underwent an immediate thoracentesis, draining a liter of fluid from the pleural cavity surrounding my right lung. The fluid compresses the lung, making it difficult to breathe. The following day they drained another liter of fluid. A new pulmonologist consulted me in the hospital and said he was having the drained fluid analyzed. He set up an appointment for a week hence because it had to be sent to California for analysis.

Dr. Nelson was very forthright. "Your results show you have adeno-carcinoma (cancer of organ tissue). I don't know what organ, but it is showing up in the pleural fluid. I am referring you to the best oncologist I know."

I have always been in good health; the worst thing I ever had was the flu and bronchitis. Every annual checkup (I got them regularly after I left the Sea Org) had ended with the doctor saying, "You're in good shape, very healthy for your age. You could lose a few pounds, but other than that, you're good." Now I knew something far more serious was wrong. I had worried that I might have lung cancer due to my many years of smoking when in scientology. Though I am usually fairly hard to rattle, the very matter-of-fact statement of the doctor took me aback. I had many questions that could not yet be answered. How advanced was the cancer? Where was it? What was the prognosis?

The only thing I was certain of was that I had another battle to wage—not the first in my life. I resolved this was a challenge I was going to overcome, in fact, had to overcome. Christie and the boys needed me and I at least had to see Jack through to adulthood. It's no time to lose your father when you are eleven. Additionally, my job with scientology was not yet done: The abuses continue and I had vowed to expose them until they were forced by whatever means to stop destroying their purported enemies.

Christie was incredible. She became my nurse, secretary for scheduling appointments, and tireless advocate. She has been a pit bull—fighting the apparently endless red tape and bureaucracy of the health system in this country to get me the treatments I need. Until you experience something like this you really have no idea how difficult it is to negotiate such a confusing, arbitrary, and uncoordinated world.

The oncologist immediately scheduled a PET scan, an imaging test that uses radioactive material to locate cancer cells. When I say "immediately" that means in a week or two. The only way to get faster action is to admit yourself through the ER, another reality of medical treatment I have come to learn through now hard-won experience.

The PET scan showed cancerous cells concentrated in my lower esophagus. After three endoscopies, one in the lungs and two in the esophagus, it was confirmed as stage 4 esophageal cancer. It is defined as stage 4 because the cancer cells also showed up in the fluid in my pleural cavity and thus have spread.

The oncologist said the tests also showed I had a specific blood mutation that made me a candidate for a targeted oral drug that had recently been FDA approved. This is in place of chemotherapy. It was the height of irony when I learned the drug is manufactured by Eli Lilly—the company that makes the anti-depression drug Prozac, which I had been part of targeting while I was still in scientology. Now their cancer drug had the potential of curing me. One catch: It cost $22,000 a month for the pills. When Aaron Smith-Levin did a YouTube video about this, there was an overwhelming avalanche response. Literally thousands of people from all over the world began donating money and sending me message of love and support.

I got onto the drug, but unfortunately it had serious side effects, raising my liver toxicity to dangerous levels (about 50 percent of patients cannot tolerate the side effects). We had to discontinue it and pivot to a new solution and a different targeted drug. This one costs $25,000 per month, but Christie, through some miracle, managed to get the manufacturer to include us in their benefit program, even though the drug is not yet FDA approved for anything beyond lung cancer. As of this writing, the drug has no meaningful side effects and my most recent PET scan shows no indication of the cancer that had shown up on the first scan. So, the news is very hopeful, and even if the cancer builds an immunity to this treatment, according to the doctor my tests show I will be very receptive to chemo/immunotherapy.

The cancer battle continues—but progress is occurring. After a few months' hiatus, I returned to the scientology whistleblowing side of life. Obviously, scientology noticed, sending PI's out to watch my home and follow me again, something we had not seen for many years. Naturally, I took videos of them to document the harassment and put it on YouTube for everyone to see. It was soon added into Leah's lawsuit as evidence of the ongoing activities of scientology trying to destroy their "enemies."

I remain more determined than ever to bring an end to the abuses of scientology and to beat the cancer. I also remain forever thankful for the friends, family, and complete strangers who have reached out to support me on both fronts. The sheer volume of outpouring of love and support in numerous forms has been incredibly humbling and gratifying.

I don't plan to let you down.

From left to right, standing: Shane Collbran and Jack Rinder
From left to right, sitting: Mike Rinder and Christie Collbran
(Photo courtesy of Will Miller Photo, LLC)

ACKNOWLEDGMENTS

Eternal thanks to the love of my life, Christie, for always encouraging, always supporting, and always insisting I sit down and write.

To the two boys who make my world entertaining and fun, Shane and Jack.

Leah Remini, my sister of choice and a source of constant inspiration for her courage, compassion, and loyalty. And to her family: Angelo, Sofia, Vicki, George, Shannon, Nicole, William, and Brianne for welcoming me into their lives as if I had always been there. My family and home away from home.

Thanks always for the support and friendship of the Headley clan, David and Mary Kahn, and Aaron and Heather Smith-Levin. Many others have helped to make life easier and/or more fulfilling in numerous ways: Luis and Rocio, Paul and Jacki, Karen and Jeff, Amy and Mat, "Grandma" Rachel, Jackson, Jefferson, Ray, Tony O., Dave and Rosemary, Shel, Carla and Don, "Uncle" Dave, Jim and Betsy, Ashley, Chris S., Stefani, Janis, Peggy, Marti, Robert, Jan, Jamie, Rafi—thank you all.

There are a number of journalists—people I was once taught were evil—who have played a significant role in my journey: two of the best, and one of the funniest, who I thankfully call friends today, Sarah Mole and John Sweeney. Joe Childs and Tom Tobin, who bravely reported on scientology for so many years and were the catalyst for me emerging as a whistleblower. Lawrence Wright, a national treasure whose advice and guidance helped me finally make this book a reality. Alex Gibney, a brilliant documentarian who has changed the world.

My friends who helped me with unreserved kindness and generosity when I had nowhere to go: Tom DeVocht, Ronnie and Bitty Miscavige, and Jim and Sarah Mortland.

And finally, my agent, Steve Fisher, my most trusted "editorial sherpa" Kathy Huck, and the amazing team at Gallery: Jennifer Bergstrom, Jennifer Long, Sally Marvin, Jennifer Robinson, Laura Cherkas, Sarah Wright, and most of all my editors extraordinaire, Aimee Bell and Max Meltzer, who not only made my book better, they made me feel at home and supported. This team is the best anyone could hope for.

GLOSSARY OF SCIENTOLOGY TERMINOLOGY

acceptable truth: A lie. Not the whole truth.

Action Chief: A Sea Org post in charge of the department that sends Sea Org Missions.

auditing: Counseling in scientology using procedures developed by L. Ron Hubbard designed to eradicate the reactive mind and make Operating Thetans. Most auditing uses an E-Meter. Auditing sessions are delivered by an auditor.

ASI (Author Services Inc.): A for-profit literary agency for Hubbard created to hide his control over scientology. Staffed exclusively by Sea Org members, ASI, though not part of the corporate hierarchy, directed and controlled scientology organizations on behalf of Hubbard.

blowing: Leaving without authorization. Usually used when someone escapes the Sea Org. Blowing often results in being labeled a Suppressive Person.

body thetans (BTs): Disembodied thetans that were created in the cataclysm Hubbard describes in OT III. BTs cause all sorts of problems, including illness.

Bosun's Party: A traditional Sea Org party on Christmas Eve with a pirate theme (the bosun is in charge of the ship's decks and equipment).

Bridge: Shortened name for "The Bridge to Total Freedom," the series of steps created by Hubbard that every scientologist must ascend to achieve the state of Operating Thetan and "full spiritual freedom." It is divided into two parts: auditing (counseling) and training (the study of Hubbard materials to learn how to be an auditor).

bulletin: Hubbard Communications Office Bulletin (HCO B). A directive written by Hubbard concerning the tech of scientology—how to audit.

cadet: A Sea Org member who is a child.

Case Supervisor (C/S): The person who oversees auditors and directs them on how to audit their clients.

CCHR: Citizen's Commission on Human Rights, a scientology organization dedicated to exposing abuses of psychiatry and seeking its total eradication.

Clear: A thetan who has eradicated their reactive mind through dianetic and scientology auditing. A Clear is supposed to be a new type of man (dubbed "homo novis" by Hubbard)—rational, healthy, and happy.

CMO: See Commodore's Messenger Org.

COB: Chairman of the Board RTC. David Miscavige's assumed title as undisputed leader of scientology.

Command Intention: Originally, what Hubbard wanted done, but now it's what David Miscavige wants done.

Committee of Evidence (Comm Ev): A scientology "justice" procedure akin to a trial. There is a list of charges based on scientology "crimes" and "high crimes" and an appointed panel is supposed to gather and review evidence, determine guilt, and recommend punishment.

Commodore: L. Ron Hubbard. Hubbard appointed himself Commodore of the Sea Org when he lived aboard a ship in the late 1960s and early 1970s, from which he ran his scientology empire.

Commodore's Messengers: Originally Sea Org cadets who ran messages for Hubbard. The Messengers eventually became the most senior officials in scientology.

Commodore's Messenger Org: The internal organization for Messengers separate from other Sea Org members and with its own chain of command.

condition formulas: Steps laid out by Hubbard to "improve conditions in life." For "lower conditions" (when someone has violated scientology rules) they include penalties and requirements to make amends.

Creston: A small town in central California, outside of which Hubbard bought a ranch where he hid during the last years of his life.

CSI: Church of Scientology International, the "Mother Church" of scientology, headquartered in Los Angeles, staffed exclusively by Sea Org members. CSI manages scientology organizations around the world.

CST: Church of Spiritual Technology, an organization created to preserve the words of L. Ron Hubbard for eternity in secret underground nuclear-proof bunkers. Only the highest-level Sea Org members are permitted access to CST operations.

declared: To be labeled a Suppressive Person. Scientologists in good standing may not have any contact with someone who has been declared.

Dianetics: The book by Hubbard outlining his "discovery" of the reactive mind and his system for eradicating it, originally published in 1950. In 1952 he lost the rights to the subject in a bankruptcy case and invented scientology to take its place. Eventually, he regained control of dianetics copyrights. In 1955 he "joined" the two and dianetics became a substudy of scientology.

disconnection: The enforced severing of ties with anyone declared a Suppressive Person.

Ethics: Hubbard's "technology" of moral choices, right and wrong, and the rules of conduct followed by scientologists.

E-Meter: A scientology device used in auditing and security checking. It's an electronic measuring device that records the level of resistance of a small electrical current passed through the body. According to Hubbard, it can read your thoughts and tell when you are lying.

Fair Game: The policy of scientology to destroy enemies through tricks, lies, smears, and harassment.

Flag: Derived from the nautical term for the lead ship of a flotilla. Originally Flag was the *Apollo*, which included all the highest-level activities of scientology—running the organizations around the world and providing the most advanced auditing and training. Flag's operations moved to Clearwater in 1975. Today, Clearwater is the "spiritual headquarters" of scientology, also called the Flag Land Base, providing auditing and training. The management activities from the *Apollo* (the Flag Bureau) subsequently moved to Los Angeles.

Flag Bureau: The scientology organization that manages the day-to-day affairs of scientology organizations around the world, located on Hollywood Boulevard in Los Angeles.

Flag Land Base: The scientology operations in Clearwater, Florida, also often referred to as Flag or Flag Service Org (FSO).

Flag Service Org (FSO): Scientology's "spiritual headquarters" in Clearwater, Florida, where high-level Bridge services are made available. Scientology's largest and most lucrative organization.

Gilman: Gilman Hot Springs, a five-hundred-acre property in Riverside County near Hemet, California, that houses Gold and International Management. Also known as the Int Base and Gold.

GO: See Guardian's Office.

Gold: Golden Era Productions, the scientology organization created to make Hubbard's instructional and promotional films, located at Gilman Hot Springs. Also used interchangeably with Int Base to denote the property at Gilman.

Guardian's Office (GO): The former department in scientology organizations that dealt with governments, media, and "attackers." It was headed by Hubbard's wife, Mary Sue. She and ten other GO officials pleaded guilty to infiltrating the US government and stealing documents. The GO was then disbanded—but replaced by the Office of Special Affairs in the early '80s.

HGB: Hollywood Guaranty Building on Hollywood Boulevard, Los Angeles, which was bought by scientology in 1988 to house management organizations, including OSA Int. The official corporate address of CSI and RTC.

IAS: See International Association of Scientologists.

INCOMM: International Network of Computer Organized Management. Scientology's internal computerization and email network.

Int Base: Gilman Hot Springs, California. See Gold and International Management.

International Association of Scientologists (IAS): The membership organization of scientology—all scientologists are required to be members in order to qualify for discounts on books, meters, and services. It is also a major fundraising organization for scientology that has amassed a war chest to protect scientology. Originally formed to keep money out of the reach of the IRS in foreign bank accounts.

International Management (Int): The top of the international scientology organizational hierarchy, located at Gilman. It includes CMO International and the International Executive Strata organizations.

Int Ranch: A property seven miles from Gilman where children of Int Base Sea Org members lived and worked until it was finally disbanded in 2000.

La Quinta: Hubbard's home and makeshift movie studio in the late 1970s, twenty miles southeast of Palm Springs, California. Operations were moved to Gilman in 1979.

MEST: Acronym for matter, energy, space, and time, used to refer to the physical (as opposed to spiritual) universe.

MEST work: Manual labor.

missions: Small organizations intended to recruit new people into scientology. Formerly called franchises.

Mission Ops: A specially trained person who runs Sea Org Missions.

MU: Misunderstood word. Hubbard claimed a not- or misunderstood word is the primary barrier to learning, and that what one reads after a word that is not fully understood is blank.

Office of Special Affairs (OSA): The department of scientology that replaced the Guardian's Office. It deals with governments, media, and "enemies."

OGH: Old Gilman House. A ramshackle old house at the edge of the Gold Base where troublemakers were sent to segregate them from the rest of the crew.

Off-Source: Altering, or not following, the teachings of L. Ron Hubbard. The opposite of On-Source. A very bad thing.

On-Source: Following the teachings of Source (Hubbard) exactly. Being deemed On-Source is high praise for any scientologist.

Operating Thetan (OT): The advanced spiritual state promised after one attains the state of Clear. OTs supposedly have superhuman powers and are free from the problems that plague *Homo sapiens*. One achieves these abilities by advancing through the confidential "OT levels" I through VIII on the auditing side of the Bridge.

Organizing Board (Org Board): The chart of a scientology organization showing seniority, functions, and assignments. Hubbard claimed the organization of scientology is derived from an ancient galactic organizational structure but improved upon by him.

orgs: Scientology organizations. The preferred term for churches of scientology or related entities.

OT III: The "Wall of Fire." A level on the Bridge based on Hubbard's space opera story of the evil galactic overlord, Xenu, who solved an overpopulation problem seventy-five million years ago by rounding up billions of people, freezing their souls in glycol, and transporting them to Earth, where they were dumped in volcanoes and blown up by H-bombs. These spiritual beings are now stuck to humans in the form of body thetans (BTs). One gets rid of BTs on the upper OT levels;

they are the cause of unhappiness, unwanted emotions, and physical ailments.

OTC: Operation and Transport Corporation, the shore story name used by the *Apollo* to obscure its connection to scientology.

OT levels: The highest steps of the auditing side of the Bridge.

overt: A sin or a crime.

O/Ws: Overts and withholds—crimes and secrets.

policy letter: Directive written by Hubbard concerning the administration of scientology organizations.

post: A position in a scientology organization. One's job title.

processes/processing: The specific steps laid out by Hubbard to be taken in auditing.

PTS: Potential Trouble Source, used to describe somebody connected to a Suppressive Person.

reactive mind: The unconscious stimulus/response mind Hubbard described in *Dianetics: The Modern Science of Mental Health*. The early levels of scientology are focused on erasing the reactive mind, but one of the secrets later disclosed is that you decide to "mock up" (create) your reactive mind. Someone who has "erased" their reactive mind is called a Clear.

RONY: Relay Office New York. Located near JFK airport, it relayed communications to and from the *Apollo* in the Caribbean.

RPF: Rehabilitation Project Force, a "rehabilitation" program for Sea Org members who are troublemakers or failures. They are segregated from the rest of the group, undergo security checks, and perform manual labor all day. They may not speak to others.

RTC: Religious Technology Center, the organization at the top of the scientology hierarchy, headed by David Miscavige.

Saint Hill: Hubbard's home in East Grinstead, Sussex, England, before he fled the country and formed the Sea Org. It now houses the Advanced Organization UK, delivering the OT levels, and the administrative headquarters for scientology in the UK.

Sea Org: The most dedicated scientologists who form the highest echelons of the scientology hierarchy. Sea Org members live, work, and eat communally and are paid a subsistence wage. They sign a billion-year contract dedicating themselves to achieving the aims of scientology. The Sea Org was formed by Hubbard aboard ships in the late '60s and continues to use many nautical terms.

Sea Org Mission: A "technology" unique to the Sea Org created by Hubbard involving two or more Sea Org members being sent to accomplish a specific objective, controlled by a Mission Operator (Msn Ops) located in the Action Bureau.

security check (sec check): An interrogation done using the E-Meter.

shore flap: Upset created with any locals (originally referred to those living onshore in the ports we visited on the *Apollo*).

shore story: A false explanation contrived to obscure real activities. Coined aboard Hubbard's ships as the story to be told to people in the ports they visited to hide scientology.

SHQ: Summer headquarters. Another name for Gilman Hot Springs.

Source: L. Ron Hubbard. He referred to himself as "Source"—the exclusive originator of all things in scientology.

SP: See Suppressive Person.

Suppressive Person/Suppressive (SP): Someone designated by scientology as an enemy. SPs are to be silenced or destroyed.

tech: Technology—what Hubbard called his teachings. He claimed they were researched, tested, and based on science.

thetan: Scientology term for the spirit. One of the three parts of man, according to Hubbard, along with the mind and body.

Touch Assist: A scientology procedure to relieve pain or injury by placing a finger on various locations around the body.

United Churches of Florida: The organization created to obscure scientology's move to Clearwater, Florida.

wog: Derogatory term for anyone who is not a scientologist.

X: An apartment where Hubbard briefly lived in Hemet.

Xenu: The evil galactic ruler from OT III.

RECOMMENDED FURTHER READING

A Piece of Blue Sky: Scientology, Dianetics, and L. Ron Hubbard Exposed by Jon Atack

Bare-Faced Messiah: The True Story of L. Ron Hubbard by Russell Miller

Blown for Good: Behind the Iron Curtain of Scientology by Marc Headley

Counterfeit Dreams: One Man's Journey Into and Out of the World of Scientology by Jefferson Hawkins

Fair Game: The Incredible Untold Story of Scientology in Australia by Steve Cannane

Going Clear: Scientology, Hollywood, and the Prison of Belief by Lawrence Wright

Inside Scientology: The Story of America's Most Secretive Religion by Janet Reitman

Man's Search for Meaning by Viktor Frankl

Ron the War Hero: The True Story of L Ron Hubbard's Calamitous Military Career by Chris Owen

Ruthless: Scientology, My Son David Miscavige, and Me by Ron Miscavige

Scientology: Abuse at the Top by Amy Scobee

Scientology: A to Xenu by Chris Shelton

The Church of Fear: Inside the Weird World of Scientology by John Sweeney

The Sociopath Next Door by Martha Stout

The Unbreakable Miss Lovely: How the Church of Scientology Tried to Destroy Paulette Cooper by Tony Ortega

Troublemaker: Surviving Hollywood and Scientology by Leah Remini

INDEX